# Le Malade imaginaire

DU MÊME AUTEUR

*Dom Juan ou le Festin de pierre*, Librio n° 14
*Les Fourberies de Scapin*, Librio n° 181
*Le Bourgeois gentilhomme*, Librio n° 235
*L'École des femmes*, Librio n° 277
*L'Avare*, Librio n° 339
*Tartuffe*, Librio n° 476
*Le Malade imaginaire*, Librio n° 536
*Les Femmes savantes*, Librio n° 585
*Le Misanthrope*, Librio n° 647
*Les Précieuses ridicules*, Librio n° 776
*George Dandin*, Librio n° 1071

# Molière

# Le Malade imaginaire

Comédie
mêlée de musique et de danses
représentée pour la première fois
sur le théâtre de la salle du Palais-Royal
le 10 février 1673
par la troupe du roi

*Texte intégral*

## PERSONNAGES

ARGAN, malade imaginaire.
BÉLINE, seconde femme d'Argan.
ANGÉLIQUE, fille d'Argan, et amante de Cléante.
LOUISON, petite fille d'Argan, et sœur d'Angélique.
BÉRALDE, frère d'Argan.
CLÉANTE, amant d'Angélique.
MONSIEUR DIAFOIRUS, médecin.
THOMAS DIAFOIRUS, son fils, et amant d'Angélique.
MONSIEUR PURGON, médecin d'Argan.
MONSIEUR FLEURANT, apothicaire d'Argan.
MONSIEUR BONNEFOY, notaire.
TOINETTE, servante.

*La scène est à Paris.*

# LE PROLOGUE

Après les glorieuses fatigues et les exploits victorieux de notre auguste monarque, il est bien juste que tous ceux qui se mêlent d'écrire travaillent ou à ses louanges, ou à son divertissement. C'est ce qu'ici l'on a voulu faire, et ce prologue est un essai des louanges de ce grand prince, qui donne entrée à la comédie du *Malade imaginaire*, dont le projet a été fait pour le délasser de ses nobles travaux.

*La décoration représente un lieu champêtre fort agréable.*

# ÉGLOGUE EN MUSIQUE ET EN DANSE

*Flore, Pan, Climène, Daphné, Tircis, Dorilas,*
*Deux Zéphyrs, Troupe de Bergères et de Bergers.*

FLORE
*Quittez, quittez vos troupeaux,*
*Venez, Bergers, venez, Bergères,*
10   *Accourez, accourez sous ces tendres ormeaux ;*
*Je viens vous annoncer des nouvelles bien chères,*
*Et réjouir tous ces hameaux.*
*Quittez, quittez vos troupeaux,*
*Venez, Bergers, venez, Bergères,*
15   *Accourez, accourez sous ces tendres ormeaux.*

CLIMÈNE ET DAPHNÉ
*Berger, laissons là tes feux,*
*Voilà Flore qui nous appelle.*

TIRCIS ET DORILAS
*Mais au moins dis-moi, cruelle,*

TIRCIS
*Si d'un peu d'amitié tu payeras mes vœux.*

DORILAS
20   *Si tu seras sensible à mon ardeur fidèle.*

CLIMÈNE ET DAPHNÉ
*Voilà Flore qui nous appelle.*

TIRCIS ET DORILAS
*Ce n'est qu'un mot, un mot, un seul mot que je veux.*

TIRCIS
*Languirai-je toujours dans ma peine mortelle ?*

DORILAS
*Puis-je espérer qu'un jour tu me rendras heureux ?*

CLIMÈNE ET DAPHNÉ
25     *Voilà Flore qui nous appelle.*

## Entrée de ballet

*Toute la troupe des Bergers et des Bergères va se placer en cadence autour de Flore.*

CLIMÈNE
*Quelle nouvelle parmi nous,*
*Déesse, doit jeter tant de réjouissance ?*

DAPHNÉ
*Nous brûlons d'apprendre de vous*
*Cette nouvelle d'importance.*

DORILAS
30     *D'ardeur nous en soupirons tous.*

TOUS
*Nous en mourons d'impatience.*

FLORE

*La voici : silence, silence !*
*Vos vœux sont exaucés, LOUIS est de retour ;*
*Il ramène en ces lieux les plaisirs et l'amour,*
35 *Et vous voyez finir vos mortelles alarmes.*
*Par ses vastes exploits son bras voit tout soumis,*
*Il quitte les armes*
*Faute d'ennemis.*


TOUS

*Ah ! quelle douce nouvelle !*
40 *Qu'elle est grande ! qu'elle est belle !*
*Que de plaisirs ! que de ris ! que de jeux !*
*Que de succès heureux !*
*Et que le Ciel a bien rempli nos vœux !*
*Ah ! quelle douce nouvelle !*
45 *Qu'elle est grande ! qu'elle est belle !*


**Autre entrée de ballet**

*Tous les Bergers et Bergères expriment par des danses les transports de leur joie.*


FLORE

*De vos flûtes bocagères*
*Réveillez les plus beaux sons :*
*LOUIS offre à vos chansons*
*La plus belle des matières.*
50 *Après cent combats,*
*Où cueille son bras*
*Une ample victoire,*
*Formez entre vous*
*Cent combats plus doux,*
55 *Pour chanter sa gloire.*

TOUS

*Formons entre nous*
*Cent combats plus doux,*
*Pour chanter sa gloire.*

FLORE

*Mon jeune amant, dans ce bois,*
60 *Des présents de mon empire*
*Prépare un prix à la voix*
*Qui saura le mieux nous dire*
*Les vertus et les exploits*
*Du plus auguste des rois.*

CLIMÈNE

65 *Si Tircis a l'avantage,*

DAPHNÉ

*Si Dorilas est vainqueur,*

CLIMÈNE

*À le chérir je m'engage.*

DAPHNÉ

*Je me donne à son ardeur.*

TIRCIS

*Ô trop chère espérance !*

DORILAS

70 *Ô mot plein de douceur !*

TOUS DEUX

*Plus beau sujet, plus belle récompense*
*Peuvent-ils animer un cœur ?*

*Les violons jouent un air pour animer les deux Bergers au combat,*
*tandis que Flore, comme juge, va se placer au pied de l'arbre, avec deux*
*Zéphyrs.*

### TIRCIS

Quand la neige fondue enfle un torrent fameux,
Contre l'effort soudain de ses flots écumeux
75         Il n'est rien d'assez solide ;
        Digues, châteaux, villes, et bois,
        Hommes et troupeaux à la fois,
        Tout cède au courant qui le guide.
        Tel, et plus fier, et plus rapide,
80         Marche LOUIS dans ses exploits.

### Ballet

Les Bergers et Bergères de son côté dansent autour de lui, sur une ritournelle, pour exprimer leurs applaudissements.

### DORILAS

Le foudre, menaçant, qui perce avec fureur
L'affreuse obscurité de la nue enflammée,
        Fait d'épouvante et d'horreur
        Trembler le plus ferme cœur ;
85         Mais à la tête d'une armée
        LOUIS jette plus de terreur.

### Ballet

Les Bergers et Bergères font de même que les autres.

### TIRCIS

Des fabuleux exploits que la Grèce a chantés,
Par un brillant amas de belles vérités
        Nous voyons la gloire effacée,
90         Et tous ces fameux demi-dieux
        Que vante l'histoire passée
        Ne sont point à notre pensée
        Ce que LOUIS est à nos yeux.

## Ballet

*Les Bergers et Bergères de son côté font encore la même chose.*

DORILAS

  LOUIS *fait à nos temps, par ses faits inouïs,*
95 *Croire tous les beaux faits que nous chante l'histoire*
    *Des siècles évanouis ;*
    *Mais nos neveux, dans leur gloire,*
    *N'auront rien qui fasse croire*
    *Tous les beaux faits de* LOUIS.

## Ballet

*Les Bergères de son côté font encore de même, après quoi les deux partis se mêlent.*

PAN, suivi des six Faunes.

100 *Laissez, laissez, Bergers, ce dessein téméraire.*
    *Hé ! que voulez-vous faire ?*
    *Chanter sur vos chalumeaux*
    *Ce qu'Apollon sur sa lyre,*
    *Avec ses chants les plus beaux,*
105    *N'entreprendrait pas de dire,*
 *C'est donner trop d'essor au feu qui vous inspire,*
 *C'est monter vers les cieux sur des ailes de cire,*
    *Pour tomber dans le fond des eaux.*
 *Pour chanter de* LOUIS *l'intrépide courage,*
110    *Il n'est point d'assez docte voix,*
 *Point de mots assez grands pour en tracer l'image ;*
    *Le silence est le langage*
    *Qui doit louer ses exploits.*
 *Consacrez d'autres soins à sa pleine victoire ;*
115 *Vos louanges n'ont rien qui flatte ses désirs ;*
    *Laissez, laissez là sa gloire,*
    *Ne songez qu'à ses plaisirs.*

**TOUS**

*Laissons, laissons là sa gloire,*
*Ne songeons qu'à ses plaisirs.*

**FLORE**

120 *Bien que, pour étaler ses vertus immortelles,*
*La force manque à vos esprits,*
*Ne laissez pas tous deux de recevoir le prix :*
*Dans les choses grandes et belles*
*Il suffit d'avoir entrepris.*

## Entrée de ballet

*Les deux Zéphyrs dansent avec deux couronnes de fleurs à la main,*
*qu'ils viennent ensuite donner aux deux Bergers.*

**CLIMÈNE ET DAPHNÉ, en leur donnant la main.**

125 *Dans les choses grandes et belles*
*Il suffit d'avoir entrepris.*

**TIRCIS ET DORILAS**

*Ha ! que d'un doux succès notre audace est suivie !*

**FLORE ET PAN**

*Ce qu'on fait pour LOUIS, on ne le perd jamais.*

**LES QUATRE AMANTS**

*Au soin de ses plaisirs donnons-nous désormais.*

**FLORE ET PAN**

130 *Heureux, heureux qui peut lui consacrer sa vie !*

**TOUS**

*Joignons tous dans ces bois*
*Nos flûtes et nos voix,*
*Ce jour nous y convie ;*

*Et faisons aux échos redire mille fois :*
135         *« LOUIS est le plus grand des rois ;*
*Heureux, heureux qui peut lui consacrer sa vie ! »*

### Dernière et grande entrée de ballet

*Faunes, Bergers et Bergères, tous se mêlent, et il se fait entre eux des jeux de danse ; après quoi ils se vont préparer pour la Comédie.*

# AUTRE PROLOGUE

*Le théâtre représente une forêt.*

*L'ouverture du théâtre se fait par un bruit agréable d'instruments. Ensuite une Bergère vient se plaindre tendrement de ce qu'elle ne trouve aucun remède pour soulager les peines qu'elle endure. Plusieurs Faunes et Ægipans, assemblés pour des fêtes et des jeux qui leur sont particuliers, rencontrent la Bergère. Ils écoutent ses plaintes et forment un spectacle très divertissant.*

## PLAINTE DE LA BERGÈRE

*Votre plus haut savoir n'est que pure chimère,*
   *Vains et peu sages médecins ;*
*Vous ne pouvez guérir par vos grands mots latins*
   *La douleur qui me désespère :*
5 *Votre plus haut savoir n'est que pure chimère.*

   *Hélas ! je n'ose découvrir*
   *Mon amoureux martyre*
  *Au Berger pour qui je soupire,*
   *Et qui seul peut me secourir.*
10   *Ne prétendez pas le finir,*
*Ignorants médecins, vous ne sauriez le faire :*
*Votre plus haut savoir n'est que pure chimère.*

*Ces remèdes peu sûrs dont le simple vulgaire*
*Croit que vous connaissez l'admirable vertu,*
15 *Pour les maux que je sens n'ont rien de salutaire ;*
*Et tout votre caquet ne peut être reçu*

*Que d'un Malade imaginaire.*

*Votre plus haut savoir n'est que pure chimère,*
    *Vains et peu sages médecins ;*
20  *Vous ne pouvez guérir par vos grands mots latins*
    *La douleur qui me désespère :*
*Votre plus haut savoir n'est que pure chimère.*

*Le théâtre change et représente une chambre.*

corroborer →plus de force

# ACTE PREMIER

## Scène première

ARGAN, *seul dans sa chambre assis, une table devant lui, compte des parties d'apothicaire avec des jetons ; il fait, parlant à lui-même, les dialogues suivants.* – Trois et deux font cinq, et cinq font dix, et dix font vingt. Trois et deux font cinq. « Plus, du vingt-quatrième, un petit clystère insinuatif, préparatif, et rémollient, pour amollir, humecter, et rafraîchir les entrailles de Monsieur. » Ce qui me plaît de Monsieur Fleurant, mon apothicaire, c'est que ses parties sont toujours fort civiles : « les entrailles de Monsieur, trente sols ». Oui, mais, Monsieur Fleurant, ce n'est pas tout que d'être civil, il faut être aussi raisonnable, et ne pas écorcher les malades. Trente sols un lavement ! Je suis votre serviteur, je vous l'ai déjà dit. Vous ne me les avez mis dans les autres parties qu'à vingt sols, et vingt sols en langage d'apothicaire, c'est-à-dire dix sols ; les voilà, dix sols. « Plus, dudit jour, un bon clystère détersif, composé avec catholicon double, rhubarbe, miel rosat, et autres, suivant l'ordonnance, pour balayer, laver et nettoyer le bas-ventre de Monsieur, trente sols. » Avec votre permission, dix sols. « Plus, dudit jour le soir, un julep hépatique, soporatif et somnifère, composé pour faire dormir Monsieur, trente-cinq sols. » Je ne me plains pas de celui-là, car il me fit bien dormir. Dix, quinze, seize et dix-sept sols, six deniers. « Plus, du vingt-cinquième, une bonne médecine purgative et corroborative, composée de casse récente avec séné levantin, et autres, suivant l'ordonnance de Monsieur Purgon, pour expulser et évacuer la bile de Monsieur, quatre livres. » Ah ! Monsieur Fleurant, c'est se moquer ; il faut vivre avec les malades. Monsieur Purgon ne vous a pas ordonné de mettre quatre francs. Mettez, mettez trois livres, s'il vous plaît. Vingt et trente sols. « Plus, dudit jour,

17

une potion anodine et astringente, pour faire reposer Monsieur, trente sols. » Bon, dix et quinze sols. « Plus, du vingt-sixième, un clystère carminatif, pour chasser les vents de Monsieur, trente sols. » Dix sols, Monsieur Fleurant. « Plus, le clystère de Monsieur réitéré le soir, comme dessus, trente sols. » Monsieur Fleurant, dix sols. « Plus, du vingt-septième, une bonne médecine composée pour hâter d'aller, et chasser dehors les mauvaises humeurs de Monsieur, trois livres. » Bon, vingt et trente sols. Je suis bien aise que vous soyez raisonnable. « Plus, du vingt-huitième, une prise de petit-lait clarifié, et édulcoré, pour adoucir, lénifier, tempérer, et rafraîchir le sang de Monsieur, vingt sols. » Bon, dix sols. « Plus, une potion cordiale et préservative, composée avec douze grains de bézoard, sirops de limon et grenade, et autres, suivant l'ordonnance, cinq livres. » Ah ! Monsieur Fleurant, tout doux, s'il vous plaît ; si vous en usez comme cela, on ne voudra plus être malade ; contentez-vous de quatre francs. Vingt et quarante sols. Trois et deux font cinq, et cinq font dix, et dix font vingt. Soixante et trois livres, quatre sols, six deniers. Si bien donc que de ce mois j'ai pris une, deux, trois, quatre, cinq, six, sept et huit médecines ; et un, deux, trois, quatre, cinq, six, sept, huit, neuf, dix, onze et douze lavements ; et l'autre mois il y avait douze médecines, et vingt lavements. Je ne m'étonne pas si je ne me porte pas si bien ce mois-ci que l'autre. Je le dirai à Monsieur Purgon, afin qu'il mette ordre à cela. Allons, qu'on m'ôte tout ceci. Il n'y a personne. J'ai beau dire, on me laisse toujours seul ; il n'y a pas moyen de les arrêter ici. *(Il sonne une sonnette pour faire venir ses gens.)* Ils n'entendent point, et ma sonnette ne fait pas assez de bruit. Drelin, drelin, drelin. Point d'affaire ! Drelin, drelin, drelin : ils sont sourds. Toinette ! Drelin, drelin, drelin. Tout comme si je ne sonnais point. Chienne, coquine ! Drelin, drelin, drelin. J'enrage. *(Il ne sonne plus mais il crie.)* Drelin, drelin, drelin. Carogne, à tous les diables ! Est-il possible qu'on laisse comme cela un pauvre malade tout seul ! Drelin, drelin, drelin. Voilà qui est pitoyable ! Drelin, drelin, drelin. Ah, mon Dieu ! ils me laisseront ici mourir. Drelin, drelin, drelin.

## Scène II

*Toinette, Argan*

TOINETTE, *en entrant dans la chambre.* – On y va.

ARGAN. – Ah ! chienne ! ah ! carogne… !

TOINETTE, *faisant semblant de s'être cogné la tête.* – Diantre soit fait de votre impatience ! Vous pressez si fort les personnes, que je me suis donné un grand coup de la tête contre la carne d'un volet.

ARGAN, *en colère.* – Ah ! traîtresse… !

TOINETTE, *pour l'interrompre et l'empêcher de crier, se plaint toujours en disant :* – Ha !

ARGAN. – Il y a…

TOINETTE. – Ha !

ARGAN. – Il y a une heure…

TOINETTE. – Ha !

ARGAN. – Tu m'as laissé…

TOINETTE. – Ha !

ARGAN. – Tais-toi donc, coquine, que je te querelle.

TOINETTE. – Çamon, ma foi ! j'en suis d'avis, après ce que je me suis fait.

ARGAN. – Tu m'as fait égosiller, carogne.

TOINETTE. – Et vous m'avez fait, vous, casser la tête ; l'un vaut bien l'autre ; quitte à quitte, si vous voulez.

ARGAN. – Quoi ! coquine…

TOINETTE. – Si vous querellez, je pleurerai.

ARGAN. – Me laisser, traîtresse…

TOINETTE, *toujours pour l'interrompre.* – Ha !

ARGAN. – Chienne, tu veux...

TOINETTE. – Ha !

ARGAN. – Quoi ! il faudra encore que je n'aie pas le plaisir de la quereller ?

TOINETTE. – Querellez tout votre soûl, je le veux bien.

ARGAN. – Tu m'en empêches, chienne, en m'interrompant à tous coups.

TOINETTE. – Si vous avez le plaisir de quereller, il faut bien que, de mon côté, j'aie le plaisir de pleurer : chacun le sien, ce n'est pas trop. Ha !

ARGAN. – Allons, il faut en passer par là. Ôte-moi ceci, coquine, ôte-moi ceci. *(Argan se lève de sa chaise et lui donne les jetons et ses parties d'apothicaire.)* Mon lavement d'aujourd'hui a-t-il bien opéré ?

TOINETTE. – Votre lavement ?

ARGAN. – Oui. Ai-je bien fait de la bile ?

TOINETTE. – Ma foi ! je ne mêle point de ces affaires-là. C'est à Monsieur Fleurant à y mettre le nez, puisqu'il en a le profit.

ARGAN. – Qu'on ait soin de me tenir un bouillon prêt pour l'autre que je dois tantôt prendre.

TOINETTE. – Ce Monsieur Fleurant-là et ce Monsieur Purgon s'égayent bien sur votre corps ; ils ont en vous une bonne vache à lait ; et je voudrais bien leur demander quel mal vous avez, pour vous faire tant de remèdes.

ARGAN. – Taisez-vous, ignorante, ce n'est pas à vous à contrôler les ordonnances de la médecine. Qu'on me fasse venir ma fille Angélique, j'ai à lui dire quelque chose.

TOINETTE. – La voici qui vient d'elle-même ; elle a deviné votre pensée.

## Scène III

*Angélique, Toinette, Argan*

ARGAN. – Approchez, Angélique ; vous venez à propos ; je voulais vous parler.

ANGÉLIQUE. – Me voilà prête à vous ouïr.

ARGAN, *courant au bassin.* – Attendez. Donnez-moi mon bâton. Je vais revenir tout à l'heure.

TOINETTE, *en le raillant.* – Allez vite, Monsieur, allez. Monsieur Fleurant nous donne des affaires. → se moque de lui

→ IL DOIT FAIRE CACA

## Scène IV

*Angélique, Toinette*

ANGÉLIQUE, *la regardant d'un œil languissant, lui dit confidemment :* – Toinette.

TOINETTE. – Quoi ?

ANGÉLIQUE. – Regarde-moi un peu.

TOINETTE. – Hé bien ! je vous regarde.

ANGÉLIQUE. – Toinette.

TOINETTE. – Hé bien, quoi, Toinette ? → se moque d'Angélique

ANGÉLIQUE. – Ne devines-tu point de quoi je veux parler ?

TOINETTE. – Je m'en doute assez : de notre jeune amant ; car c'est sur lui, depuis six jours, que roulent tous nos entretiens ; et vous n'êtes point bien si vous n'en parlez à toute heure.

ANGÉLIQUE. – Puisque tu connais cela, que n'es-tu donc la première à m'en entretenir, et que ne m'épargnes-tu la peine de te jeter sur ce discours ?

TOINETTE. – Vous ne m'en donnez pas le temps, et vous avez des soins là-dessus qu'il est difficile de prévenir.

ANGÉLIQUE. – Je t'avoue que je ne saurais me lasser de te parler de lui, et que mon cœur profite avec chaleur de tous les moments de s'ouvrir à toi. Mais dis-moi, condamnes-tu, Toinette, les sentiments que j'ai pour lui ?

TOINETTE. – Je n'ai garde.

ANGÉLIQUE. – Ai-je tort de m'abandonner à ces douces impressions ?

TOINETTE. – Je ne dis pas cela.

ANGÉLIQUE. – Et voudrais-tu que je fusse insensible aux tendres protestations de cette passion ardente qu'il témoigne pour moi ?

TOINETTE. – À Dieu ne plaise !

ANGÉLIQUE. – Dis-moi un peu, ne trouves-tu pas, comme moi, quelque chose du Ciel, quelque effet du destin, dans l'aventure inopinée de notre connaissance ?

TOINETTE. – Oui.

ANGÉLIQUE. – Ne trouves-tu pas que cette action d'embrasser ma défense sans me connaître est tout à fait d'un honnête homme ?

TOINETTE. – Oui.

ANGÉLIQUE. – Que l'on ne peut pas en user plus généreusement ?

TOINETTE. – D'accord.

ANGÉLIQUE. – Et qu'il fit tout cela de la meilleure grâce du monde ?

TOINETTE. – Oh ! oui.

ANGÉLIQUE. – Ne trouves-tu pas, Toinette, qu'il est bien fait de sa personne ?

TOINETTE. – Assurément.

ANGÉLIQUE. – Qu'il a l'air le meilleur du monde ?

TOINETTE. – Sans doute.

ANGÉLIQUE. – Que ses discours, comme ses actions, ont quelque chose de noble ?

TOINETTE. – Cela est sûr.

ANGÉLIQUE. – Qu'on ne peut rien entendre de plus passionné que tout ce qu'il me dit ?

TOINETTE. – Il est vrai.

ANGÉLIQUE. – Et qu'il n'est rien de plus fâcheux que la contrainte où l'on me tient, qui bouche tout commerce aux doux empressements de cette mutuelle ardeur que le Ciel nous inspire ?

TOINETTE. – Vous avez raison.

ANGÉLIQUE. – Mais, ma pauvre Toinette, crois-tu qu'il m'aime autant qu'il me le dit ?

TOINETTE. – Eh, eh ! ces choses-là, parfois, sont un peu sujettes àcaution. Les grimaces d'amour ressemblent fort à la vérité ; et j'ai vu de grands comédiens là-dessus.

ANGÉLIQUE. – Ah ! Toinette, que dis-tu là ? Hélas ! de la façon qu'il parle, serait-il bien possible qu'il ne me dît pas vrai ?

TOINETTE. – En tout cas, vous en serez bientôt éclaircie ; et la résolution où il vous écrivit hier qu'il était de vous faire demander en mariage est une prompte voie à vous faire connaître s'il vous dit vrai, ou non. C'en sera là la bonne preuve.

ANGÉLIQUE. – Ah ! Toinette, si celui-là me trompe, je ne croirai de ma vie aucun homme.

TOINETTE. – Voilà votre père qui revient.

## Scène v

*Argan, Angélique, Toinette*

ARGAN *se met dans sa chaise.*– Ô çà, ma fille, je vais vous dire une nouvelle, où peut-être ne vous attendez-vous pas. On vous demande en mariage. Qu'est-ce que cela ? Vous riez. Cela est plaisant, oui, ce mot de mariage ; il n'y a rien de plus drôle pour les jeunes filles. Ah ! nature, nature ! À ce que je puis voir, ma fille, je n'ai que faire de vous demander si vous voulez bien vous marier.

ANGÉLIQUE. – Je dois faire, mon père, tout ce qu'il vous plaira de m'ordonner.

ARGAN. – Je suis bien aise d'avoir une fille si obéissante. La chose est donc conclue, et je vous ai promise.

ANGÉLIQUE. – C'est à moi, mon père, de suivre aveuglément toutes vos volontés.

ARGAN. – Ma femme, votre belle-mère, avait envie que je vous fisse religieuse, et votre petite sœur LOUISON aussi ; et de tout temps elle a été aheurtée à cela.

TOINETTE, *tout bas*. – La bonne bête a ses raisons. *moquerie !*

ARGAN. – Elle ne voulait point consentir à ce mariage, mais je l'ai emporté, et ma parole est donnée.

ANGÉLIQUE.–Ah ! mon père, que je vous suis obligée de toutes vos bontés.

TOINETTE. – En vérité, je vous sais bon gré de cela, et voilà l'action la plus sage que vous ayez faite de votre vie.

ARGAN. – Je n'ai point encore vu la personne, mais on m'a dit que j'en serais content, et toi aussi.

ANGÉLIQUE. – Assurément, mon père.

ARGAN. – Comment l'as-tu vu ?

ANGÉLIQUE. – Puisque votre consentement m'autorise à vous pouvoir ouvrir mon cœur, je ne feindrai point de vous dire que le hasard nous a fait connaître il y a six jours, et que la demande qu'on vous a faite est un effet de l'inclination que, dès cette première vue, nous avons prise l'un pour l'autre.

ARGAN. – Ils ne m'ont pas dit cela ; mais j'en suis bien aise, et c'est tant mieux que les choses soient de la sorte. Ils disent que c'est un grand jeune garçon bien fait.

ANGÉLIQUE. – Oui, mon père.

ARGAN. – De belle taille.

ANGÉLIQUE. – Sans doute.

ARGAN. – Agréable de sa personne.

ANGÉLIQUE. – Assurément.

ARGAN. – De bonne physionomie.

ANGÉLIQUE. – Très bonne.

ARGAN. – Sage, et bien né.

ANGÉLIQUE. – Tout à fait.

ARGAN. – Fort honnête.

ANGÉLIQUE. – Le plus honnête du monde.

ARGAN. – Qui parle bien latin et grec.

ANGÉLIQUE. – C'est ce que je ne sais pas.

ARGAN. – Et qui sera reçu médecin dans trois jours.

ANGÉLIQUE. – Lui, mon père ?

ARGAN. – Oui. Est-ce qu'il ne te l'a pas dit ?

ANGÉLIQUE. – Non vraiment. Qui vous l'a dit à vous ?

ARGAN. – Monsieur Purgon.

ANGÉLIQUE. – Est-ce que Monsieur Purgon le connaît ?

ARGAN. – La belle demande ! il faut bien qu'il le connaisse, puisque c'est son neveu.

ANGÉLIQUE. – Cléante, neveu de Monsieur Purgon ?

ARGAN. – Quel Cléante ? Nous parlons de celui pour qui l'on t'a demandée en mariage.

ANGÉLIQUE. – Hé ! oui.

ARGAN. – Hé bien, c'est le neveu de Monsieur Purgon qui est le fils de son beau-frère le médecin, Monsieur Diafoirus ; et ce fils s'appelle Thomas Diafoirus, et non pas Cléante ; et nous avons conclu ce mariage-là ce matin, Monsieur Purgon, Monsieur Fleurant et moi, et demain ce gendre prétendu doit m'être amené par son père. Qu'est-ce ? Vous voilà tout ébaubie ?

ANGÉLIQUE. – C'est, mon père, que je connais que vous avez parlé d'une personne, et que j'ai entendu une autre.

TOINETTE. – Quoi ! Monsieur, vous auriez fait ce dessein burlesque ? Et avec tout le bien que vous avez, vous voudriez marier votre fille avec un médecin ?

ARGAN. – Oui. De quoi te mêles-tu, coquine, impudente que tu es ?

TOINETTE. – Mon Dieu ! tout doux. Vous allez d'abord aux invectives. Est-ce que nous ne pouvons pas raisonner ensemble sans nous emporter ? Là, parlons de sang-froid. Quelle est votre raison, s'il vous plaît, pour un tel mariage ?

ARGAN. – Ma raison est que, me voyant infirme et malade comme je suis, je veux me faire un gendre et des alliés médecins, afin de m'appuyer de bons secours contre ma maladie, d'avoir dans ma famille les sources des remèdes qui me sont nécessaires, et d'être à même des consultations et des ordonnances.

TOINETTE. – Hé bien ! voilà dire une raison, et il y a plaisir à se répondre doucement les uns aux autres. Mais, Monsieur, mettez la main à la conscience. Est-ce que vous êtes malade ?

ARGAN. – Comment, coquine, si je suis malade ? si je suis malade, impudente ?

*→ moquerie*

TOINETTE. – Hé bien ! oui, Monsieur, vous êtes malade, n'ayons point de querelle là-dessus. Oui, vous êtes fort malade, j'en demeure d'accord, et plus malade que vous ne pensez. Voilà qui est fait. Mais votre fille doit épouser un mari pour elle ; et, n'étant point malade, il n'est pas nécessaire de lui donner un médecin.

ARGAN. – C'est pour moi que je lui donne ce médecin ; et une fille de bon naturel doit être ravie d'épouser ce qui est utile à la santé de son père.

TOINETTE. – Ma foi ! Monsieur, voulez-vous qu'en amie je vous donne un conseil ?

ARGAN. – Quel est-il, ce conseil ?

TOINETTE. – De ne point songer à ce mariage-là.

ARGAN. – Hé, la raison ?

TOINETTE. – La raison ? C'est que votre fille n'y consentira point.

ARGAN. – Elle n'y consentira point ?

TOINETTE. – Non.

ARGAN. – Ma fille ?

TOINETTE. – Votre fille. Elle vous dira qu'elle n'a que faire de Monsieur Diafoirus, ni de son fils Thomas Diafoirus, ni de tous les Diafoirus du monde.

ARGAN. – J'en ai affaire, moi, outre que le parti est plus avantageux qu'on ne pense. Monsieur Diafoirus n'a que ce fils-là pour tout héritier ; et, de plus, Monsieur Purgon, qui n'a ni femme, ni enfants, lui donne tout son bien, en faveur de ce mariage ; et Monsieur Purgon est un homme qui a huit mille bonnes livres de rente.

TOINETTE. – Il faut qu'il ait tué bien des gens, pour s'être fait si riche. *C'est un docteur*

ARGAN. – Huit mille livres de rente sont quelque chose, sans compter le bien du père.

TOINETTE. – Monsieur, tout cela est bel et bon ; mais j'en reviens toujours là. Je vous conseille, entre nous, de lui choisir un autre mari, et elle n'est point faite pour être Madame Diafoirus.

ARGAN. – Et je veux, moi, que cela soit.

TOINETTE. – Eh fi ! ne dites pas cela.

ARGAN. – Comment, que je ne dise pas cela ?

TOINETTE. – Hé non !

ARGAN. – Et pourquoi ne le dirai-je pas ?

TOINETTE. – On dira que vous ne songez pas à ce que vous dites.

ARGAN. – On dira ce qu'on voudra ; mais je vous dis que je veux qu'elle exécute la parole que j'ai donnée.

TOINETTE. – Non : je suis sûre qu'elle ne le fera pas.

ARGAN. – Je l'y forcerai bien.

TOINETTE. – Elle ne le fera pas, vous dis-je.

ARGAN. – Elle le fera, ou je la mettrai dans un couvent.

TOINETTE. – Vous ?

ARGAN. – Moi.

TOINETTE. – Bon !

ARGAN. – Comment, « bon » ?

TOINETTE. – Vous ne la mettrez point dans un couvent.

ARGAN. – Je ne la mettrai point dans un couvent ?

TOINETTE. – Non.

ARGAN. – Non ?

TOINETTE. – Non.

ARGAN. – Ouais ! voici qui est plaisant. Je ne mettrai pas ma fille dans un couvent, si je veux ?

TOINETTE. – Non, vous dis-je.

ARGAN. – Qui m'en empêchera ?

TOINETTE. – Vous-même.

ARGAN. – Moi ?

TOINETTE. – Oui, vous n'aurez pas ce cœur-là.

ARGAN. – Je l'aurai.

TOINETTE. – Vous vous moquez.

ARGAN. – Je ne me moque point.

TOINETTE. – La tendresse paternelle vous prendra.

ARGAN. – Elle ne me prendra point.

TOINETTE. – Une petite larme ou deux, des bras jetés au cou, un « mon petit papa mignon », prononcé tendrement, sera assez pour vous toucher.

ARGAN. – Tout cela ne fera rien.

TOINETTE. – Oui, oui.

ARGAN. – Je vous dis que je n'en démordrai point.

TOINETTE. – Bagatelles.

ARGAN. – Il ne faut point dire « bagatelles ».

TOINETTE. – Mon Dieu ! je vous connais, vous êtes bon naturellement.

ARGAN, *avec emportement*. – Je ne suis point bon, et je suis méchant quand je veux.

TOINETTE. – Doucement, Monsieur, vous ne songez pas que vous êtes malade.

ARGAN. – Je lui commande absolument de se préparer à prendre le mari que je dis.

TOINETTE. – Et moi, je lui défends absolument d'en faire rien.

ARGAN. – Où est-ce donc que nous sommes ? et quelle audace

est-ce là à une coquine de servante de parler de la sorte devant son maître ?

TOINETTE. – Quand un maître ne songe pas à ce qu'il fait, une servante bien sensée est en droit de le redresser.

ARGAN *court après Toinette.* – Ah ! insolente, il faut que je t'assomme.

TOINETTE *se sauve de lui.* – Il est de mon devoir de m'opposer aux choses qui vous peuvent déshonorer.

ARGAN, *en colère, court après elle autour de sa chaise, son bâton à la main.* – Viens, viens, que je t'apprenne à parler.

TOINETTE, *courant, et se sauvant du côté de la chaise où n'est pas Argan.* – Je m'intéresse, comme je dois, à ne vous point laisser faire de folie.

ARGAN. – Chienne !

TOINETTE. – Non, je ne consentirai jamais à ce mariage.

ARGAN. – Pendarde !

TOINETTE. – Je ne veux point qu'elle épouse votre Thomas Diafoirus.

ARGAN. – Carogne ! →

TOINETTE. – Et elle m'obéira plutôt qu'à vous.

ARGAN. – Angélique, tu ne veux pas m'arrêter cette coquine-là ?

ANGÉLIQUE. – Eh ! mon père, ne vous faites point malade.

ARGAN. – Si tu ne me l'arrêtes, je te donnerai ma malédiction.

TOINETTE. – Et moi, je la déshériterai, si elle vous obéit.

ARGAN *se jette dans sa chaise, étant las de courir après elle.* – Ah ! ah ! je n'en puis plus. Voilà pour me faire mourir.

## Scène VI

*Béline, Angélique, Toinette, Argan*

ARGAN. – Ah ! ma femme, approchez.

BÉLINE. – Qu'avez-vous, mon pauvre mari ?

ARGAN. – Venez-vous-en ici à mon secours.

BÉLINE. – Qu'est-ce que c'est donc qu'il y a, mon petit fils ?

ARGAN. – Mamie.

BÉLINE. – Mon ami.

ARGAN. – On vient de me mettre en colère !

BÉLINE. – Hélas ! pauvre petit mari. Comment donc, mon ami ?

ARGAN. – Votre coquine de Toinette est devenue plus insolente que jamais.

BÉLINE. – Ne vous passionnez donc point.

ARGAN. – Elle m'a fait enrager, mamie.

BÉLINE. – Doucement, mon fils.

ARGAN. – Elle a contrecarré, une heure durant, les choses que je veux faire.

BÉLINE. – Là, là, tout doux.

ARGAN. – Et a eu l'effronterie de me dire que je ne suis point malade.

BÉLINE. – C'est une impertinente.

ARGAN. – Vous savez, mon cœur, ce qui en est.

BÉLINE. – Oui, mon cœur, elle a tort.

ARGAN. – Mamour, cette coquine-là me fera mourir.

BÉLINE. – Eh là, eh là !

ARGAN. – Elle est cause de toute la bile que je fais.

BÉLINE. – Ne vous fâchez point tant.

ARGAN. – Et il y a je ne sais combien que je vous dis de me la chasser.

BÉLINE. – Mon Dieu ! mon fils, il n'y a point de serviteurs et de servantes qui n'aient leurs défauts. On est contraint parfois de souffrir leurs mauvaises qualités à cause des bonnes. Celle-ci est adroite, soigneuse, diligente, et surtout fidèle ; et vous savez qu'il faut maintenant de grandes précautions pour les gens que l'on prend. Holà ! Toinette !

TOINETTE. – Madame.

BÉLINE. – Pourquoi donc est-ce que vous mettez mon mari en colère ?

TOINETTE, *d'un ton doucereux*. – Moi, Madame ? Hélas ! Je ne sais pas ce que vous me voulez dire, et je ne songe qu'à complaire à Monsieur en toutes choses.

ARGAN. – Ah ! la traîtresse !

TOINETTE. – Il nous a dit qu'il voulait donner sa fille en mariage au fils de Monsieur Diafoirus ; je lui ai répondu que je trouvais le parti avantageux pour elle, mais que je croyais qu'il ferait mieux de la mettre dans un couvent.

BÉLINE. – Il n'y a pas grand mal à cela, et je trouve qu'elle a raison.

ARGAN. – Ah ! mamour, vous la croyez. C'est une scélérate ; elle m'a dit cent insolences.

BÉLINE. – Hé bien ! je vous crois, mon ami. Là, remettez-vous. Écoutez, Toinette, si vous fâchez jamais mon mari, je vous mettrai dehors. Çà, donnez-moi son manteau fourré et des oreillers, que je l'accommode dans sa chaise. Vous voilà je ne sais comment. Enfoncez bien votre bonnet jusque sur vos oreilles ; il n'y a rien qui enrhume tant que de prendre l'air par les oreilles.

ARGAN. – Ah ! mamie, que je vous suis obligé de tous les soins que vous prenez de moi !

BÉLINE, *accommodant les oreillers qu'elle met autour d'Argan.* – Levez-vous, que je mette ceci sous vous. Mettons celui-ci pour vous appuyer, et celui-là de l'autre côté. Mettons celui-ci derrière votre dos, et cet autre-là pour soutenir votre tête.

TOINETTE, *lui mettant rudement un oreiller sur la tête, et puis fuyant.* – Et celui-ci pour vous garder du serein.

ARGAN *se lève en colère, et jette tous les oreillers à Toinette.* – Ah ! coquine, tu veux m'étouffer.

BÉLINE. – Eh là, eh là ! Qu'est-ce que c'est donc ?

ARGAN, *tout essoufflé, se jette dans sa chaise.* – Ah, ah, ah ! je n'en puis plus.

BÉLINE. – Pourquoi vous emporter ainsi ? Elle a cru faire bien.

ARGAN. – Vous ne connaissez pas, mamour, la malice de la pendarde. Ah ! elle m'a mis tout hors de moi ; et il faudra plus de huit médecines et de douze lavements, pour réparer tout ceci.

BÉLINE. – Là, là, mon petit ami, apaisez-vous un peu.

ARGAN. – Mamie, vous êtes toute ma consolation.

BÉLINE. – Pauvre petit fils !

ARGAN. – Pour tâcher de reconnaître l'amour que vous me portez, je veux, mon cœur, comme je vous ai dit, faire mon testament.

BÉLINE. – Ah ! mon ami, ne parlons point de cela, je vous prie. Je ne saurais souffrir cette pensée ; et le seul mot de testament me fait tressaillir de douleur.

ARGAN. – Je vous avais dit de parler pour cela à votre notaire.

BÉLINE. – Le voilà là-dedans, que j'ai amené avec moi.

ARGAN. – Faites-le donc entrer, mamour.

BÉLINE. – Hélas ! mon ami, quand on aime bien un mari, on n'est guère en état de songer à tout cela.

## Scène VII

*Le Notaire, Béline, Argan*

ARGAN. – Approchez, Monsieur de Bonnefoy, approchez. Prenez un siège, s'il vous plaît. Ma femme m'a dit, Monsieur, que vous étiez fort honnête homme, et tout à fait de ses amis ; et je l'ai chargée de vous parler pour un testament que je veux faire.

BÉLINE. – Hélas ! je ne suis point capable de parler de ces choses-là.

LE NOTAIRE. – Elle m'a, Monsieur, expliqué vos intentions et le dessein où vous êtes pour elle ; et j'ai à vous dire là-dessus que vous ne sauriez rien donner à votre femme par votre testament.

ARGAN. – Mais pourquoi ?

LE NOTAIRE. – La coutume y résiste. Si vous étiez en pays de droit écrit, cela se pourrait faire ; mais à Paris et dans les pays coutumiers, au moins dans la plupart, c'est ce qui ne se peut, et la disposition serait nulle. Tout l'avantage qu'homme et femme conjoints par mariage se peuvent faire l'un à l'autre, c'est un don mutuel entre-vifs ; encore faut-il qu'il n'y ait enfants, soit des deux conjoints, ou de l'un d'eux, lors du décès du premier mourant.

ARGAN. – Voilà une coutume bien impertinente, qu'un mari ne puisse rien laisser à une femme dont il est aimé tendrement, et qui prend de lui tant de soin. J'aurais envie de consulter mon avocat pour voir comment je pourrais faire.

LE NOTAIRE. – Ce n'est point à des avocats qu'il faut aller, car ils sont d'ordinaire sévères là-dessus, et s'imaginent que c'est un grand crime que de disposer en fraude de la loi. Ce sont gens de difficultés, et qui sont ignorants des détours de la conscience. Il y a d'autres personnes à consulter, qui sont bien plus accommodantes ; qui ont des expédients pour passer doucement par-dessus la loi, et rendre juste ce qui n'est pas permis ; qui savent aplanir les difficultés d'une affaire, et trouver des moyens d'éluder la coutume par quelque avantage indirect. Sans cela, où en serions-nous tous les jours ? Il faut de la facilité dans les choses ; autrement nous ne ferions rien, et je ne donnerais pas un sou de notre métier.

ARGAN. – Ma femme m'avait bien dit, Monsieur, que vous étiez fort habile, et fort honnête homme. Comment puis-je faire, s'il vous plaît, pour lui donner mon bien, et en frustrer mes enfants ?

LE NOTAIRE. – Comment vous pouvez faire ? Vous pouvez choisir doucement un ami intime de votre femme, auquel vous donnerez en bonne forme par votre testament tout ce que vous pouvez ; et cet ami ensuite lui rendra tout. Vous pouvez encore contracter un grand nombre d'obligations, non suspectes, au profit de divers créanciers, qui prêteront leur nom à votre femme, et entre les mains de laquelle ils mettront leur déclaration que ce qu'ils en ont fait n'a été que pour lui faire plaisir. Vous pouvez aussi, pendant que vous êtes en vie, mettre entre ses mains de l'argent comptant, ou des billets que vous pourrez avoir, payables au porteur.

BÉLINE. – Mon Dieu ! il ne faut point vous tourmenter de tout cela. S'il vient faute de vous, mon fils, je ne veux plus rester au monde.

ARGAN. – Mamie !

BÉLINE. – Oui, mon ami, si je suis assez malheureuse pour vous perdre...

ARGAN. – Ma chère femme !

BÉLINE. – La vie ne me sera plus de rien.

ARGAN. – Mamour !

BÉLINE. – Et je suivrai vos pas, pour vous faire connaître la tendresse que j'ai pour vous.

ARGAN. – Mamie, vous me fendez le cœur. Consolez-vous, je vous en prie.

LE NOTAIRE. – Ces larmes sont hors de saison, et les choses n'en sont point encore là.

BÉLINE. – Ah ! Monsieur, vous ne savez pas ce que c'est qu'un mari qu'on aime tendrement.

ARGAN. – Tout le regret que j'aurai, si je meurs, mamie, c'est de n'avoir point un enfant de vous. Monsieur Purgon m'avait dit qu'il m'en ferait faire un.

LE NOTAIRE. – Cela pourra venir encore.

ARGAN. – Il faut faire mon testament, mamour, de la façon que Monsieur dit ; mais, par précaution, je veux vous mettre entre les mains vingt mille francs en or, que j'ai dans le lambris de mon alcôve, et deux billets payables au porteur, qui me sont dus, l'un par Monsieur Damon, et l'autre par Monsieur Gérante.

BÉLINE. – Non, non, je ne veux point de tout cela. Ah ! combien dites-vous qu'il y a dans votre alcôve ?

ARGAN. – Vingt mille francs, mamour.

BÉLINE. – Ne me parlez point de bien, je vous prie. Ah ! de combien sont les deux billets ?

ARGAN. – Ils sont, mamie, l'un de quatre mille francs, et l'autre de six.

BÉLINE. – Tous les biens du monde, mon ami, ne me sont rien au prix de vous.

LE NOTAIRE. – Voulez-vous que nous procédions au testament ?

ARGAN. – Oui, Monsieur, mais nous serons mieux dans mon petit cabinet. Mamour, conduisez-moi, je vous prie.

BÉLINE. – Allons, mon pauvre petit fils.


### Scène VIII

*Angélique, Toinette*


TOINETTE. – Les voilà avec un notaire, et j'ai ouï parler de testament. Votre belle-mère ne s'endort point, et c'est sans doute quelque conspiration contre vos intérêts où elle pousse votre père.

Angélique. – Qu'il dispose de son bien à sa fantaisie, pourvu qu'il ne dispose point de mon cœur. Tu vois, Toinette, les desseins violents que l'on fait sur lui. Ne m'abandonne point, je te prie, dans l'extrémité où je suis.

Toinette. – Moi, vous abandonner ? j'aimerais mieux mourir. Votre belle-mère a beau me faire sa confidente, et me vouloir jeter dans ses intérêts, je n'ai jamais pu avoir d'inclination pour elle, et j'ai toujours été de votre parti. Laissez-moi faire, j'emploierai toute chose pour vous servir ; mais pour vous servir avec plus d'effet, je veux changer de batterie, couvrir le zèle que j'ai pour vous, et feindre d'entrer dans les sentiments de votre père et de votre belle-mère.

Angélique. – Tâche, je t'en conjure, de faire donner avis à Cléante du mariage qu'on a conclu.

Toinette. – Je n'ai personne à employer à cet office que le vieux usurier Polichinelle, mon amant, et il m'en coûtera pour cela quelques paroles de douceur, que je veux bien dépenser pour vous. Pour aujourd'hui il est trop tard ; mais demain, du grand matin, je l'enverrai quérir, et il sera ravi de...

Béline. – Toinette !

Toinette, *à Angélique*. – Voilà qu'on m'appelle. Bonsoir. Reposez-vous sur moi.


*Le théâtre change et représente une ville.*

# PREMIER INTERMÈDE

*Polichinelle, dans la nuit, vient pour donner une sérénade à sa maî-
tresse. Il est interrompu d'abord par des violons, contre lesquels il se met
en colère, et ensuite par le guet, composé de musiciens et de danseurs.*

### POLICHINELLE

*Ô amour, amour, amour, amour ! Pauvre Polichinelle, quelle diable
de fantaisie t'es-tu allé mettre dans la cervelle ? À quoi t'amuses-tu,
misérable insensé que tu es ? Tu quittes le soin de ton négoce, et tu
laisses aller tes affaires à l'abandon. Tu ne manges plus, tu ne bois
presque plus, tu perds le repos de la nuit ; et tout cela pour qui ? Pour
une dragonne, franche dragonne, une diablesse qui te rembarre, et se
moque de tout ce que tu peux lui dire. Mais il n'y a point à raisonner
là-dessus : tu le veux, amour ; il faut être fou comme beaucoup
d'autres. Cela n'est pas le mieux du monde à un homme de mon âge ;
mais qu'y faire ? On n'est pas sage quand on veut, et les vieilles cer-
velles se démontent comme les jeunes. Je viens voir si je ne pourrai
point adoucir ma tigresse par une sérénade. Il n'y a rien parfois qui
soit si touchant qu'un amant qui vient chanter ses doléances aux
gonds et aux verrous de la porte de sa maîtresse. Voici de quoi accom-
pagner ma voix. Ô nuit ! ô chère nuit ! porte mes plaintes amoureuses
jusque dans le lit de mon inflexible.*

*Il chante ces paroles :*

|  | [TRADUCTION] |
|---|---|
| *Notte e dì v'amo e v'adoro.* | *Nuit et jour, je vous aime et* |
| | *[vous adore.* |
| 20 *Cerco un sì per mio ristoro ;* | *Je demande un oui pour mon* |
| | *[réconfort ;* |

| | |
|---|---|
| *Ma se voi dite di no,* | *Mais si vous dites un non,* |
| *Bell' ingrata, io morirò.* | *Belle ingrate, je mourrai.* |
| | |
| *Fra la speranza* | *Au sein de l'espérance,* |
| *S'afflige il cuore,* | *Le cœur s'afflige,* |
| *In lontananza* | *Dans l'absence,* |
| *Consuma l'hore ;* | *Il consume tristement les heures.* |
| *Si dolce inganno* | *Ah ! la douce illusion* |
| *Che mi figura* | *Qui me fait apercevoir* |
| *Breve l'affanno* | *La fin prochaine de mon tourment* |
| *Ahi ! troppo dura !* | *Dure trop longtemps.* |
| *Cosi per tropp'amar languisco* | *Pour trop vous aimer,* |
| *[e muoro.* | *[je languis, je meurs.* |
| | |
| *Notte e dì v'amo e v'adoro,* | *Nuit et jour, je vous aime et* |
| | *[vous adore.* |
| *Cerco un sì per mio ristoro ;* | *Je demande un oui pour mon* |
| | *[réconfort ;* |
| *Ma se voi dite di no,* | *Mais si vous dites un non,* |
| *Bell' ingrata, io morirò.* | *Belle ingrate, je mourrai.* |
| | |
| *Se non dormite,* | *Si vous ne dormez pas,* |
| *Almen pensate* | *Au moins pensez* |
| *Alle ferite* | *Aux blessures* |
| *Ch'al cuor mi fate ;* | *Que vous faites à mon cœur ;* |
| *Deh ! almen fingete,* | *Si vous me faites périr, ah !* |
| *Per mio conforto,* | *Pour ma consolation,* |
| *Se m'uccidete,* | *Feignez au moins* |
| *D'haver il torto :* | *De vous le reprocher ;* |
| *Vostra pietà mi scemerà il* | *Votre pitié diminuera mon* |
| *[martoro.* | *[martyre.* |
| | |
| *Notte e dì v'amo e v'adoro.* | *Nuit et jour, je vous aime et* |
| | *[vous adore.* |
| *Cerco un sì per mio ristoro ;* | *Je demande un oui pour mon* |
| | *[réconfort ;* |
| *Ma se voi dite di no,* | *Mais si vous dites un non,* |
| *Bell' ingrata, io morirò.* | *Belle ingrate, je mourrai.* |

UNE VIEILLE *se présente à la fenêtre,*
*et répond au signor Polichinelle en se moquant de lui.*

*Zerbinetti, ch'ogn' hor con*
    *[finti sguardi,*

50  *Mentiti desiri,*
    *Fallaci sospiri,*
    *Accenti bugiardi,*
    *Di fede vi pregiate,*
    *Ah ! che non m'ingannate,*
55  *Che già so per prova*
    *Ch'in voi non si trova*
    *Constanza ne fede ;*
    *Oh ! quanto è pazza colei che*
        *[vi crede !*

    *Quei sguardi languidi*
60  *Non m'innamorano,*
    *Quei sospir fervidi*
    *Più non m'infiammano ;*
    *Vel giuro a fè.*
    *Zerbino misero,*
65  *Del vostro piangere*
    *Il mio cor libero*
    *Vuol sempre ridere.*
    *Credet' a me*
    *Che già so per prova*
70  *Ch' in voi non si trova*
    *Constanza ne fede ;*
    *Oh ! quanto è pazza colei che*
        *[vi crede !*

*Petits galants, qui à chaque*
    *[instant avec des regards*
        *[trompeurs,*
*Des désirs mensongers,*
*Des soupirs fallacieux,*
*Et des serments perfides,*
*Vous vantez d'être fidèles ;*
*Ah ! vous ne me trompez plus.*
*Je sais par expérience,*
*Qu'on ne trouve en vous*
*Ni constance ni foi ;*
*Oh ! combien est folle celle qui*
        *[vous croit !*

*Ces regards languissants*
*Ne m'attendrissent plus ;*
*Ces soupirs brûlants*
*Ne m'enflamment plus ;*
*Je vous le jure sur ma foi.*
*Pauvre galant,*
*Mon cœur rendu à la liberté*
*Veut toujours rire de vos*
        *[plaintes.*
*Croyez-moi,*
*Je sais par expérience,*
*Qu'on ne trouve en vous*
*Ni constance ni foi ;*
*Oh ! combien est folle celle qui*
        *[vous croit !*

VIOLONS

POLICHINELLE

*Quelle impertinente harmonie vient interrompre ici ma voix ?*

VIOLONS

POLICHINELLE

*Paix là ! taisez-vous, violons. Laissez-moi me plaindre à mon aise
des cruautés de mon inexorable.*

VIOLONS

POLICHINELLE

*Taisez-vous, vous dis-je. C'est moi qui veux chanter.*

VIOLONS

POLICHINELLE

*Paix donc !*

VIOLONS

POLICHINELLE

*Ouais !*

VIOLONS

POLICHINELLE

*Ahi !*

VIOLONS

POLICHINELLE

*Est-ce pour rire ?*

VIOLONS

POLICHINELLE

*Ah ! que de bruit !*

VIOLONS

POLICHINELLE

*Le diable vous emporte !*

VIOLONS

POLICHINELLE

J'enrage !

VIOLONS

POLICHINELLE

Vous ne vous tairez pas ? Ah, Dieu soit loué !

VIOLONS

POLICHINELLE

Encore ?

VIOLONS

POLICHINELLE

Peste des violons !

VIOLONS

POLICHINELLE

La sotte musique que voilà !

VIOLONS

POLICHINELLE

La, la, la, la, la, la.

VIOLONS

POLICHINELLE

La, la, la, la, la, la.

VIOLONS

POLICHINELLE

La, la, la, la, la, la, la, la.

VIOLONS

POLICHINELLE

*La, la, la, la, la.*

VIOLONS

POLICHINELLE

*La, la, la, la, la, la.*

VIOLONS

POLICHINELLE

*Par ma foi ! cela me divertit. Poursuivez, Messieurs les Violons, vous me ferez plaisir. Allons donc, continuez, je vous en prie. Voilà le moyen de les faire taire. La musique est accoutumée à ne point faire ce qu'on veut. Ho ! sus à nous ! Avant que de chanter, il faut que je prélude un peu, et joue quelque pièce, afin de mieux prendre mon ton. Plan, plan, plan. Plin, plin, plin. Voilà un temps fâcheux pour mettre un luth d'accord. Plin, plin, plin. Plin tan plan. Plin, plin. Les cordes ne tiennent point par ce temps-là. Plin, plan. J'entends du bruit, mettons mon luth contre la porte.*

ARCHERS

*Qui va là, qui va là ?*

POLICHINELLE

*Qui diable est-ce là ? Est-ce que c'est la mode de parler en musique ?*

ARCHERS

*Qui va là, qui va là, qui va là ?*

POLICHINELLE

*Moi, moi, moi.*

ARCHERS

*Qui va là, qui va là ? vous dis-je.*

POLICHINELLE

*Moi, moi, vous dis-je.*

ARCHERS

*Et qui toi ? et qui toi ?*

POLICHINELLE

*Moi, moi, moi, moi, moi, moi.*

ARCHERS

*Dis ton nom, dis ton nom, sans davantage attendre.*

POLICHINELLE

*Mon nom est : « Va te faire pendre. »*

ARCHERS

*Ici, camarades, ici.*
*Saisissons l'insolent qui nous répond ainsi.*

## Entrée de ballet

*Tout le guet vient, qui cherche Polichinelle dans la nuit.*

VIOLONS ET DANSEURS

POLICHINELLE

*Qui va là ?*

VIOLONS ET DANSEURS

POLICHINELLE

*Qui sont les coquins que j'entends ?*

VIOLONS ET DANSEURS

POLICHINELLE

*Euh ?*

VIOLONS ET DANSEURS

POLICHINELLE

*Holà ! mes laquais, mes gens !*

VIOLONS ET DANSEURS

POLICHINELLE

*Par la mort !*

VIOLONS ET DANSEURS

POLICHINELLE

*Par le sang !*

VIOLONS ET DANSEURS

POLICHINELLE

*J'en jetterai par terre.*

VIOLONS ET DANSEURS

POLICHINELLE

*Champagne, Poitevin, Picard, Basque, Breton !*

VIOLONS ET DANSEURS

POLICHINELLE

*Donnez-moi mon mousqueton.*

VIOLONS ET DANSEURS

POLICHINELLE, *faisant semblant de tirer un coup de pistolet.*
*Poue !*

*Ils tombent tous et s'enfuient.*

POLICHINELLE

*Ah ! ah ! ah ! ah ! comme je leur ai donné l'épouvante ! Voilà de
sottes gens d'avoir peur de moi, qui ai peur des autres. Ma foi ! il
n'est que de jouer d'adresse en ce monde. Si je n'avais tranché du*

*grand seigneur, et n'avais fait le brave, ils n'auraient pas manqué de me happer. Ah ! ah ! ah !*

ARCHERS

*Nous le tenons. À nous, camarades, à nous !*
*Dépêchez, de la lumière.*

## Ballet

*Tout le guet vient avec des lanternes.*

ARCHERS

*Ah, traître ! ah, fripon ! c'est donc vous ?*
*Faquin, maraud, pendard, impudent, téméraire,*
*Insolent, effronté, coquin, filou, voleur !*
*Vous osez nous faire peur ?*

POLICHINELLE

*Messieurs, c'est que j'étais ivre.*

ARCHERS

*Non, non, non, point de raison :*
*Il faut vous apprendre à vivre.*
*En prison, vite, en prison.*

POLICHINELLE

*Messieurs, je ne suis point voleur.*

ARCHERS

*En prison.*

POLICHINELLE

*Je suis un bourgeois de la ville.*

ARCHERS

*En prison.*

POLICHINELLE

*Qu'ai-je fait ?*

ARCHERS

*En prison, vite, en prison.*

POLICHINELLE

*Messieurs, laissez-moi aller.*

ARCHERS

*Non.*

POLICHINELLE

*Je vous prie.*

ARCHERS

*Non.*

POLICHINELLE

*Eh !*

ARCHERS

*Non.*

POLICHINELLE

*De grâce.*

ARCHERS

*Non, non.*

POLICHINELLE

*Messieurs.*

ARCHERS

*Non, non, non.*

POLICHINELLE

*S'il vous plaît.*

ARCHERS

*Non, non.*

POLICHINELLE

*Par charité.*

ARCHERS

*Non, non.*

POLICHINELLE

*Au nom du Ciel !*

ARCHERS

*Non, non.*

POLICHINELLE

*Miséricorde !*

ARCHERS

*Non, non, non, point de raison :*
*Il faut vous apprendre à vivre.*
*En prison, vite, en prison.*

POLICHINELLE

*Hé ! n'est-il rien, Messieurs, qui soit capable d'attendrir vos âmes ?*

ARCHERS

*Il est aisé de nous toucher,*
*Et nous sommes humains plus qu'on ne saurait croire :*
*Donnez-nous doucement six pistoles pour boire,*
170 *Nous allons vous lâcher.*

POLICHINELLE

*Hélas ! Messieurs, je vous assure que je n'ai pas un sou sur moi.*

ARCHERS

*Au défaut de six pistoles,*
*Choisissez donc sans façon*

D'avoir trente croquignoles
Ou douze coups de bâton.

75

POLICHINELLE

Si c'est une nécessité, et qu'il faille en passer par là, je choisis les croquignoles.

ARCHERS

Allons, préparez-vous,
Et comptez bien les coups.

**Ballet**

Les Archers danseurs lui donnent des croquignoles en cadence.

POLICHINELLE

Un et deux, trois et quatre, cinq et six, sept et huit, neuf et dix, onze et douze, et treize, et quatorze, et quinze.

ARCHERS

Ah, ah ! vous en voulez passer :
Allons, c'est à recommencer.

POLICHINELLE

Ah ! Messieurs, ma pauvre tête n'en peut plus, et vous venez de me la rendre comme une pomme cuite. J'aime mieux encore les coups de bâton que de recommencer.

ARCHERS

Soit ! puisque le bâton est pour vous plus charmant,
Vous aurez contentement.

**Ballet**

Les Archers danseurs lui donnent des coups de bâton en cadence.

POLICHINELLE

*Un, deux, trois, quatre, cinq, six, ah ! ah ! ah ! je n'y saurais plus résister. Tenez, Messieurs, voilà six pistoles que je vous donne.*

ARCHERS

*Ah, l'honnête homme ! Ah, l'âme noble et belle !*
*Adieu, Seigneur, adieu, Seigneur Polichinelle.*

POLICHINELLE

*Messieurs, je vous donne le bonsoir.*

ARCHERS

*Adieu, Seigneur, adieu, Seigneur Polichinelle.*

POLICHINELLE

*Votre serviteur.*

ARCHERS

*Adieu, Seigneur, adieu, Seigneur Polichinelle.*

POLICHINELLE

*Très humble valet.*

ARCHERS

*Adieu, Seigneur, adieu, Seigneur Polichinelle.*

POLICHINELLE

*Jusqu'au revoir.*

**Ballet**

*Ils dansent tous, en réjouissance de l'argent qu'ils ont reçu.*
*Le théâtre change et représente la même chambre.*

# ACTE II

## Scène première

*Toinette, Cléante*

TOINETTE. – Que demandez-vous, Monsieur ?

CLÉANTE. – Ce que je demande ?

TOINETTE. – Ah, ah, c'est vous ? Quelle surprise ! Que venez-vous faire céans ?

CLÉANTE. – Savoir ma destinée, parler à l'aimable Angélique, consulter les sentiments de son cœur, et lui demander ses résolutions sur ce mariage fatal dont on m'a averti.

TOINETTE. – Oui, mais on ne parle pas comme cela de but en blanc à Angélique. Il faut des mystères, et l'on vous a dit l'étroite garde où elle est retenue, qu'on ne la laisse ni sortir, ni parler à personne, et que ce ne fut que la curiosité d'une vieille tante qui nous fit accorder la liberté d'aller à cette comédie qui donna lieu à la naissance de votre passion ; et nous nous sommes bien gardées de parler de cette aventure.

CLÉANTE. – Aussi ne viens-je pas ici comme Cléante et sous l'apparence de son amant, mais comme ami de son maître de musique, dont j'ai obtenu le pouvoir de dire qu'il m'envoie à sa place.

TOINETTE. – Voici son père. Retirez-vous un peu, et me laissez lui dire que vous êtes là.

## Scène II

*Argan, Toinette, Cléante*

ARGAN. – Monsieur Purgon m'a dit de me promener le matin dans ma chambre, douze allées et douze venues ; mais j'ai oublié à lui demander si c'est en long, ou en large.

TOINETTE. – Monsieur, voilà un...

ARGAN. – Parle bas, pendarde ! tu viens m'ébranler tout le cerveau, et tu ne songes pas qu'il ne faut point parler si haut à des malades.

TOINETTE. – Je voulais vous dire, Monsieur...

ARGAN. – Parle bas, te dis-je.

TOINETTE. – Monsieur...

*Elle fait semblant de parler.*

ARGAN. – Eh ?

TOINETTE. – Je vous dis que...

*Elle fait semblant de parler.*

ARGAN. – Qu'est-ce que tu dis ?

TOINETTE, *haut.* – Je dis que voilà un homme qui veut parler à vous.

ARGAN. – Qu'il vienne.

*Toinette fait signe à Cléante d'avancer.*

CLÉANTE. – Monsieur...

TOINETTE, *raillant.* – Ne parlez pas si haut, de peur d'ébranler le cerveau de Monsieur.

CLÉANTE. – Monsieur, je suis ravi de vous trouver debout et de voir que vous vous portez mieux.

TOINETTE, *feignant d'être en colère.* – Comment « qu'il se porte mieux » ? Cela est faux : Monsieur se porte toujours mal.

CLÉANTE. – J'ai ouï dire que Monsieur était mieux, et je lui trouve bon visage.

TOINETTE. – Que voulez-vous dire avec votre bon visage ? Monsieur l'a fort mauvais, et ce sont des impertinents qui vous ont dit qu'il était mieux. Il ne s'est jamais si mal porté.

ARGAN. – Elle a raison.

TOINETTE. – Il marche, dort, mange, et boit tout comme les autres ; mais cela n'empêche pas qu'il ne soit fort malade.

ARGAN. – Cela est vrai.

CLÉANTE. – Monsieur, j'en suis au désespoir. Je viens de la part du maître à chanter de Mademoiselle votre fille. Il s'est vu obligé d'aller à la campagne pour quelques jours ; et comme son ami intime, il m'envoie à sa place, pour lui continuer ses leçons, de peur qu'en les interrompant elle ne vînt à oublier ce qu'elle sait déjà.

ARGAN. – Fort bien. Appelez Angélique.

TOINETTE. – Je crois, Monsieur, qu'il sera mieux de mener Monsieur à sa chambre.

ARGAN. – Non ; faites-la venir.

TOINETTE. – Il ne pourra lui donner leçon comme il faut, s'ils ne sont en particulier.

ARGAN. – Si fait, si fait.

TOINETTE. – Monsieur, cela ne fera que vous étourdir, et il ne faut rien pour vous émouvoir en l'état où vous êtes, et vous ébranler le cerveau.

ARGAN. – Point, point, j'aime la musique, et je serai bien aise de… Ah ! la voici. Allez-vous-en voir, vous, si ma femme est habillée.

## Scène III

*Argan, Angélique, Cléante*

ARGAN. – Venez, ma fille. Votre maître de musique est allé aux champs, et voilà une personne qu'il envoie à sa place pour vous montrer.

ANGÉLIQUE. – Ah, Ciel !

ARGAN. – Qu'est-ce ? D'où vient cette surprise ?

ANGÉLIQUE. – C'est...

ARGAN. – Quoi ! Qui vous émeut de la sorte ?

ANGÉLIQUE. – C'est, mon père, une aventure surprenante qui se rencontre ici.

ARGAN. – Comment ?

ANGÉLIQUE. – J'ai songé cette nuit que j'étais dans le plus grand embarras du monde, et qu'une personne faite tout comme Monsieur s'est présentée à moi, à qui j'ai demandé secours, et qui m'est venue tirer de la peine où j'étais ; et ma surprise a été grande de voir inopinément en arrivant ici ce que j'ai eu dans l'idée toute la nuit.

CLÉANTE. – Ce n'est pas être malheureux que d'occuper votre pensée, soit en dormant, soit en veillant, et mon bonheur serait grand sans doute, si vous étiez dans quelque peine dont vous me jugeassiez digne de vous tirer ; et il n'y a rien que je ne fisse pour...

## Scène IV

*Toinette, Cléante, Angélique, Argan*

TOINETTE, *par dérision.* – Ma foi, Monsieur, je suis pour vous maintenant, et je me dédis de tout ce que je disais hier. Voici Monsieur Diafoirus le père, et Monsieur Diafoirus le fils, qui viennent vous rendre visite. Que vous serez bien engendré ! Vous allez voir le garçon le mieux fait du monde et le plus spirituel. Il n'a dit que deux mots, qui m'ont ravie, et votre fille va être charmée de lui.

ARGAN, *à Cléante, qui feint de vouloir s'en aller.* – Ne vous en allez point, Monsieur. C'est que je marie ma fille ; et voilà qu'on lui amène son prétendu mari, qu'elle n'a point encore vu.

CLÉANTE. – C'est m'honorer beaucoup, Monsieur, de vouloir que je sois témoin d'une entrevue si agréable.

ARGAN. – C'est le fils d'un habile médecin, et le mariage se fera dans quatre jours.

CLÉANTE. – Fort bien.

ARGAN. – Mandez-le un peu à son maître de musique, afin qu'il se trouve à la noce.

CLÉANTE. – Je n'y manquerai pas.

ARGAN. – Je vous y prie aussi.

CLÉANTE. – Vous me faites beaucoup d'honneur.

TOINETTE. – Allons, qu'on se range, les voici.


### Scène v

*Monsieur Diafoirus, Thomas Diafoirus,*
*Argan, Angélique, Cléante, Toinette*

ARGAN, *mettant la main à son bonnet sans l'ôter.* – Monsieur Purgon, Monsieur, m'a défendu de découvrir ma tête. Vous êtes du métier, vous savez les conséquences.

MONSIEUR DIAFOIRUS. – Nous sommes dans toutes nos visites pour porter secours aux malades, et non pour leur porter de l'incommodité.

ARGAN. – Je reçois, Monsieur...

*Ils parlent tous deux en même temps, s'interrompent et confondent.*

MONSIEUR DIAFOIRUS. – Nous venons ici, Monsieur...

ARGAN. – Avec beaucoup de joie...

MONSIEUR DIAFOIRUS. – Mon fils Thomas, et moi...

ARGAN. – L'honneur que vous me faites...

MONSIEUR DIAFOIRUS. – Vous témoigner, Monsieur...

ARGAN. – Et j'aurais souhaité...

MONSIEUR DIAFOIRUS. – Le ravissement où nous sommes...

ARGAN. – De pouvoir aller chez vous...

MONSIEUR DIAFOIRUS. – De la grâce que vous nous faites...

ARGAN. – Pour vous en assurer...

MONSIEUR DIAFOIRUS. – De vouloir bien nous recevoir...

ARGAN. – Mais vous savez, Monsieur...

MONSIEUR DIAFOIRUS. – Dans l'honneur, Monsieur...

ARGAN. – Ce que c'est qu'un pauvre malade...

MONSIEUR DIAFOIRUS. – De votre alliance...

ARGAN. – Qui ne peut faire autre chose...

MONSIEUR DIAFOIRUS. – Et vous assurer...

ARGAN. – Que de vous dire ici...

MONSIEUR DIAFOIRUS. – Que dans les choses qui dépendront de notre métier...

ARGAN. – Qu'il cherchera toutes les occasions...

MONSIEUR DIAFOIRUS. – De même qu'en toute autre...

ARGAN. – De vous faire connaître, Monsieur...

MONSIEUR DIAFOIRUS. – Nous serons toujours prêts, Monsieur...

ARGAN. – Qu'il est tout à votre service...

MONSIEUR DIAFOIRUS. – À vous témoigner notre zèle. *(Il se retourne vers son fils et lui dit :)* Allons, Thomas, avancez. Faites vos compliments.

THOMAS DIAFOIRUS *est un grand benêt, nouvellement sorti des Écoles, qui fait toutes choses de mauvaise grâce et à contretemps.* – N'est-ce pas par le père qu'il convient commencer ?

MONSIEUR DIAFOIRUS. – Oui.

THOMAS DIAFOIRUS. – Monsieur, je viens saluer, reconnaître, chérir, et révérer en vous un second père ; mais un second père auquel j'ose dire que je me trouve plus redevable qu'au premier. Le premier m'a engendré, mais vous m'avez choisi. Il m'a reçu par nécessité, mais vous m'avez accepté par grâce. Ce que je tiens de lui est un ouvrage de son corps, mais ce que je tiens de vous est un ouvrage de votre volonté ; et d'autant plus que les facultés spirituelles sont au-dessus des corporelles, d'autant plus je vous dois, et d'autant plus je tiens précieuse cette future filiation, dont je viens aujourd'hui vous rendre par avance les très humbles et très respectueux hommages.

TOINETTE. – Vivent les collèges, d'où l'on sort si habile homme !

THOMAS DIAFOIRUS. – Cela a-t-il bien été, mon père ?

MONSIEUR DIAFOIRUS. – *Optime.* → très bien

ARGAN, *à Angélique.* – Allons, saluez Monsieur.

THOMAS DIAFOIRUS. – Baiserai-je ?

MONSIEUR DIAFOIRUS. – Oui, oui.

THOMAS DIAFOIRUS, *à Angélique.* – Madame, c'est avec justice que le Ciel vous a concédé le nom de belle-mère, puisque l'on...

ARGAN. – Ce n'est pas ma femme, c'est ma fille à qui vous parlez.

THOMAS DIAFOIRUS. – Où donc est-elle ?

ARGAN. – Elle va venir.

THOMAS DIAFOIRUS. – Attendrai-je, mon père, qu'elle soit venue ?

*ambiance inconfortable*

*attendre le plaisir*

MONSIEUR DIAFOIRUS. – Faites toujours le compliment de Mademoiselle.

THOMAS DIAFOIRUS. – Mademoiselle, ne plus ne moins que la statue de Memnon rendait un son harmonieux, lorsqu'elle venait à être éclairée des rayons du soleil ; tout de même me sens-je animé d'un doux transport à l'apparition du soleil de vos beautés. Et comme les naturalistes remarquent que la fleur nommée héliotrope tourne sans cesse vers cet astre du jour, aussi mon cœur dores-en-avant tournera-t-il toujours vers les astres resplendissants de vos yeux adorables, ainsi que vers son pôle unique. Souffrez donc, Mademoiselle, que j'appende aujourd'hui à l'autel de vos charmes l'offrande de ce cœur, qui ne respire et n'ambitionne autre gloire que d'être toute sa vie, Mademoiselle, votre très humble, très obéissant et très fidèle serviteur et mari.

TOINETTE, *en le raillant.* – Voilà ce que c'est que d'étudier, on apprend à dire de belles choses.

ARGAN. – Eh ! que dites-vous de cela ?

CLÉANTE. – Que Monsieur fait merveilles, et que s'il est aussi bon médecin qu'il est bon orateur, il y aura plaisir à être de ses malades.

TOINETTE. – Assurément. Ce sera quelque chose d'admirable s'il fait d'aussi belles cures qu'il fait de beaux discours.

ARGAN. – Allons vite, ma chaise, et des sièges à tout le monde. Mettez-vous là, ma fille. Vous voyez, Monsieur, que tout le monde admire Monsieur votre fils, et je vous trouve bien heureux de vous voir un garçon comme cela.

MONSIEUR DIAFOIRUS. – Monsieur, ce n'est pas parce que je suis son père, mais je puis dire que j'ai sujet d'être content de lui, et que tous ceux qui le voient en parlent comme d'un garçon qui n'a point de méchanceté. Il n'a jamais eu l'imagination bien vive, ni ce feu d'esprit qu'on remarque dans quelques-uns ; mais c'est par là que j'ai toujours bien auguré de sa judiciaire, qualité requise pour l'exercice de notre art. Lorsqu'il était petit, il n'a jamais été ce qu'on appelle mièvre et éveillé. On le voyait toujours doux, paisible, et taciturne, ne disant jamais mot, et ne jouant jamais à tous ces petits jeux que l'on nomme enfantins. On eut toutes les peines du monde à lui apprendre à lire, et il avait neuf ans, qu'il ne connaissait pas encore ses lettres. « Bon, disais-je en moi-même, les arbres tardifs sont ceux qui portent les meilleurs fruits ; on grave sur le marbre bien plus malaisément que sur le sable ; mais les choses y sont conservées bien plus longtemps ; et cette lenteur à comprendre, cette pesanteur d'imagination, est la marque d'un bon jugement à venir. » Lorsque je l'envoyai au collège, il trouva de la peine ; mais il se raidissait contre les difficultés, et ses régents se louaient toujours à moi de son assiduité, et de son travail. Enfin, à force de battre le fer, il en est venu glorieusement à avoir ses licences ; et je puis dire sans vanité que depuis deux ans qu'il est sur les bancs, il n'y a point de candidat qui ait fait plus de bruit que lui dans toutes les disputes de notre École. Il s'y est rendu redoutable, et il ne s'y passe point d'acte où il n'aille argumenter à outrance pour la proposition contraire. Il est ferme dans la dispute, fort comme un Turc sur ses principes, ne démord jamais de son opinion, et poursuit un raisonnement jusque dans les derniers recoins de la logique. Mais sur toute chose ce qui me plaît en lui, et en quoi il suit mon exemple, c'est qu'il s'attache aveuglément aux opinions de nos anciens, et que jamais il n'a voulu comprendre ni écouter les raisons et les expériences des prétendues découvertes de notre siècle, touchant la circulation du sang, et autres opinions de même farine.

THOMAS DIAFOIRUS. *Il tire une grande thèse roulée de sa poche, qu'il présente à Angélique.* – J'ai contre les circulateurs soutenu une thèse, qu'avec la permission de Monsieur, j'ose présenter à Mademoiselle, comme un hommage que je lui dois des prémices de mon esprit.

ANGÉLIQUE. – Monsieur, c'est pour moi un meuble inutile, et je ne me connais pas à ces choses-là.

TOINETTE. – Donnez, donnez, elle est toujours bonne à prendre pour l'image ; cela servira à parer notre chambre.

THOMAS DIAFOIRUS. – Avec la permission aussi de Monsieur, je vous invite à venir voir l'un de ces jours pour vous divertir la dissection d'une femme, sur quoi je dois raisonner.

TOINETTE. – Le divertissement sera agréable. Il y en a qui donnent la comédie à leurs maîtresses ; mais donner une dissection est quelque chose de plus galant.

MONSIEUR DIAFOIRUS. – Au reste, pour ce qui est des qualités requises pour le mariage et la propagation, je vous assure que, selon les règles de nos docteurs, il est tel qu'on le peut souhaiter, qu'il possède en un degré louable la vertu prolifique, et qu'il est du tempérament qu'il faut pour engendrer et procréer des enfants bien conditionnés.

ARGAN. – N'est-ce pas votre intention, Monsieur, de le pousser à la cour, et d'y ménager pour lui une charge de médecin ?

MONSIEUR DIAFOIRUS. – À vous en parler franchement, notre métier auprès des grands ne m'a jamais paru agréable, et j'ai toujours trouvé qu'il valait mieux, pour nous autres, demeurer au public. Le public est commode. Vous n'avez à répondre de vos actions à personne ; et pourvu que l'on suive le courant des règles de l'art, on ne se met point en peine de tout ce qui peut arriver. Mais ce qu'il y a de fâcheux auprès des grands, c'est que, quand ils viennent à être malades, ils veulent absolument que leurs médecins les guérissent.

TOINETTE. – Cela est plaisant, et ils sont bien impertinents de vouloir que vous autres Messieurs vous les guérissiez. Vous n'êtes point auprès d'eux pour cela ; vous n'y êtes que pour recevoir vos pensions, et leur ordonner des remèdes ; c'est à eux à guérir s'ils peuvent.

MONSIEUR DIAFOIRUS. – Cela est vrai. On n'est obligé qu'à traiter les gens dans les formes.

ARGAN, à *Cléante*. – Monsieur, faites un peu chanter ma fille devant la compagnie.

CLÉANTE. – J'attendais vos ordres, Monsieur, et il m'est venu en pensée, pour divertir la compagnie, de chanter avec Mademoiselle une scène d'un petit opéra qu'on a fait depuis peu. Tenez, voilà votre partie.

ANGÉLIQUE. – Moi ?

CLÉANTE. – Ne vous défendez point, s'il vous plaît, et me laissez vous faire comprendre ce que c'est que la scène que nous devons chanter. Je n'ai pas une voix à chanter ; mais il suffit ici que je me fasse entendre, et l'on aura la bonté de m'excuser par la nécessité où je me trouve de faire chanter Mademoiselle.

ARGAN. – Les vers en sont-ils beaux ?

CLÉANTE. – C'est proprement ici un petit opéra impromptu, et vous n'allez entendre chanter que de la prose cadencée, ou des manières de vers libres, tels que la passion et la nécessité peuvent faire trouver à deux personnes qui disent les choses d'eux-mêmes, et parlent sur-le-champ.

ARGAN. – Fort bien. Écoutons.

CLÉANTE *sous le nom d'un Berger, explique à sa maîtresse son amour depuis leur rencontre, et ensuite ils s'appliquent leurs pensées l'un à l'autre en chantant.* – Voici le sujet de la scène. Un Berger était attentif aux beautés d'un spectacle, qui ne faisait que de commencer, lorsqu'il fut tiré de son attention par un bruit qu'il entendit à ses côtés. Il se retourne, et voit un brutal qui de paroles insolentes maltraitait une Bergère. D'abord il prend les intérêts d'un sexe à qui tous les hommes doivent hommage ; et après avoir donné au brutal le châtiment de son insolence, il vient à la Bergère, et voit une jeune personne qui, des deux plus beaux yeux qu'il eût jamais vus, versait des larmes, qu'il trouva les plus belles du monde. « Hélas ! dit-il en lui-même, est-on capable d'outrager une personne si aimable ? Et quel inhumain, quel barbare ne serait touché par de telles larmes ? » Il prend soin de les arrêter, ces larmes, qu'il trouve si belles ; et l'aimable Bergère prend soin en même temps de le remercier de son léger service, mais d'une manière si charmante, si tendre et si passionnée, que le Berger n'y peut résister ; et chaque mot, chaque regard, est un trait plein de flamme, dont son cœur se sent pénétré. « Est-il, disait-il, quelque chose qui puisse mériter les aimables paroles d'un tel remerciement ? Et que ne voudrait-on pas faire, à quels services, à quels dangers, ne serait-on pas ravi de courir, pour s'attirer un seul moment des touchantes douceurs d'une âme si reconnaissante ? » Tout le spectacle passe sans qu'il y donne aucune attention ; mais il se plaint qu'il est trop court, parce qu'en finissant il le sépare de son adorable Bergère ; et de cette première vue, de ce premier moment, il emporte chez lui tout ce qu'un amour de plusieurs années peut avoir de plus violent. Le voilà aussitôt à sentir tous les maux de l'absence, et il est tourmenté de ne plus voir ce qu'il a si peu vu. Il fait tout ce qu'il peut pour se redonner cette vue, dont il conserve nuit et jour une si chère idée ; mais la grande contrainte où l'on tient sa Bergère lui en ôte tous les moyens. La violence de sa passion le fait résoudre à demander en mariage l'adorable beauté sans laquelle il ne peut plus vivre, et il en obtient d'elle la permission par un billet qu'il a l'adresse de lui faire tenir. Mais dans le même temps on l'avertit que le père de cette belle a conclu son mariage avec un autre, et que tout se dispose pour en célébrer la cérémonie. Jugez quelle atteinte cruelle au cœur de ce triste Berger. Le voilà accablé d'une mortelle douleur. Il ne peut souffrir l'effroyable idée de voir tout ce qu'il aime entre les bras d'un autre, et son amour au désespoir lui fait trouver moyen de s'introduire dans la maison de sa Bergère, pour apprendre ses sentiments et savoir d'elle la destinée à laquelle il doit se résoudre. Il y rencontre les apprêts de tout ce qu'il craint ; il y voit venir l'indigne rival que le caprice d'un père oppose aux tendresses de son amour. Il le voit triomphant, ce rival ridicule, auprès de l'aimable Bergère, ainsi qu'auprès d'une conquête qui lui est assurée ; et cette vue le remplit d'une colère dont il a peine à se rendre le maître. Il jette de douloureux regards sur celle qu'il adore ; et son respect et la présence de son père l'empêchent de lui rien dire que des yeux. Mais enfin il force toute contrainte, et le transport de son amour l'oblige à lui parler ainsi :

*il décrit son histoire d'amour avec Angélique*

*Il chante.*

— *Belle Philis, c'est trop, c'est trop souffrir ;*
  *Rompons ce dur silence, et m'ouvrez vos pensées.*
245  *Apprenez-moi ma destinée :*
  *Faut-il vivre ? Faut-il mourir ?*

ANGÉLIQUE *répond en chantant :*
— *Vous me voyez, Tircis, triste et mélancolique,*
  *Aux apprêts de l'hymen dont vous vous alarmez,*
  *Je lève au ciel les yeux, je vous regarde, je soupire,*
250  *C'est vous en dire assez.*

ARGAN. – Ouais ! je ne croyais pas que ma fille fût si habile que de chanter ainsi à livre ouvert, sans hésiter.

CLÉANTE
— *Hélas ! belle Philis,*
*Se pourrait-il que l'amoureux Tircis*
55     *Eût assez de bonheur,*
*Pour avoir quelque place dans votre cœur ?*

ANGÉLIQUE
— *Je ne m'en défends point dans cette peine extrême :*
*Oui, Tircis, je vous aime.*

CLÉANTE
— *Ô parole pleine d'appas !*
60     *Ai-je bien entendu, hélas !*
*Redites-la, Philis, que je n'en doute pas.*

ANGÉLIQUE
— *Oui, Tircis, je vous aime.*

CLÉANTE
— *De grâce, encor, Philis.*

ANGÉLIQUE
— *Je vous aime.*

CLÉANTE
65 — *Recommencez cent fois, ne vous en lassez pas.*

ANGÉLIQUE
— *Je vous aime, je vous aime,*
*Oui, Tircis, je vous aime.*

CLÉANTE
— *Dieux, rois, qui sous vos pieds regardez tout le monde,*
*Pouvez-vous comparer votre bonheur au mien ?*

*Mais, Philis, une pensée*
*Vient troubler ce doux transport :*
*Un rival, un rival...* → Thomas

LOL

ANGÉLIQUE

— *Ah ! je le hais plus que la mort ;* → Thomas
*Et sa présence, ainsi qu'à vous,* → Thomas
275 *M'est un cruel supplice.*

CLÉANTE

— *Mais un père à ses vœux vous veut assujettir.*

ANGÉLIQUE

— *Plutôt, plutôt mourir*
*Que de jamais y consentir ;*
*Plutôt, plutôt mourir, plutôt mourir !*

ARGAN. — Et que dit le père à tout cela ?

CLÉANTE. — Il ne dit rien.

ARGAN. — Voilà un sot père que ce père-là, de souffrir toutes ces sottises-là sans rien dire. c'est lui !

CLÉANTE

— *Ah ! mon amour...*

ARGAN. — Non, non, en voilà assez. Cette comédie-là est de fort mauvais exemple. Le berger Tircis est un impertinent, et la bergère Philis une impudente, de parler de la sorte devant son père. Montrez-moi ce papier. Ha ! ha ! Où sont donc les paroles que vous avez dites ? Il n'y a là que de la musique écrite.

CLÉANTE. — Est-ce que vous ne savez pas, Monsieur, qu'on a trouvé depuis peu l'invention d'écrire les paroles avec les notes mêmes ?

ARGAN. — Fort bien. Je suis votre serviteur, Monsieur ; jusqu'au revoir. Nous nous serions bien passés de votre impertinent d'opéra.

il le croit !

CLÉANTE. – J'ai cru vous divertir.

ARGAN. – Les sottises ne divertissent point. Ah ! voici ma femme.

### Scène VI

*Béline, Argan, Toinette, Angélique,*
*Monsieur Diafoirus, Thomas Diafoirus*

ARGAN. – Mamour, voilà le fils de Monsieur Diafoirus.

THOMAS DIAFOIRUS *commence un compliment qu'il avait étudié, et la mémoire lui manquant, il ne peut le continuer.* – Madame, c'est avec justice que le Ciel vous a concédé le nom de belle-mère, puisque l'on voit sur votre visage...

BÉLINE. – Monsieur, je suis ravie d'être venue ici à propos pour avoir l'honneur de vous voir.

THOMAS DIAFOIRUS. – Puisque l'on voit sur votre visage... puisque l'on voit sur votre visage... Madame, vous m'avez interrompu dans le milieu de ma période, et cela m'a troublé la mémoire.

MONSIEUR DIAFOIRUS. – Thomas, réservez cela pour une autre fois.

ARGAN. – Je voudrais, mamie, que vous eussiez été ici tantôt.

TOINETTE. – Ah ! Madame, vous avez bien perdu de n'avoir point été au second père, à la statue de Memnon, et à la fleur nommée héliotrope.

ARGAN. – Allons, ma fille, touchez dans la main de Monsieur, et lui donnez votre foi comme à votre mari.

ANGÉLIQUE. – Mon père !

ARGAN. – Hé bien ! « Mon père » ? Qu'est-ce que cela veut dire ?

ANGÉLIQUE. – De grâce, ne précipitez pas les choses. Donnez-nous au moins le temps de nous connaître, et de voir naître en nous l'un pour l'autre cette inclination si nécessaire à composer une union parfaite.

THOMAS DIAFOIRUS. – Quant à moi, Mademoiselle, elle est déjà toute née en moi, et je n'ai pas besoin d'attendre davantage.

ANGÉLIQUE. – Si vous êtes si prompt, Monsieur, il n'en est pas de même de moi, et je vous avoue que votre mérite n'a pas encore fait assez d'impression dans mon âme.

ARGAN. – Ho ! bien, bien ! cela aura tout le loisir de se faire, quand vous serez mariés ensemble.

ANGÉLIQUE. – Eh ! mon père, donnez-moi du temps, je vous prie. Le mariage est une chaîne où l'on ne doit jamais soumettre un cœur par force ; et si Monsieur est honnête homme, il ne doit point vouloir accepter une personne qui serait à lui par contrainte.

THOMAS DIAFOIRUS. – *Nego consequentiam*, Mademoiselle, et je puis être honnête homme et vouloir bien vous accepter des mains de Monsieur votre père.

ANGÉLIQUE. – C'est un méchant moyen de se faire aimer de quelqu'un que de lui faire violence.

THOMAS DIAFOIRUS. – Nous lisons des anciens, Mademoiselle, que leur coutume était d'enlever par force de la maison des pères les filles qu'on menait marier, afin qu'il ne semblât pas que ce fût de leur consentement qu'elles convolaient dans les bras d'un homme.

ANGÉLIQUE. – Les anciens, Monsieur, sont les anciens, et nous sommes les gens de maintenant. Les grimaces ne sont point nécessaires dans notre siècle ; et quand un mariage nous plaît, nous savons fort bien y aller, sans qu'on nous y traîne. Donnez-vous patience ; si vous m'aimez, Monsieur, vous devez vouloir tout ce que je veux.

THOMAS DIAFOIRUS. – Oui, Mademoiselle, jusqu'aux intérêts de mon amour exclusivement.

ANGÉLIQUE. – Mais la grande marque d'amour, c'est d'être soumis aux volontés de celle qu'on aime.

THOMAS DIAFOIRUS. — *Distinguo*, Mademoiselle : dans ce qui ne regarde point sa possession, *concedo* ; mais dans ce qui la regarde, *nego*.

TOINETTE. — Vous avez beau raisonner ; Monsieur est frais émoulu du collège, et il vous donnera toujours votre reste. Pourquoi tant résister, et refuser la gloire d'être attachée au corps de la Faculté ?

BÉLINE. — Elle a peut-être quelque inclination en tête.

ANGÉLIQUE. — Si j'en avais, Madame, elle serait telle que la raison et l'honnêteté pourraient me la permettre.

ARGAN. — Ouais ! je joue ici un plaisant personnage.

BÉLINE. — Si j'étais que de vous, mon fils, je ne la forcerais point à se marier, et je sais bien ce que je ferais.

ANGÉLIQUE. — Je sais, Madame, ce que vous voulez dire, et les bontés que vous avez pour moi ; mais peut-être que vos conseils ne seront pas assez heureux pour être exécutés.

BÉLINE. — C'est que les filles bien sages et bien honnêtes comme vous se moquent d'être obéissantes, et soumises aux volontés de leurs pères. Cela était bon autrefois.

ANGÉLIQUE. — Le devoir d'une fille a des bornes, Madame, et la raison et les lois ne l'étendent point à toutes sortes de choses.

BÉLINE. — C'est-à-dire que vos pensées ne sont que pour le mariage ; mais vous voulez choisir un époux à votre fantaisie.

ANGÉLIQUE. — Si mon père ne veut pas me donner un mari qui me plaise, je le conjurerai, au moins, de ne me point forcer à en épouser un que je ne puisse pas aimer.

ARGAN. — Messieurs, je vous demande pardon de tout ceci.

ANGÉLIQUE. — Chacun a son but en se mariant. Pour moi, qui ne veux un mari que pour l'aimer véritablement, et qui prétends en faire tout l'attachement de ma vie, je vous avoue que j'y cherche quelque précaution. Il y en a d'aucunes qui prennent des maris seulement pour se tirer de la contrainte de leurs parents, et se mettre en état de faire tout ce qu'elles voudront. Il y en a d'autres, Madame, qui font du mariage un commerce de pur intérêt, qui ne se marient que pour gagner des douaires, que pour s'enrichir par la mort de ceux qu'elles épousent, et courent sans scrupule de mari en mari, pour s'approprier leurs dépouilles. Ces personnes-là, à la vérité, n'y cherchent pas tant de façons et regardent peu la personne.

BÉLINE. – Je vous trouve aujourd'hui bien raisonnante, et je voudrais bien savoir ce que vous voulez dire par là.

ANGÉLIQUE. – Moi, Madame, que voudrais-je dire que ce que je dis ?

BÉLINE. – Vous êtes si sotte, mamie, qu'on ne saurait plus vous souffrir.

ANGÉLIQUE. – Vous voudriez bien, Madame, m'obliger à vous répondre quelque impertinence, mais je vous avertis que vous n'aurez pas cet avantage.

BÉLINE. – Il n'est rien d'égal à votre insolence.

ANGÉLIQUE. – Non, Madame, vous avez beau dire.

BÉLINE. – Et vous avez un ridicule orgueil, une impertinente présomption qui fait hausser les épaules à tout le monde.

ANGÉLIQUE. – Tout cela, Madame, ne servira de rien. Je serai sage en dépit de vous ; et, pour vous ôter l'espérance de pouvoir réussir dans ce que vous voulez, je vais m'ôter de votre vue.

ARGAN. – Écoute, il n'y a point de milieu à cela. Choisis d'épouser dans quatre jours, ou Monsieur, ou un couvent. *(À Béline.)* Ne vous mettez pas en peine, je la rangerai bien.

BÉLINE. – Je suis fâchée de vous quitter, mon fils, mais j'ai une affaire en ville, dont je ne puis me dispenser. Je reviendrai bientôt.

ARGAN. – Allez, mamour, et passez chez votre notaire, afin qu'il expédie ce que vous savez.

BÉLINE. – Adieu, mon petit ami.

ARGAN. – Adieu, mamie. Voilà une femme qui m'aime… Cela n'est pas croyable.

MONSIEUR DIAFOIRUS. – Nous allons, Monsieur, prendre congé de vous.

ARGAN. – Je vous prie, Monsieur, de me dire un peu comment je suis.

MONSIEUR DIAFOIRUS *lui tâte le pouls.* – Allons, Thomas, prenez l'autre bras de Monsieur, pour voir si vous saurez porter un bon jugement de son pouls. *Quid dicis ?*

THOMAS DIAFOIRUS. – *Dico,* que le pouls de Monsieur est le pouls d'un homme qui ne se porte point bien.

MONSIEUR DIAFOIRUS. – Bon.

THOMAS DIAFOIRUS. – Qu'il est duriuscule, pour ne pas dire dur.

MONSIEUR DIAFOIRUS. – Fort bien.

THOMAS DIAFOIRUS. – Repoussant.

MONSIEUR DIAFOIRUS. – *Bene.*

THOMAS DIAFOIRUS. – Et même un peu caprisant.

MONSIEUR DIAFOIRUS. – *Optime.*

THOMAS DIAFOIRUS. – Ce qui marque une intempérie dans le *parenchyme splénique*, c'est-à-dire la rate.

MONSIEUR DIAFOIRUS. – Fort bien.

ARGAN. – Non ; Monsieur Purgon dit que c'est mon foie qui est malade.

MONSIEUR DIAFOIRUS. – Eh ! oui ; qui dit *parenchyme*, dit l'un et l'autre, à cause de l'étroite sympathie qu'ils ont ensemble, par le moyen du *vas breve du pylore*, et souvent des *méats cholidoques*. Il vous ordonne sans doute de manger force rôti ?

ARGAN. – Non, rien que du bouilli.

MONSIEUR DIAFOIRUS. – Eh ! oui ; rôti, bouilli, même chose. Il vous ordonne fort prudemment, et vous ne pouvez être en de meilleures mains.

ARGAN. – Monsieur, combien est-ce qu'il faut mettre de grains de sel dans un œuf ?

MONSIEUR DIAFOIRUS. – Six, huit, dix, par les nombres pairs ; comme dans les médicaments, par les nombres impairs.

ARGAN. – Jusqu'au revoir, Monsieur. *niaiseries*


## Scène VII

*Béline, Argan*

BÉLINE. – Je viens, mon fils, avant que de sortir, vous donner avis d'une chose à laquelle il faut que vous preniez garde. En passant par-devant la chambre d'Angélique, j'ai vu un jeune homme avec elle, qui s'est sauvé d'abord qu'il m'a vue.

ARGAN. – Un jeune homme avec ma fille ?

BÉLINE. – Oui. Votre petite fille Louison était avec eux, qui pourra vous en dire des nouvelles.

ARGAN. – Envoyez-la ici, mamour, envoyez-la ici. Ah, l'effrontée ! je ne m'étonne plus de sa résistance.


## Scène VIII

*Louison, Argan*

LOUISON. – Qu'est-ce que vous voulez, mon papa ? Ma belle-maman m'a dit que vous me demandez.

ARGAN. – Oui, venez çà, avancez là. Tournez-vous, levez les yeux, regardez-moi. Eh !

LOUISON. – Quoi, mon papa ?

ARGAN. – Là.

LOUISON. – Quoi ?

ARGAN. – N'avez-vous rien à me dire ?

LOUISON. – Je vous dirai, si vous voulez, pour vous désennuyer, le conte de *Peau d'âne*, ou bien la fable du *Corbeau et du Renard*, qu'on m'a apprise depuis peu.

ARGAN. – Ce n'est pas là ce que je demande.

LOUISON. – Quoi donc ?

ARGAN. – Ah ! rusée, vous savez bien ce que je veux dire.

LOUISON. – Pardonnez-moi, mon papa.

ARGAN. – Est-ce là comme vous m'obéissez ?

LOUISON. – Quoi ?

ARGAN. – Ne vous ai-je pas recommandé de me venir dire d'abord tout ce que vous voyez ?

LOUISON. – Oui, mon papa.

ARGAN. – L'avez-vous fait ?

LOUISON. – Oui, mon papa. Je vous suis venue dire tout ce que j'ai vu.

ARGAN. – Et n'avez-vous rien vu aujourd'hui ?

LOUISON. – Non, mon papa.

ARGAN. – Non ?

LOUISON. – Non, mon papa.

ARGAN. – Assurément ?

LOUISON. – Assurément.

ARGAN. – Oh çà ! je m'en vais vous faire voir quelque chose, moi.

*Il va prendre une poignée de verges.*

LOUISON. – Ah ! mon papa.

ARGAN. – Ah, ah ! petite masque, vous ne me dites pas que vous avez vu un homme dans la chambre de votre sœur ?

LOUISON. – Mon papa !

ARGAN. – Voici qui vous apprendra à mentir.

LOUISON *se jette à genoux.* – Ah ! mon papa, je vous demande pardon. C'est que ma sœur m'avait dit de ne pas vous le dire, mais je m'en vais vous dire tout.

ARGAN. – Il faut premièrement que vous ayez le fouet pour avoir menti. Puis après nous verrons au reste.

LOUISON. – Pardon, mon papa !

ARGAN. – Non, non.

LOUISON. – Mon pauvre papa, ne me donnez pas le fouet !

ARGAN. – Vous l'aurez.

LOUISON. – Au nom de Dieu ! mon papa, que je ne l'aie pas.

ARGAN, *la prenant pour la fouetter.* – Allons, allons.

LOUISON. – Ah ! mon papa, vous m'avez blessée. Attendez, je suis morte. *(Elle contrefait la morte.)*

ARGAN. – Holà ! Qu'est-ce là ? Louison, Louison ! Ah, mon Dieu ! Louison ! Ah ! ma fille ! Ah ! malheureux, ma pauvre fille est morte. Qu'ai-je fait, misérable ? Ah ! chiennes de verges. La peste soit des verges ! Ah ! ma pauvre fille, ma pauvre petite LOUISON.

LOUISON. – Là, là, mon papa, ne pleurez point tant, je ne suis pas morte tout à fait.

ARGAN. – Voyez-vous la petite rusée ! Oh çà, çà ! je vous pardonne pour cette fois-ci, pourvu que vous me disiez bien tout.

LOUISON. – Oh ! oui, mon papa.

ARGAN. – Prenez-y bien garde au moins, car voilà un petit doigt qui sait tout, qui me dira si vous mentez.

LOUISON. – Mais, mon papa, ne dites pas à ma sœur que je vous l'ai dit.

ARGAN. – Non, non.

LOUISON. – C'est, mon papa, qu'il est venu un homme dans la chambre de ma sœur comme j'y étais.

ARGAN. – Hé bien ?

LOUISON. – Je lui ai demandé ce qu'il demandait, et il m'a dit qu'il était son maître à chanter.

ARGAN. – Hon, hon ! Voilà l'affaire. Hé bien ?

LOUISON. – Ma sœur est venue après.

ARGAN. – Hé bien ?

LOUISON. – Elle lui a dit : « Sortez, sortez, sortez ! mon Dieu ! sortez ! vous me mettez au désespoir. »

ARGAN. – Hé bien ?

LOUISON. – Et lui, il ne voulait pas sortir.

ARGAN. – Qu'est-ce qu'il lui disait ?

LOUISON. – Il lui disait je ne sais combien de choses.

ARGAN. – Et quoi encore ?

LOUISON. – Il lui disait tout ci, tout ça, qu'il l'aimait bien, et qu'elle était la plus belle du monde.

ARGAN. – Et puis après ?

LOUISON. – Et puis après, il se mettait à genoux devant elle.

ARGAN. – Et puis après ?

LOUISON. – Et puis après, il lui baisait les mains.

ARGAN. – Et puis après ?

LOUISON. – Et puis après, ma belle-maman est venue à la porte, et il s'est enfui.

ARGAN. – Il n'y a point autre chose ?

LOUISON. – Non, mon papa.

ARGAN. – Voilà mon petit doigt pourtant qui gronde quelque chose. *(Il met son doigt à son oreille.)* Attendez. Eh ! ah, ah ! Oui ? Oh, oh ! voilà mon petit doigt qui me dit quelque chose que vous avez vu, et que vous ne m'avez pas dit.

LOUISON. – Ah ! mon papa, votre petit doigt est un menteur.

ARGAN. – Prenez garde.

LOUISON. – Non, mon papa, ne le croyez pas, il ment, je vous assure.

ARGAN. – Oh bien, bien ! nous verrons cela. Allez-vous-en, et prenez bien garde à tout, allez. Ah ! il n'y a plus d'enfants. Ah ! que d'affaires ! je n'ai pas seulement le loisir de songer à ma maladie. En vérité, je n'en puis plus.

*Il se remet dans sa chaise.*

### Scène 9

*Béralde, Argan*

BÉRALDE. – Hé bien ! mon frère, qu'est-ce ? comment vous portez-vous ?

ARGAN. – Ah ! mon frère, fort mal.

BÉRALDE. – Comment, « fort mal » ?

ARGAN. – Oui, je suis dans une faiblesse si grande, que cela n'est pas croyable.

BÉRALDE. – Voilà qui est fâcheux.

ARGAN. – Je n'ai pas seulement la force de pouvoir parler.

BÉRALDE. – J'étais venu ici, mon frère, vous proposer un parti pour ma nièce Angélique.

ARGAN, *parlant avec emportement, et se levant de sa chaise.* – Mon frère, ne me parlez point de cette coquine-là. C'est une friponne, une impertinente, une effrontée, que je mettrai dans un couvent avant qu'il soit deux jours.

BÉRALDE. – Ah ! voilà qui est bien. Je suis bien aise que la force vous revienne un peu, et que ma visite vous fasse du bien. Oh çà ! nous parlerons d'affaires tantôt. Je vous amène ici un divertissement, que j'ai rencontré, qui dissipera votre chagrin, et vous rendra l'âme mieux disposée aux choses que nous avons à dire. Ce sont des Égyptiens, vêtus en Mores, qui font des danses mêlées de chansons, où je suis sûr que vous prendrez plaisir ; et cela vaudra bien une ordonnance de Monsieur Purgon. Allons.

# SECOND INTERMÈDE

*Le frère du Malade imaginaire lui amène, pour le divertir, plusieurs Égyptiens et Égyptiennes, vêtus en Mores, qui font des danses entremêlées de chansons.*

PREMIÈRE FEMME MORE

      *Profitez du printemps*
        *De vos beaux ans,*
         *Aimable jeunesse !*
      *Profitez du printemps*
5        *De vos beaux ans,*
      *Donnez-vous à la tendresse !*

      *Les plaisirs les plus charmants,*
      *Sans l'amoureuse flamme,*
      *Pour contenter une âme*
10   *N'ont point d'attraits assez puissants.*

      *Profitez du printemps*
        *De vos beaux ans,*
         *Aimable jeunesse !*
      *Profitez du printemps*
15      *De vos beaux ans,*
      *Donnez-vous à la tendresse !*

      *Ne perdez point ces précieux moments ;*
        *La beauté passe,*
        *Le temps l'efface,*
20      *L'âge de glace*
        *Vient à sa place,*
*Qui nous ôte le goût de ces doux passe-temps.*

*Profitez du printemps*
*De vos beaux ans,*
25    *Aimable jeunesse !*
*Profitez du printemps*
*De vos beaux ans,*
*Donnez-vous à la tendresse !*

SECONDE FEMME MORE

*Quand d'aimer on nous presse*
30    *À quoi songez-vous ?*
*Nos cœurs, dans la jeunesse,*
*N'ont vers la tendresse*
*Qu'un penchant trop doux ;*
*L'amour a pour nous prendre,*
35    *De si doux attraits,*
*Que de soi, sans attendre,*
*On voudrait se rendre*
*À ses premiers traits ;*
*Mais tout ce qu'on écoute*
40    *Des vives douleurs*
*Et des pleurs*
*Qu'il nous coûte,*
*Fait qu'on en redoute*
*Toutes les douceurs.*

TROISIÈME FEMME MORE

45    *Il est doux, à notre âge,*
*D'aimer tendrement*
*Un amant*
*Qui s'engage ;*
*Mais s'il est volage,*
50    *Hélas ! quel tourment !*

QUATRIÈME FEMME MORE

*L'amant qui se dégage*
*N'est pas le malheur ;*
*La douleur*
*Et la rage,*

55      *C'est que le volage*
        *Garde notre cœur.*


                    SECONDE FEMME MORE
        *Quel parti faut-il prendre*
            *Pour nos jeunes cœurs ?*


                    QUATRIÈME FEMME MORE
        *Devons-nous nous y rendre*
60          *Malgré ses rigueurs ?*


                    ENSEMBLE
        *Oui, suivons ses ardeurs,*
        *Ses transports, ses caprices,*
            *Ses douces langueurs ;*
        *S'il a quelques supplices,*
65          *Il a cent délices*
            *Qui charment les cœurs.*


### Entrée de ballet


*Tous les Mores dansent ensemble et font sauter des singes qu'ils ont amenés avec eux.*

comique de gestes

comique de situation

comique de mots

Comique de Daractères

# ACTE III

## Scène première

*Béralde, Argan, Toinette*

BÉRALDE. – Hé bien ! mon frère, qu'en dites-vous ? cela ne vaut-il pas bien une prise de casse ?

TOINETTE. – Hon ! de bonne casse est bonne.

BÉRALDE. – Oh çà ! voulez-vous que nous parlions un peu ensemble ?

ARGAN. – Un peu de patience, mon frère, je vais revenir.

TOINETTE. – Tenez, Monsieur, vous ne songez pas que vous ne sauriez marcher sans bâton.

ARGAN. – Tu as raison.

## Scène II

*Béralde, Toinette*

TOINETTE. – N'abandonnez pas, s'il vous plaît, les intérêts de votre nièce.

BÉRALDE. – J'emploierai toutes choses pour lui obtenir ce qu'elle souhaite.

TOINETTE. – Il faut absolument empêcher ce mariage extravagant qu'il s'est mis dans la fantaisie, et j'avais songé en moi-même que ç'aurait été une bonne affaire de pouvoir introduire ici un médecin à notre poste, pour le dégoûter de son Monsieur Purgon, et lui décrier sa conduite. Mais, comme nous n'avons personne en main pour cela, j'ai résolu de jouer un tour de ma tête.

BÉRALDE. – Comment ?

TOINETTE. – C'est une imagination burlesque. Cela sera peut-être plus heureux que sage. Laissez-moi faire ; agissez de votre côté. Voici notre homme.

### Scène III

*Argan, Béralde*

BÉRALDE. – Vous voulez bien, mon frère, que je vous demande, avant toute chose, de ne vous point échauffer l'esprit dans notre conversation.

ARGAN. – Voilà qui est fait.

BÉRALDE. – De répondre sans nulle aigreur aux choses que je pourrai vous dire.

ARGAN. – Oui.

BÉRALDE. – Et de raisonner ensemble, sur les affaires dont nous avons à parler, avec un esprit détaché de toute passion.

ARGAN. – Mon Dieu ! oui. Voilà bien du préambule.

BÉRALDE. – D'où vient, mon frère, qu'ayant le bien que vous avez, et n'ayant d'enfants qu'une fille, car je ne compte pas la petite ; d'où vient, dis-je, que vous parlez de la mettre dans un couvent ?

ARGAN. – D'où vient, mon frère, que je suis maître dans ma famille pour faire ce que bon me semble ?

BÉRALDE. – Votre femme ne manque pas de vous conseiller de vous défaire ainsi de vos deux filles, et je ne doute point que, par un esprit de charité, elle ne fût ravie de les voir toutes deux bonnes religieuses.

ARGAN. – Oh çà ! nous y voici. Voilà d'abord la pauvre femme en jeu. C'est elle qui fait tout le mal, et tout le monde lui en veut.

BÉRALDE. – Non, mon frère ; laissons-la là : c'est une femme qui a les meilleures intentions du monde pour votre famille, et qui est détachée de toute sorte d'intérêt, qui a pour vous une tendresse merveilleuse, et qui montre pour vos enfants une affection et une bonté qui n'est pas concevable : cela est certain. N'en parlons point, et revenons à votre fille. Sur quelle pensée, mon frère, la voulez-vous donner en mariage au fils d'un médecin ?

ARGAN. – Sur la pensée, mon frère, de me donner un gendre tel qu'il me faut.

BÉRALDE. – Ce n'est point là, mon frère, le fait de votre fille, et il se présente un parti plus sortable pour elle.

ARGAN. – Oui, mais celui-ci, mon frère, est plus sortable pour moi.

BÉRALDE. – Mais le mari qu'elle doit prendre doit-il être, mon frère, ou pour elle, ou pour vous ?

ARGAN. – Il doit être, mon frère, et pour elle, et pour moi, et je veux mettre dans ma famille les gens dont j'ai besoin.

BÉRALDE. – Par cette raison-là, si votre petite était grande, vous lui donneriez en mariage un apothicaire ?

ARGAN. – Pourquoi non ?

BÉRALDE. – Est-il possible que vous serez toujours embéguiné de vos apothicaires et de vos médecins, et que vous vouliez être malade en dépit des gens et de la nature ?

ARGAN. – Comment l'entendez-vous, mon frère ?

BÉRALDE. – J'entends, mon frère, que je ne vois point d'homme qui soit moins malade que vous, et que je ne demanderais point une meilleure constitution que la vôtre. Une grande marque que vous vous portez bien, et que vous avez un corps parfaitement bien composé, c'est qu'avec tous les soins que vous avez pris, vous n'avez pu parvenir encore à gâter la bonté de votre tempérament, et que vous n'êtes point crevé de toutes les médecines qu'on vous a fait prendre.

ARGAN. – Mais savez-vous, mon frère, que c'est cela qui me conserve, et que Monsieur Purgon dit que je succomberais, s'il était seulement trois jours sans prendre soin de moi ?

BÉRALDE. – Si vous n'y prenez garde, il prendra tant de soin de vous qu'il vous enverra en l'autre monde.

ARGAN. – Mais raisonnons un peu, mon frère. Vous ne croyez donc point à la médecine ?

BÉRALDE. – Non, mon frère, et je ne vois pas que pour son salut il soit nécessaire d'y croire.

ARGAN. – Quoi ! vous ne tenez pas véritable une chose établie par tout le monde, et que tous les siècles ont révérée ?

BÉRALDE. – Bien loin de la tenir véritable, je la trouve, entre nous, une des plus grandes folies qui soit parmi les hommes ; et, à regarder les choses en philosophe, je ne vois point de plus plaisante momerie, je ne vois rien de plus ridicule qu'un homme qui se veut mêler d'en guérir un autre.

ARGAN. – Pourquoi ne voulez-vous pas, mon frère, qu'un homme en puisse guérir un autre ?

BÉRALDE. – Par la raison, mon frère, que les ressorts de notre machine sont des mystères, jusques ici, où les hommes ne voient goutte, et que la nature nous a mis au-devant des yeux des voiles trop épais pour y connaître quelque chose.

ARGAN. – Les médecins ne savent donc rien, à votre compte ?

BÉRALDE. – Si fait, mon frère. Ils savent la plupart de fort belles humanités, savent parler en beau latin, savent nommer en grec toutes les maladies, les définir et les diviser ; mais, pour ce qui est de les guérir, c'est ce qu'ils ne savent point du tout.

ARGAN. – Mais toujours faut-il demeurer d'accord que, sur cette matière, les médecins en savent plus que les autres.

BÉRALDE. – Ils savent, mon frère, ce que je vous ai dit, qui ne guérit pas de grand'chose ; et toute l'excellence de leur art consiste en un pompeux galimatias, en un spécieux babil, qui vous donne des mots pour des raisons et des promesses pour des effets.

ARGAN. – Mais enfin, mon frère, il y a des gens aussi sages et aussi habiles que vous ; et nous voyons que, dans la maladie, tout le monde a recours aux médecins.

BÉRALDE. – C'est une marque de la faiblesse humaine, et non pas de la vérité de leur art.

ARGAN. – Mais il faut bien que les médecins croient leur art véritable, puisqu'ils s'en servent pour eux-mêmes.

BÉRALDE. – C'est qu'il y en a parmi eux qui sont eux-mêmes dans l'erreur populaire, dont ils profitent, et d'autres qui en profitent sans y être. Votre Monsieur Purgon, par exemple, n'y sait point de finesse ; c'est un homme tout médecin, depuis la tête jusqu'aux pieds ; un homme qui croit à ses règles plus qu'à toutes les démonstrations des mathématiques, et qui croirait du crime à les vouloir examiner ; qui ne voit rien d'obscur dans la médecine, rien de douteux, rien de difficile, et qui, avec une impétuosité de prévention, une raideur de confiance, une brutalité de sens commun et de raison, donne au travers des purgations et des saignées, et ne balance aucune chose. Il ne lui faut point vouloir mal de tout ce qu'il pourra vous faire ; c'est de la meilleure foi du monde qu'il vous expédiera, et il ne fera, en vous tuant, que ce qu'il a fait à sa femme et à ses enfants, et ce qu'en un besoin il ferait à lui-même.

ARGAN. – C'est que vous avez, mon frère, une dent de lait contre lui. Mais enfin venons au fait. Que faire donc quand on est malade ?

BÉRALDE. – Rien, mon frère.

ARGAN. – Rien ?

BÉRALDE. – Rien. Il ne faut que demeurer en repos. La nature, d'elle-même, quand nous la laissons faire, se tire doucement du désordre où elle est tombée. C'est notre inquiétude, c'est notre impatience qui gâte tout, et presque tous les hommes meurent de leurs remèdes, et non pas de leurs maladies.

ARGAN. – Mais il faut demeurer d'accord, mon frère, qu'on peut aider cette nature par de certaines choses.

BÉRALDE. – Mon Dieu ! mon frère, ce sont pures idées, dont nous aimons à nous repaître ; et, de tout temps, il s'est glissé parmi les hommes de belles imaginations, que nous venons à croire, parce qu'elles nous flattent et qu'il serait à souhaiter qu'elles fussent véritables. Lorsqu'un médecin vous parle d'aider, de secourir, de soulager la nature, de lui ôter ce qui lui nuit, et lui donner ce qui lui manque, de la rétablir et de la remettre dans une pleine facilité de ses fonctions ; lorsqu'il vous parle de rectifier le sang, de tempérer les entrailles et le cerveau, de dégonfler la rate, de raccommoder la poitrine, de réparer le foie, de fortifier le cœur, de rétablir et conserver la chaleur naturelle, et d'avoir des secrets pour étendre la vie à de longues années ; il vous dit justement le roman de la médecine. Mais quand vous en venez à la vérité et à l'expérience, vous ne trouvez rien de tout cela, et il en est comme de ces beaux songes qui ne vous laissent au réveil que le déplaisir de les avoir crus.

ARGAN. – C'est-à-dire que toute la science du monde est renfermée dans votre tête, et vous voulez en savoir plus que tous les grands médecins de notre siècle.

BÉRALDE. – Dans les discours et dans les choses, ce sont deux sortes de personnes que vos grands médecins. Entendez-les parler : les plus habiles gens du monde. Voyez-les faire : les plus ignorants de tous les hommes.

ARGAN. – Hoy ! Vous êtes un grand docteur, à ce que je vois, et je voudrais bien qu'il y eût ici quelqu'un de ces Messieurs pour rembarrer vos raisonnements et rabaisser votre caquet.

BÉRALDE. – Moi, mon frère, je ne prends point à tâche de combattre la médecine ; et chacun, à ses périls et fortune, peut croire tout ce qu'il lui plaît. Ce que j'en dis n'est qu'entre nous, et j'aurais souhaité de pouvoir un peu vous tirer de l'erreur où vous êtes, et, pour vous divertir, vous mener voir sur ce chapitre quelqu'une des comédies de Molière.

ARGAN. – C'est un bon impertinent que votre Molière avec ses comédies, et je le trouve bien plaisant d'aller jouer d'honnêtes gens comme les médecins.

BÉRALDE. – Ce ne sont point les médecins qu'il joue, mais le ridicule de la médecine.

ARGAN. – C'est bien à lui à faire de se mêler de contrôler la médecine ; voilà un bon nigaud, un bon impertinent, de se moquer des consultations et des ordonnances, de s'attaquer au corps des médecins, et d'aller mettre sur son théâtre des personnes vénérables comme ces messieurs-là.

BÉRALDE. – Que voulez-vous qu'il y mette que les diverses professions des hommes ? On y met bien tous les jours les princes et les rois, qui sont d'aussi bonne maison que les médecins.

ARGAN. – Par la mort non de diable ! si j'étais que des médecins, je me vengerais de son impertinence ; et quand il sera malade, je le laisserais mourir sans secours. Il aurait beau faire et beau dire, je ne lui ordonnerais pas la moindre petite saignée, le moindre petit lavement, et je lui dirais : « Crève, crève ! cela t'apprendra une autre fois à te jouer à la Faculté. »

BÉRALDE. – Vous voilà bien en colère contre lui.

ARGAN. – Oui, c'est un malavisé, et si les médecins sont sages, ils feront ce que je dis.

BÉRALDE. – Il sera encore plus sage que vos médecins, car il ne leur demandera point de secours.

ARGAN. – Tant pis pour lui s'il n'a point recours aux remèdes.

BÉRALDE. – Il a ses raisons pour n'en point vouloir, et il soutient que cela n'est permis qu'aux gens vigoureux et robustes, et qui ont des forces de reste pour porter les remèdes avec la maladie ; mais que, pour lui, il n'a justement de la force que pour porter son mal.

ARGAN. – Les sottes raisons que voilà ! Tenez, mon frère, ne parlons point de cet homme-là davantage, car cela m'échauffe la bile, et vous me donneriez mon mal.

BÉRALDE. – Je le veux bien, mon frère ; et, pour changer de discours, je vous dirai que, sur une petite répugnance que vous témoigne votre fille, vous ne devez point prendre les résolutions violentes de la mettre dans un couvent ; que, pour le choix d'un gendre, il ne vous faut pas suivre aveuglément la passion qui vous emporte, et qu'on doit, sur cette matière, s'accommoder un peu à l'inclination d'une fille, puisque c'est pour toute la vie, et que de là dépend tout le bonheur d'un mariage.

## Scène IV

*Monsieur Fleurant, Argan, Béralde*

ARGAN. – Ah ! mon frère, avec votre permission.

BÉRALDE. – Comment ! que voulez-vous faire ?

ARGAN. – Prendre ce petit lavement-là ; ce sera bientôt fait.

BÉRALDE. – Vous vous moquez. Est-ce que vous ne sauriez être un moment sans lavement ou sans médecine ? Remettez cela à une autre fois, et demeurez un peu en repos.

ARGAN. – Monsieur Fleurant, à ce soir, ou à demain au matin.

MONSIEUR FLEURANT. – De quoi vous mêlez-vous de vous opposer aux ordonnances de la médecine, et d'empêcher Monsieur de prendre mon clystère ? Vous êtes bien plaisant d'avoir cette hardiesse-là !

BÉRALDE. – Allez, Monsieur, on voit bien que vous n'avez pas accoutumé de parler à des visages.

MONSIEUR FLEURANT. – On ne doit point ainsi se jouer des remèdes, et me faire perdre mon temps. Je ne suis venu ici que sur une bonne ordonnance, et je vais dire à Monsieur Purgon comme on m'a empêché d'exécuter ses ordres et de faire ma fonction. Vous verrez, vous verrez...

ARGAN. – Mon frère, vous serez cause ici de quelque malheur.

BÉRALDE. – Le grand malheur de ne pas prendre un lavement que Monsieur Purgon a ordonné. Encore un coup, mon frère, est-il possible qu'il n'y ait pas moyen de vous guérir de la maladie des médecins, et que vous vouliez être toute votre vie enseveli dans leurs remèdes ?

ARGAN. – Mon Dieu ! mon frère, vous en parlez comme un homme qui se porte bien ; mais, si vous étiez à ma place, vous changeriez bien de langage. Il est aisé de parler contre la médecine quand on est en pleine santé.

BÉRALDE. – Mais quel mal avez-vous ?

ARGAN. – Vous me feriez enrager. Je voudrais que vous l'eussiez, mon mal, pour voir si vous jaseriez tant. Ah ! voici Monsieur Purgon.

### Scène v

*Monsieur Purgon, Argan, Béralde, Toinette*

MONSIEUR PURGON. – Je viens d'apprendre là-bas, à la porte, de jolies nouvelles : qu'on se moque ici de mes ordonnances, et qu'on a fait refus de prendre le remède que j'avais prescrit.

ARGAN. – Monsieur, ce n'est pas...

MONSIEUR PURGON. – Voilà une hardiesse bien grande, une étrange rébellion d'un malade contre son médecin.

TOINETTE. – Cela est épouvantable.

MONSIEUR PURGON. – Un clystère que j'avais pris plaisir à composer moi-même.

ARGAN. – Ce n'est pas moi...

MONSIEUR PURGON. – Inventé et formé dans toutes les règles de l'art.

TOINETTE. – Il a tort.

MONSIEUR PURGON. – Et qui devait faire dans des entrailles un effet merveilleux…

ARGAN. – Mon frère ?

MONSIEUR PURGON. – Le renvoyer avec mépris !

ARGAN. – C'est lui…

MONSIEUR PURGON. – C'est une action exorbitante.

TOINETTE. – Cela est vrai.

MONSIEUR PURGON. – Un attentat énorme contre la médecine.

ARGAN. – Il est cause…

MONSIEUR PURGON. – Un crime de lèse-Faculté, qui ne se peut assez punir.

TOINETTE. – Vous avez raison.

MONSIEUR PURGON. – Je vous déclare que je romps commerce avec vous.

ARGAN. – C'est mon frère…

MONSIEUR PURGON. – Que je ne veux plus d'alliance avec vous.

TOINETTE. – Vous ferez bien.

MONSIEUR PURGON. – Et que, pour finir toute liaison avec vous, voilà la donation que je faisais à mon neveu, en faveur du mariage.

ARGAN. – C'est mon frère qui a fait tout le mal.

MONSIEUR PURGON. – Mépriser mon clystère !

ARGAN. – Faites-le venir, je m'en vais le prendre.

MONSIEUR PURGON. – Je vous aurais tiré d'affaire avant qu'il fût peu.

TOINETTE. – Il ne le mérite pas.

MONSIEUR PURGON. – J'allais nettoyer votre corps et en évacuer entièrement les mauvaises humeurs.

ARGAN. – Ah, mon frère !

MONSIEUR PURGON. – Et je ne voulais plus qu'une douzaine de médecines, pour vider le fond du sac.

TOINETTE. – Il est indigne de vos soins.

MONSIEUR PURGON. – Mais puisque vous n'avez pas voulu guérir par mes mains…

ARGAN. – Ce n'est pas ma faute.

MONSIEUR PURGON. – Puisque vous vous êtes soustrait de l'obéissance que l'on doit à son médecin…

TOINETTE. – Cela crie vengeance.

MONSIEUR PURGON. – Puisque vous vous êtes déclaré rebelle aux remèdes que je vous ordonnais…

ARGAN. – Hé ! point du tout.

MONSIEUR PURGON. – J'ai à vous dire que je vous abandonne à votre mauvaise constitution, à l'intempérie de vos entrailles, à la corruption de votre sang, à l'âcreté de votre bile et à la féculence de vos humeurs.

TOINETTE. – C'est fort bien fait.

ARGAN. – Mon Dieu !

MONSIEUR PURGON. – Et je veux qu'avant qu'il soit quatre jours vous deveniez dans un état incurable.

ARGAN. – Ah ! miséricorde !

MONSIEUR PURGON. – Que vous tombiez dans la bradypepsie.

ARGAN. – Monsieur Purgon.

MONSIEUR PURGON. – De la bradypepsie dans la dyspepsie.

ARGAN. – Monsieur Purgon.

MONSIEUR PURGON. – De la dyspepsie dans l'apepsie.

ARGAN. – Monsieur Purgon.

MONSIEUR PURGON. – De l'apepsie dans la lienterie.

ARGAN. – Monsieur Purgon.

MONSIEUR PURGON. – De la lienterie dans la dysenterie.

ARGAN. – Monsieur Purgon.

MONSIEUR PURGON. – De la dysenterie dans l'hydropisie.

ARGAN. – Monsieur Purgon.

MONSIEUR PURGON. – Et de l'hydropisie dans la privation de la vie, où vous aura conduit votre folie.

## Scène VI

*Argan, Béralde*

ARGAN. – Ah, mon Dieu ! je suis mort. Mon frère, vous m'avez perdu.

BÉRALDE. – Quoi ? qu'y a-t-il ?

ARGAN. – Je n'en puis plus. Je sens déjà que la médecine se venge.

BÉRALDE. – Ma foi ! mon frère, vous êtes fou, et je ne voudrais pas, pour beaucoup de choses, qu'on vous vît faire ce que vous faites. Tâtez-vous un peu, je vous prie, revenez à vous-même, et ne donnez point tant à votre imagination.

ARGAN. – Vous voyez, mon frère, les étranges maladies dont il m'a menacé.

BÉRALDE. – Le simple homme que vous êtes !

ARGAN. – Il dit que je deviendrai incurable avant qu'il soit quatre jours.

BÉRALDE. – Et ce qu'il dit, que fait-il à la chose ? Est-ce un oracle qui a parlé ? Il me semble, à vous entendre, que Monsieur Purgon tienne dans ses mains le filet de vos jours, et que, d'autorité suprême, il vous l'allonge et vous le raccourcisse comme il lui plaît. Songez que les principes de votre vie sont en vous-même, et que le courroux de Monsieur Purgon est aussi peu capable de vous faire mourir que ses remèdes de vous faire vivre. Voici une aventure, si vous voulez, à vous défaire des médecins ; ou, si vous êtes né à ne pouvoir vous en passer, il est aisé d'en avoir un autre, avec lequel, mon frère, vous puissiez courir un peu moins de risque.

ARGAN. – Ah ! mon frère, il sait tout mon tempérament et la manière dont il faut me gouverner.

BÉRALDE. – Il faut vous avouer que vous êtes un homme d'une grande prévention, et que vous voyez les choses avec d'étranges yeux.

### Scène VII

*Toinette, Argan, Béralde*

TOINETTE. – Monsieur, voilà un médecin qui demande à vous voir.

ARGAN. – Et quel médecin ?

TOINETTE. – Un médecin de la médecine.

ARGAN. – Je te demande qui il est ?

TOINETTE. – Je ne le connais pas ; mais il me ressemble comme deux gouttes d'eau, et si je n'étais sûre que ma mère était honnête femme, je dirais que ce serait quelque petit frère qu'elle m'aurait donné depuis le trépas de mon père.

ARGAN. – Fais-le venir.

BÉRALDE. – Vous êtes servi à souhait. Un médecin vous quitte, un autre se présente.

ARGAN. – J'ai bien peur que vous ne soyez cause de quelque malheur.

BÉRALDE. – Encore ! Vous en revenez toujours là ?

ARGAN. – Voyez-vous, j'ai sur le cœur toutes ces maladies-là que je ne connais point, ces...

## Scène VIII

*Toinette, en médecin ; Argan, Béralde*

TOINETTE. – Monsieur, agréez que je vienne vous rendre visite et vous offrir mes petits services pour toutes les saignées et les purgations dont vous aurez besoin.

ARGAN. – Monsieur, je vous suis fort obligé. Par ma foi ! voilà Toinette elle-même.

TOINETTE. – Monsieur, je vous prie de m'excuser, j'ai oublié de donner une commission à mon valet ; je reviens tout à l'heure.

ARGAN. – Eh ! ne diriez-vous pas que c'est effectivement Toinette ?

BÉRALDE. – Il est vrai que la ressemblance est tout à fait grande. Mais ce n'est pas la première fois qu'on a vu de ces sortes de choses, et les histoires ne sont pleines que de ces jeux de la nature.

ARGAN. – Pour moi, j'en suis surpris, et...

## Scène IX

*Toinette, Argan, Béralde*

TOINETTE *quitte son habit de médecin si promptement qu'il est difficile de croire que ce soit elle qui a paru en médecin.* – Que voulez-vous, Monsieur ?

ARGAN. – Comment ?

TOINETTE. – Ne m'avez-vous pas appelée ?

ARGAN. – Moi ? non.

TOINETTE. – Il faut donc que les oreilles m'aient corné.

ARGAN. – Demeure un peu ici pour voir comme ce médecin te ressemble.

TOINETTE, *en sortant, dit :* – Oui, vraiment, j'ai affaire là-bas, et je l'ai assez vu.

ARGAN. – Si je ne les voyais tous deux, je croirais que ce n'est qu'un.

BÉRALDE. – J'ai lu des choses surprenantes de ces sortes de ressemblances, et nous en avons vu de notre temps où tout le monde s'est trompé.

ARGAN. – Pour moi, j'aurais été trompé à celle-là, et j'aurais juré que c'est la même personne.


## Scène x

*Toinette, en médecin ; Argan, Béralde*

TOINETTE. – Monsieur, je vous demande pardon de tout mon cœur.

ARGAN. – Cela est admirable !

TOINETTE. – Vous ne trouverez pas mauvaise, s'il vous plaît, la curiosité que j'ai eue de voir un illustre malade comme vous êtes ; et votre réputation, qui s'étend partout, peut excuser la liberté que j'ai prise.

ARGAN. – Monsieur, je suis votre serviteur.

TOINETTE. – Je vois, Monsieur, que vous me regardez fixement. Quel âge croyez-vous bien que j'aie ?

ARGAN. – Je crois que tout au plus vous pouvez avoir vingt-six, ou vingt-sept ans.

TOINETTE. – Ah, ah, ah, ah, ah ! j'en ai quatre-vingt-dix.

ARGAN. – Quatre-vingt-dix ?

TOINETTE. – Oui. Vous voyez un effet des secrets de mon art, de me conserver ainsi frais et vigoureux.

ARGAN. – Par ma foi ! voilà un beau jeune vieillard pour quatre-vingt-dix ans.

TOINETTE. – Je suis médecin passager, qui vais de ville en ville, de province en province, de royaume en royaume, pour chercher d'illustres matières à ma capacité, pour trouver des malades dignes de m'occuper, capables d'exercer les grands et beaux secrets que j'ai trouvés dans la médecine. Je dédaigne de m'amuser à ce menu fatras de maladies ordinaires, à ces bagatelles de rhumatismes et de fluxions, à ces fiévrottes, à ces vapeurs, et à ces migraines. Je veux des maladies d'impor-tance : de bonnes fièvres continues avec des transports au cerveau, de bonnes fièvres pourprées, de bonnes pestes, de bonnes hydropisies formées, de bonnes pleurésies avec des inflammations de poitrine : c'est là que je me plais, c'est là que je triomphe. Et je voudrais, Monsieur, que vous eussiez toutes les maladies que je viens de dire, que vous fussiez abandonné de tous les médecins, désespéré, à l'agonie, pour vous montrer l'excellence de mes remèdes, et l'envie que j'aurais de vous rendre service.

ARGAN. – Je vous suis obligé, Monsieur, des bontés que vous avez pour moi.

TOINETTE. – Donnez-moi votre pouls. Allons donc, que l'on batte comme il faut. Ahy ! je vous ferai bien aller comme vous devez. Hoy ! ce pouls-là fait l'impertinent ; je vois bien que vous ne me connaissez pas encore. Qui est votre médecin ?

ARGAN. – Monsieur Purgon.

TOINETTE. – Cet homme-là n'est point écrit sur mes tablettes entre les grands médecins. De quoi dit-il que vous êtes malade ?

ARGAN. – Il dit que c'est du foie, et d'autres disent que c'est de la rate.

TOINETTE. – Ce sont tous des ignorants. C'est du poumon que vous êtes malade.

ARGAN. – Du poumon ?

TOINETTE. – Oui. Que sentez-vous ?

ARGAN. – Je sens de temps en temps des douleurs de tête.

TOINETTE. – Justement, le poumon.

ARGAN. – Il me semble parfois que j'ai un voile devant les yeux.

TOINETTE. – Le poumon.

ARGAN. – J'ai quelquefois des maux de cœur.

TOINETTE. – Le poumon.

ARGAN. – Je sens parfois des lassitudes par tous les membres.

TOINETTE. – Le poumon.

ARGAN. – Et quelquefois il me prend des douleurs dans le ventre, comme si c'était des coliques.

TOINETTE. – Le poumon. Vous avez appétit à ce que vous mangez ?

ARGAN. – Oui, Monsieur.

TOINETTE. – Le poumon. Vous aimez à boire un peu de vin ?

ARGAN. – Oui, Monsieur.

TOINETTE. – Le poumon. Il vous prend un petit sommeil après le repas, et vous êtes bien aise de dormir ?

ARGAN. – Oui, Monsieur.

TOINETTE. – Le poumon, le poumon, vous dis-je. Que vous ordonne votre médecin pour votre nourriture ?

ARGAN. – Il m'ordonne du potage.

TOINETTE. – Ignorant.

ARGAN. – De la volaille.

TOINETTE. – Ignorant.

ARGAN. – Du veau.

TOINETTE. – Ignorant.

ARGAN. – Des bouillons.

TOINETTE. – Ignorant.

ARGAN. – Des œufs frais.

TOINETTE. – Ignorant.

ARGAN. – Et le soir de petits pruneaux pour lâcher le ventre.

TOINETTE. – Ignorant.

ARGAN. – Et surtout de boire mon vin fort trempé.

TOINETTE. – *Ignorantus, ignoranta, ignorantum.* Il faut boire votre vin pur ; et pour épaissir votre sang, qui est trop subtil, il faut manger de bon gros bœuf, de bon gros porc, de bon fromage de Hollande, du gruau et du riz, et des marrons et des oublies, pour coller et conglutiner. Votre médecin est une bête. Je veux vous en envoyer un de ma main, et je viendrai vous voir de temps en temps, tandis que je serai en cette ville.

ARGAN. – Vous m'obligez beaucoup.

TOINETTE. – Que diantre faites-vous de ce bras-là ?

ARGAN. – Comment ?

TOINETTE. – Voilà un bras que je me ferais couper tout à l'heure, si j'étais que de vous.

ARGAN. – Et pourquoi ?

TOINETTE. – Ne voyez-vous pas qu'il tire à soi toute la nourriture, et qu'il empêche ce côté-là de profiter ?

ARGAN. – Oui ; mais j'ai besoin de mon bras.

TOINETTE. – Vous avez là aussi un œil droit que je me ferais crever, si j'étais en votre place.

ARGAN. – Crever un œil ?

TOINETTE. – Ne voyez-vous pas qu'il incommode l'autre, et lui dérobe sa nourriture ? Croyez-moi, faites-vous-le crever au plus tôt, vous en verrez plus clair de l'œil gauche.

ARGAN. – Cela n'est pas pressé.

TOINETTE. – Adieu. Je suis fâché de vous quitter si tôt ; mais il faut que je me trouve à une grande consultation qui se doit faire pour un homme qui mourut hier.

ARGAN. – Pour un homme qui mourut hier ?

TOINETTE. – Oui, pour aviser, et voir ce qu'il aurait fallu lui faire pour le guérir. Jusqu'au revoir.

ARGAN. – Vous savez que les malades ne reconduisent point.

BÉRALDE. – Voilà un médecin vraiment qui paraît fort habile.

ARGAN. – Oui, mais il va un peu bien vite.

BÉRALDE. – Tous les grands médecins sont comme cela.

ARGAN. – Me couper un bras, et me crever un œil, afin que l'autre se porte mieux ! J'aime bien mieux qu'il ne se porte pas si bien. La belle opération, de me rendre borgne et manchot !

### Scène XI

*Toinette, Argan, Béralde*

TOINETTE. – Allons, allons, je suis votre servante. Je n'ai pas envie de rire.

ARGAN. – Qu'est-ce que c'est ?

TOINETTE. – Votre médecin, ma foi ! qui me voulait tâter le pouls.

ARGAN. – Voyez un peu, à l'âge de quatre-vingt-dix ans !

BÉRALDE. – Oh çà ! mon frère, puisque voilà votre Monsieur Purgon brouillé avec vous, ne voulez-vous pas bien que je vous parle du parti qui s'offre pour ma nièce ?

ARGAN. – Non, mon frère, je veux la mettre dans un couvent, puisqu'elle s'est opposée à mes volontés. Je vois bien qu'il y a quelque amourette là-dessous, et j'ai découvert certaine entrevue secrète, qu'on ne sait pas que j'ai découverte.

BÉRALDE. – Hé bien ! mon frère, quand il y aurait quelque petite inclination, cela serait-il si criminel, et rien peut-il vous offenser, quand tout ne va qu'à des choses honnêtes comme le mariage ?

ARGAN. – Quoi qu'il en soit, mon frère, elle sera religieuse, c'est une chose résolue.

BÉRALDE. – Vous voulez faire plaisir à quelqu'un.

ARGAN. – Je vous entends. Vous en revenez toujours là, et ma femme vous tient au cœur.

BÉRALDE. – Hé bien ! oui, mon frère, puisqu'il faut parler à cœur ouvert, c'est votre femme que je veux dire ; et non plus que l'entêtement de la médecine, je ne puis vous souffrir l'entêtement où vous êtes pour elle, et voir que vous donniez tête baissée dans tous les pièges qu'elle vous tend.

TOINETTE. – Ah ! Monsieur, ne parlez point de Madame. C'est une femme sur laquelle il n'y a rien à dire, une femme sans artifice, et qui aime Monsieur, qui l'aime… On ne peut pas dire cela.

ARGAN. – Demandez-lui un peu les caresses qu'elle me fait.

TOINETTE. – Cela est vrai.

ARGAN. – L'inquiétude que lui donne ma maladie.

TOINETTE. – Assurément.

ARGAN. – Et les soins et les peines qu'elle prend autour de moi.

TOINETTE. – Il est certain. Voulez-vous que je vous convainque, et vous fasse voir tout à l'heure comme Madame aime Monsieur ? Monsieur, souffrez que je lui montre son bec jaune, et le tire d'erreur.

ARGAN. – Comment ?

TOINETTE. – Madame s'en va revenir. Mettez-vous tout étendu dans cette chaise, et contrefaites le mort. Vous verrez la douleur où elle sera, quand je lui dirai la nouvelle.

ARGAN. – Je le veux bien.

TOINETTE. – Oui ; mais ne la laissez pas longtemps dans le désespoir, car elle en pourrait bien mourir.

ARGAN. – Laisse-moi faire.

TOINETTE, *à Béralde*. – Cachez-vous, vous, dans ce coin-là.

ARGAN. – N'y a-t-il point quelque danger à contrefaire le mort ?

TOINETTE. – Non, non. Quel danger y aurait-il ? Étendez-vous là seulement. *(Bas.)* Il y aura plaisir à confondre votre frère. Voici Madame. Tenez-vous bien.


### Scène XII

*Béline, Toinette, Argan, Béralde*

TOINETTE. – Ah, mon Dieu ! Ah, malheur ! Quel étrange accident !

BÉLINE. – Qu'est-ce, Toinette ?

TOINETTE. – Ah, Madame !

BÉLINE. – Qu'y a-t-il ?

TOINETTE. – Votre mari est mort.

BÉLINE. – Mon mari est mort ?

TOINETTE. – Hélas ! oui. Le pauvre défunt est trépassé.

BÉLINE. – Assurément ?

TOINETTE. – Assurément. Personne ne sait encore cet accident-là, et je me suis trouvée ici toute seule. Il vient de passer entre mes bras. Tenez, le voilà tout de son long dans cette chaise.

BÉLINE. – Le Ciel en soit loué ! Me voilà délivrée d'un grand fardeau. Que tu es sotte, Toinette, de t'affliger de cette mort !

TOINETTE. – Je pensais, Madame, qu'il fallût pleurer.

BÉLINE. – Va, va, cela n'en vaut pas la peine. Quelle perte est-ce que la sienne ? et de quoi servait-il sur la terre ? Un homme incommode à tout le monde, malpropre, dégoûtant, sans cesse un lavement ou une médecine dans le ventre, mouchant, toussant, crachant toujours, sans esprit, ennuyeux, de mauvaise humeur, fatiguant sans cesse les gens, et grondant jour et nuit servantes et valets.

TOINETTE. – Voilà une belle oraison funèbre.

BÉLINE. – Il faut, Toinette, que tu m'aides à exécuter mon dessein, et tu peux croire qu'en me servant ta récompense est sûre. Puisque, par un bonheur, personne n'est encore averti de la chose, portons-le dans son lit, et tenons cette mort cachée, jusqu'à ce que j'aie fait mon affaire. Il y a des papiers, il y a de l'argent dont je veux me saisir, et il n'est pas juste que j'aie passé sans fruit auprès de lui mes plus belles années. Viens, Toinette, prenons auparavant toutes ses clefs.

ARGAN, *se levant brusquement.* – Doucement.

BÉLINE, *surprise et épouvantée.* – Ahy !

ARGAN. – Oui, Madame ma femme, c'est ainsi que vous m'aimez ?

TOINETTE. – Ah, ah ! le défunt n'est pas mort.

ARGAN, *à Béline, qui sort.* – Je suis bien aise de voir votre amitié, et d'avoir entendu le beau panégyrique que vous avez fait de moi. Voilà un avis au lecteur qui me rendra sage à l'avenir, et qui m'empêchera de faire bien des choses.

BÉRALDE, *sortant de l'endroit où il était caché.* – Hé bien ! mon frère, vous le voyez.

TOINETTE. – Par ma foi ! Je n'aurais jamais cru cela. Mais j'entends votre fille ; remettez-vous comme vous étiez, et voyons de quelle manière elle recevra votre mort. C'est une chose qu'il n'est pas mauvais d'éprouver ; et puisque vous êtes en train, vous connaîtrez par là les sentiments que votre famille a pour vous.

### Scène XIII

*Angélique, Argan, Toinette, Béralde*

TOINETTE *s'écrie*. – Ô Ciel ! ah, fâcheuse aventure ! Malheureuse journée !

ANGÉLIQUE. – Qu'as-tu, Toinette, et de quoi pleures-tu ?

TOINETTE. – Hélas ! j'ai de tristes nouvelles à vous donner.

ANGÉLIQUE. – Hé quoi ?

TOINETTE. – Votre père est mort.

ANGÉLIQUE. – Mon père est mort, Toinette ?

TOINETTE. – Oui ; vous le voyez là. Il vient de mourir tout à l'heure d'une faiblesse qui lui a pris.

ANGÉLIQUE. – Ô Ciel ! quelle infortune ! quelle atteinte cruelle ! Hélas ! faut-il que je perde mon père, la seule chose qui me restait au monde ? et qu'encore, pour un surcroît de désespoir, je le perde dans un moment où il était irrité contre moi ? Que deviendrai-je, malheureuse, et quelle consolation trouver après une si grande perte ?

### Scène XIV et dernière

*Cléante, Angélique, Argan, Toinette, Béralde*

CLÉANTE. – Qu'avez-vous donc, belle Angélique ? et quel malheur pleurez-vous ?

ANGÉLIQUE. – Hélas ! je pleure tout ce que dans la vie je pouvais perdre de plus cher et de plus précieux. Je pleure la mort de mon père.

CLÉANTE. – Ô Ciel ! quel accident ! quel coup inopiné ! Hélas ! après la demande que j'avais conjuré votre oncle de lui faire pour moi, je venais me présenter à lui, et tâcher par mes respects et par mes prières de disposer son cœur à vous accorder à mes vœux.

ANGÉLIQUE. – Ah ! Cléante, ne parlons plus de rien. Laissons là toutes les pensées du mariage. Après la perte de mon père, je ne veux plus être du monde, et j'y renonce pour jamais. Oui, mon père, si j'ai résisté tantôt à vos volontés, je veux suivre du moins une de vos intentions, et réparer par là le chagrin que je m'accuse de vous avoir donné. Souffrez, mon père, que je vous en donne ici ma parole, et que je vous embrasse, pour vous témoigner mon ressentiment.

ARGAN. – Ah, ma fille !

ANGÉLIQUE, *épouvantée*. – Ahi !

ARGAN. – Viens. N'aie point de peur, je ne suis pas mort. Va, tu es mon vrai sang, ma véritable fille ; et je suis ravi d'avoir vu ton bon naturel.

ANGÉLIQUE. – Ah ! quelle surprise agréable, mon père ! Puisque par un bonheur extrême le Ciel vous redonne à mes vœux, souffrez qu'ici je me jette à vos pieds pour vous supplier d'une chose. Si vous n'êtes pas favorable au penchant de mon cœur, si vous me refusez Cléante pour époux, je vous conjure au moins de ne me point forcer d'en épouser un autre. C'est toute la grâce que je vous demande.

CLÉANTE *se jette à genoux*. – Eh ! Monsieur, laissez-vous toucher à ses prières et aux miennes, et ne vous montrez point contraire aux mutuels empressements d'une si belle inclination.

BÉRALDE. – Mon frère, pouvez-vous tenir là contre ?

TOINETTE. – Monsieur, serez-vous insensible à tant d'amour ?

ARGAN. – Qu'il se fasse médecin, je consens au mariage. Oui, faites-vous médecin, je vous donne ma fille.

CLÉANTE. – Très volontiers, Monsieur ; s'il ne tient qu'à cela pour être votre gendre, je me ferai médecin, apothicaire même, si vous voulez. Ce n'est pas une affaire que cela, et je ferais bien d'autres choses pour obtenir la belle Angélique.

BÉRALDE. – Mais, mon frère, il me vient une pensée. Faites-vous médecin vous-même. La commodité sera encore plus grande, d'avoir en vous tout ce qu'il vous faut.

TOINETTE. – Cela est vrai. Voilà le vrai moyen de vous guérir bientôt ; et il n'y a point de maladie si osée, que de se jouer à la personne d'un médecin.

ARGAN. – Je pense, mon frère, que vous vous moquez de moi. Est-ce que je suis en âge d'étudier ?

BÉRALDE. – Bon, étudier ! Vous êtes assez savant ; et il y en a beaucoup parmi eux qui ne sont pas plus habiles que vous.

ARGAN. – Mais il faut savoir bien parler latin, connaître les maladies, et les remèdes qu'il y faut faire.

BÉRALDE. – En recevant la robe et le bonnet de médecin, vous apprendrez tout cela, et vous serez après plus habile que vous ne voudrez.

ARGAN. – Quoi ! l'on sait discourir sur les maladies quand on a cet habit-là ?

BÉRALDE. – Oui. L'on n'a qu'à parler avec une robe et un bonnet, tout galimatias devient savant, et toute sottise devient raison.

TOINETTE. – Tenez, Monsieur, quand il n'y aurait que votre barbe, c'est déjà beaucoup, et la barbe fait plus de la moitié d'un médecin.

CLÉANTE. – En tout cas, je suis prêt à tout.

BÉRALDE. – Voulez-vous que l'affaire se fasse tout à l'heure ?

ARGAN. – Comment tout à l'heure ?

BÉRALDE. – Oui, et dans votre maison.

ARGAN. – Dans ma maison ?

BÉRALDE. – Oui. Je connais une Faculté de mes amies, qui

viendra tout à l'heure en faire la cérémonie dans votre salle. Cela ne vous coûtera rien.

ARGAN. – Mais moi, que dire, que répondre ?

BÉRALDE. – On vous instruira en deux mots, et l'on vous donnera par écrit ce que vous devez dire. Allez-vous-en vous mettre en habit décent, je vais les envoyer quérir.

ARGAN. – Allons, voyons cela.

CLÉANTE. – Que voulez-vous dire, et qu'entendez-vous avec cette Faculté de vos amies... ?

TOINETTE. – Quel est donc votre dessein ?

BÉRALDE. – De nous divertir un peu ce soir. Les comédiens ont fait un petit intermède de la réception d'un médecin, avec des danses et de la musique ; je veux que nous en prenions ensemble le divertissement, et que mon frère y fasse le premier personnage.

ANGÉLIQUE. – Mais mon oncle, il me semble que vous vous jouez un peu beaucoup de mon père.

BÉRALDE. – Mais, ma nièce, ce n'est pas tant le jouer que s'accommoder à ses fantaisies. Tout ceci n'est qu'entre nous. Nous y pouvons aussi prendre chacun un personnage, et nous donner ainsi la comédie les uns aux autres. Le carnaval autorise cela. Allons vite préparer toutes choses.

CLÉANTE. – Y consentez-vous ?

ANGÉLIQUE. – Oui, puisque mon oncle nous conduit.

# TROISIÈME INTERMÈDE

*C'est une cérémonie burlesque d'un homme qu'on fait médecin en récit, chant et danse.*

## Entrée de ballet

*Plusieurs tapissiers viennent préparer la salle et placer les bancs en cadence ; ensuite de quoi toute l'assemblée, composée de huit Porteseringues, six Apothicaires, vingt-deux Docteurs, celui qui se fait recevoir médecin, huit Chirurgiens dansant et chantant, entre et prend ses places selon les rangs.*

| PRÆSES | [TRADUCTION] |
|---|---|
| | LE PRÉSIDENT |

|  |  |
|---|---|
| Sçavantissimi doctores, | Très savants docteurs, |
| Medicinae professores, | Professeurs de médecine, |
| Qui hic assemblati estis, | Qui êtes assemblés ici, |
| Et vos, altri Messiores, | Et vous autres, Messieurs, |
| 5 Sententiarum Facultatis | Des sentences de la Faculté |
| Fideles executores, | Fidèles exécuteurs, |
| Chirurgiani et apothicari, | Chirurgiens et apothicaires, |
| Atque tota compania aussi, | Et toute la compagnie aussi, |
| Salus, honor et argentum, | Salut, honneur et argent, |
| 10 Atque bonum appetitum. | Et bon appétit ! |
| | |
| Non possum, docti Confreri, | Je ne peux, doctes confrères, |
| En moi satis admirari | En moi-même admirer assez |
| Qualis bona inventio | Quelle bonne invention |
| Est medici professio ; | Est la profession de médecin ; |

15   *Quam bella chosa est*
           *[et bene trovata,*
    *Medicina illa benedicta,*
    *Quae suo nomine solo,*
    *Surprenanti miraculo,*
    *Depuis si longo tempore,*
20   *Facit à gogo vivere*
    *Tant de gens omni genere.*

    *Per totam terram videmus*
    *Grandam vogam ubi sumus,*

    *Et quod grandes et petiti*
25   *Sunt de nobis infatuti.*
    *Totus mundus currens ad*
           *[nostros remedios,*
    *Nos regardat sicut Deos ;*
    *Et nostris ordonnanciis*
    *Principes et reges soumissos*
           *[videtis.*

30   *Donque il est nostræ*
           *[sapientiæ,*
    *Boni sensus atque prudentiæ,*

    *De fortement travaillare*
    *A nos bene conservare*
    *In tali credito, voga et honore,*

35   *Et prandere gardam à non*
           *[recevere*
    *In nostro docto corpore*
    *Quam personas capabiles,*
    *Et totas dignas ramplire*
    *Has plaças honorabiles.*

*Comme c'est une belle chose*
           *[et bien trouvée,*
*Cette médecine bénie*
*Qui, grâce à son seul nom,*
*Miracle surprenant,*
*Depuis si longtemps,*
*Fait vivre à gogo*
*Tant de gens de toute sorte.*

*Sur toute la terre nous voyons*
*La grande vogue où nous*
           *[sommes,*
*Et que les grands et les petits*
*Sont de nous infatués.*
*Le monde entier courant après*
           *[nos remèdes,*
*Nous regarde comme des dieux ;*
*Et à nos ordonnances*
*Vous voyez soumis les princes et*
           *[les rois.*

*Donc il est de notre sagesse,*

*De notre bon sens et de notre*
           *[prudence,*

*De fortement travailler*
*À nous bien conserver*
*En tels crédit, vogue et*
           *[honneur*

*Et prendre garde à ne recevoir*

*Dans notre docte corporation*
*Que des personnes capables,*
*Et tout à fait dignes de remplir*
*Ces places honorables.*

| | |
|---|---|
| 40 C'est pour cela que nunc<br>    [convocati estis ;<br>Et credo quod trovabitis<br>Dignam matieram medici<br>In sçavanti homine que voici,<br>Lequel, in chosis omnibus,<br>45 Dono ad interrogandum,<br>Et à fond examinandum<br>Vostris capacitatibus. | C'est pour cela que vous êtes<br>    [à présent convoqués ;<br>Et je crois que vous trouverez<br>Matière à faire un bon médecin<br>Dans le savant homme que voici,<br>Lequel, sur toutes choses,<br>Je vous demande d'interroger,<br>Et d'examiner à fond<br>Grâce à vos capacités. |

PRIMUS DOCTOR

| | |
|---|---|
| Si mihi licenciam dat Dominus<br>    [Prœses,<br>Et tanti docti Doctores,<br>50 Et assistantes illustres,<br>Très sçavanti Bacheliero,<br>Quem estimo et honoro,<br>Domandabo causam et<br>    [rationem quare<br>Opium facit dormire. | |

LE PREMIER DOCTEUR

Si me le permettent Monsieur
    [le Président
Et tous les doctes docteurs,
Et leurs illustres assistants,
Au très savant bachelier,
Que j'estime et honore,
Je demanderai la cause et la
    [raison qui font
Que l'opium fait dormir.

BACHELIERUS

55 Mihi a docto Doctore
Domandatur causam et
    [rationem quare
Opium facit dormire :
À quoi respondeo,
Quia est in eo
60 Virtus dormitiva,
Cujus est natura
Sensus assoupire.

LE BACHELIER

À moi, le docte docteur
Demande la cause et la raison
    [qui font
Que l'opium fait dormir :
À quoi je réponds,
Qu'il y a en lui
Une vertu dormitive,
Dont c'est la nature
D'endormir les sens.

CHORUS

Bene, bene, bene, bene
    [respondere.
Dignus, dignus est entrare
65 In nostro docto corpore.

LE CHŒUR

Bien, bien, bien, bien répondu.

Il est digne, digne d'entrer
Dans notre docte corporation.

Cum permissione Domini
            [Præsidis,
Doctissimæ Facultatis,
Et totius his nostris actis
Companiæ assistantis,

70 Domandabo tibi, docte
            [Bacheliere,
Quæ sunt remedia
Quæ in maladia
Ditte hydropisia
Convenit facere.

BACHELIERUS
75 Clysterium donare,
Postea seignare,
Ensuitta purgare.

CHORUS
Bene, bene, bene, bene
            [respondere.
Dignus, dignus est entrare
80 In nostro docto corpore.

TERTIUS DOCTOR
Si bonum semblatur Domino
            [Præsidi,
Doctissimæ Facultati,
Et companiæ præsenti,
Domandabo tibi, docte
            [Bacheliere,
85 Quæ remedia eticis,
Pulmonicis, atque asmaticis,

Trovas à propos facere.

LE SECOND DOCTEUR
Avec la permission de Monsieur
            [le Président,
De la très docte Faculté,
Et de toute la compagnie
De ceux qui assistent à nos
            [actes,
Je te demanderai, docte
            [bachelier,
Quels sont les remèdes
Que pour la maladie
Qu'on nomme hydropisie
Il convient de donner.

LE BACHELIER
Il faut clystère donner,
Après saigner,
Ensuite purger.

LE CHŒUR
Bien, bien, bien, bien répondu.

Il est digne, digne d'entrer
Dans notre docte corporation.

LE TROISIÈME DOCTEUR
Si cela agrée à Monsieur
            [le Président,
De la très docte Faculté,
Et à la compagnie ici présente,
Je te demanderai, docte
            [bachelier,
Quels remèdes aux étiques,
Aux pulmoniques et aux
            [asthmatiques
Tu trouves à propos de donner.

| | |
|---|---|
| **BACHELIERUS** | **LE BACHELIER** |
| *Clysterium donare,* | *Il faut clystère donner,* |
| *Postea seignare,* | *Après saigner,* |
| 90 *Ensuitta purgare.* | *Ensuite purger.* |

<br>

**CHORUS**

*Bene, bene, bene, bene*
                *[respondere.*
*Dignus, dignus est entrare*
*In nostro docto corpore.*

**LE CHŒUR**

*Bien, bien, bien, bien répondu.*

*Il est digne, digne d'entrer*
*Dans notre docte corporation.*

<br>

**QUARTUS DOCTOR**

*Super illas maladias*
95 *Doctus Bachelierus dixit*
                *[maravillas,*
*Mais si non ennuyo Dominum*
                *[Præsidem,*
*Doctissimam Facultatem,*
*Et totam honorabilem*
*Companiam écoutantem,*
100 *Faciam illi unam*
                *[quæstionem.*
*De hiero maladus unus*
*Tombavit in meas manus :*
*Habet grandam fievram cum*
                *[redoublamentis,*
*Grandam dolorem capitis,*
105 *Et grandum malum au côté,*
*Cum granda difficultate*
*Et pena de respirare :*
*Veillas mihi dire,*
*Docte Bacheliere,*
110 *Quid illi facere ?*

**LE QUATRIÈME DOCTEUR**

*Sur ces maladies,*
*Le docte bachelier a dit des*
                *[merveilles,*
*Mais si je n'ennuie pas*
                *[Monsieur le Président,*
*La très docte Faculté,*
*Et toute l'honorable*
*Compagnie des écoutants,*
*Je lui poserai une question :*

*Hier un malade*
*Tomba entre mes mains :*
*Il avait une grande fièvre qui*
                *[ne faisait qu'augmenter,*
*Une grande douleur à la tête,*
*Et un grand mal au côté,*
*Avec grande difficulté*
*Et grande peine à respirer :*
*Veux-tu me dire,*
*Docte bachelier,*
*Le remède qu'il faut lui*
                *[donner ?*

<br>

**BACHELIERUS**

*Clysterium donare,*
*Postea seignare,*
*Ensuitta purgare.*

**LE BACHELIER**

*Il faut clystère donner,*
*Après saigner,*
*Ensuite purger.*

QUINTUS DOCTOR
*Mais si maladia*
115 *Opiniatria*
*Non vult se garire,*
*Quid illi facere ?*

LE CINQUIÈME DOCTEUR
*Mais si la maladie*
*Obstinée*
*Ne veut pas se laisser guérir,*
*Quel remède faut-il donner ?*

BACHELIERUS
*Clysterium donare,*
*Postea seignare,*
120 *Ensuitta purgare.*

LE BACHELIER
*Il faut clystère donner,*
*Après saigner,*
*Ensuite purger.*

CHORUS
*Bene, bene, bene, bene*
*[respondere.*
*Dignus, dignus est entrare*
*In nostro docto corpore.*

LE CHŒUR
*Bien, bien, bien, bien répondu.*

*Il est digne, digne d'entrer*
*Dans notre docte corporation.*

PRÆSES
*Juras gardare statuta*
125 *Per Facultatem præscripta*
*Cum sensu et jugeamento ?*

LE PRÉSIDENT
*Tu jures d'observer les règles*
*Prescrites par la Faculté*
*Avec bon sens et jugement ?*

BACHELIERUS
*Juro.*

LE BACHELIER
*Je le jure.*

PRÆSES
*Essere in omnibus*
*Consultationibus,*
130 *Ancieni aviso,*
*Aut bono,*
*Aut mauvaiso ?*

LE PRÉSIDENT
*D'être, dans toutes*
*Les consultations,*
*De l'avis d'un ancien*
*Qu'il soit bon*
*Ou mauvais ?*

BACHELIERUS
*Juro.*

LE BACHELIER
*Je le jure.*

PRÆSES
*De non jamais te servire*
135 *De remediis aucunis*

LE PRÉSIDENT
*De ne jamais te servir*
*D'aucun autre remède*

| | |
|---|---|
| *Quam de ceux seulement* | *Que ceux seulement de la* |
|       *[doctæ Facultatis,* |       *[docte Faculté,* |
| *Maladus dût-il crevare* | *Le malade dût-il crever* |
| *Et mori de suo malo ?* | *Et mourir de son mal ?* |

BACHELIERUS        LE BACHELIER

| | |
|---|---|
| *Juro.* | *Je le jure.* |

PRÆSES        LE PRÉSIDENT

| | |
|---|---|
| 140  *Ego, cum isto boneto* | *Moi, grâce à ce bonnet* |
| *Venerabili et docto,* | *Vénérable et docte,* |
| *Dono tibi et concedo* | *Je te donne et te concède* |
| *Virtutem et puissanciam* | *La vertu et la puissance* |
| *Medicandi,* | *D'exercer la médecine,* |
| 145  *Purgandi,* | *De purger,* |
| *Seignandi,* | *De saigner,* |
| *Perçandi,* | *De percer,* |
| *Taillandi,* | *De tailler,* |
| *Coupandi,* | *De couper,* |
| 150  *Et occidendi* | *Et de tuer,* |
| *Impune per totam terram.* | *En toute impunité, dans le* |
| |       *[monde entier.* |

**Entrée de ballet**

*Tous les Chirurgiens et Apothicaires viennent lui faire la révérence en cadence.*

BACHELIERUS        LE BACHELIER

| | |
|---|---|
| *Grandes doctores doctrinæ* | *Grands docteurs de la doctrine* |
| *De la rhubarbe et du séné* | *De la rhubarbe et du séné* |
| *Ce serait sans douta à moi* | *Ce serait sans doute à moi* |
|       *[chosa folla,* |       *[chose folle,* |
| 155  *Inepta et ridicula,* | *Inepte et ridicule,* |
| *Si j'alloibam m'engageare* | *Si j'allais m'engager* |
| *Vobis louangeas donare,* | *À dresser vos louanges,* |
| *Et entreprenoibam adjoutare* | *Et si j'entreprenais d'ajouter* |

Des lumieras au soleillo,
160  Et des étoilas au cielo,
Des ondas à l'Oceano,
Et des rosas au printanno.
Agreate qu'avec uno moto,
Pro toto remercimento,
165  Rendam gratiam corpori tam
               [docto.
Vobis, vobis debeo
Bien plus qu'à naturæ et qu'à
               [patri meo :
Natura et pater meus
Hominem me habent factum ;
170  Mais vos me, ce qui est bien
               [plus,
Avetis factum medicum,
Honor, favor, et gratia
Qui, in hoc corde que voilà,
Imprimant ressentimenta
175  Qui dureront in secula.

Des lumières au soleil,
Et des étoiles au ciel,
Et des ondes à l'océan,
Et des roses au printemps.
Agréez qu'en un seul mot,
En guise de tout remerciement,
Je rende grâces à une corporation
               [si savante.
À vous, à vous je dois
Bien plus qu'à la nature et qu'à
               [mon père :
La nature et mon père
Ont fait de moi un homme ;
Mais vous, de moi, ce qui est
               [bien plus,
Vous avez fait un médecin,
Honneur, faveur et grâce
Qui, dans ce cœur que voilà,
Impriment des sentiments
Qui dureront éternellement.

### CHORUS

Vivat, vivat, vivat, vivat, cent
               [fois vivat
Novus Doctor, qui tam bene
               [parlat !
Mille, mille annis et manget
               [et bibat,
Et seignet et tuat !

### LE CHŒUR

Vive, vive, vive, vive, vive
               [cent fois
Le nouveau docteur, qui parle
               [si bien !
Pendant mille et mille ans, qu'il
               [mange et qu'il boive,
Et qu'il saigne et qu'il tue !


### Entrée de ballet

Tous les Chirurgiens et les Apothicaires dansent au son des instruments et des voix, et des battements de mains, et des mortiers
d'apothicaires.

|                          |                          |
|--------------------------|--------------------------|
| **CHIRURGUS**            | **LE CHIRURGIEN**        |

180 *Puisse-t-il voir doctas*     *Puisse-t-il voir*
*Suas ordonnancias*        *Ses doctes ordonnances*
*Omnium chirurgorum*      *De tous les chirurgiens*
*Et apothiquarum*        *Et les apothicaires*
*Remplire boutiquas !*      *Remplir les boutiques !*

    **CHORUS**        **LE CHŒUR**

185 *Vivat, vivat, vivat, vivat, cent*  *Vive, vive, vive, vive, cent fois*
       *[fois vivat*
*Novus Doctor, qui tam bene*   *Le nouveau docteur, qui parle*
        *[parlat !*          *[si bien !*
*Mille, mille annis et manget et*  *Pendant mille et mille ans, qu'il*
        *[bibat,*       *[mange et qu'il boive,*
*Et seignet et tuat !*      *Et qu'il saigne et qu'il tue !*

    **CHIRURGUS**      **LE CHIRURGIEN**
*Puissent toti anni*       *Puissent toutes les années*
190 *Lui essere boni*       *Lui être bonnes*
*Et favorabiles,*        *Et favorables,*
*Et n'habere jamais*      *Et n'avoir jamais*
*Quam pestas, verolas,*     *Que pestes, véroles,*
*Fievras, pluresias,*      *Fièvres, pleurésies,*
195 *Fluxus de sang et*      *Flux de sang et dysenteries !*
      *[dyssenterias !*

    **CHORUS**        **LE CHŒUR**
*Vivat, vivat, vivat, vivat, cent*   *Vive, vive, vive, vive, cent fois*
       *[fois vivat*
*Novus Doctor, qui tam bene*   *Le nouveau docteur, qui parle*
        *[parlat !*          *[si bien !*
*Mille, mille annis et manget et*  *Pendant mille et mille ans, qu'il*
        *[bibat,*       *[mange et qu'il boive,*
*Et seignet et tuat !*      *Et qu'il saigne et qu'il tue !*

## Dernière entrée de ballet

# La scène à jouer

Dossier réalisé par Guillaume Poix,
comédien, metteur en scène et dramaturge
formé au cours Florent et à l'École Nationale
Supérieure d'Arts et Techniques du Théâtre

## Molière aujourd'hui et demain

*Dans ce dossier, vous trouverez :*

**1.** Une introduction qui présente certaines des problématiques traitées par Molière dans *Le Malade imaginaire,* et étudie les enjeux de l'œuvre dans un contexte contemporain. Il s'agit avant tout d'ouvrir des pistes de réflexion, les plus larges possibles, en mettant en lumière des échos avec la littérature contemporaine, le cinéma, la sociologie ou des phénomènes de société actuels dans le but d'instaurer un véritable débat entre le texte, le professeur et les élèves. Pourquoi ? pour montrer la démarche que toute équipe artistique, désireuse de « monter » la pièce aujourd'hui, est amenée à produire pour saisir ce qui fait sa singularité, tout autant que sa modernité. Sans « abîmer » l'intégrité historique de l'œuvre, ce travail permet de la rendre plus proche, afin qu'elle ne se fige pas dans un passé littéraire patrimonial, mais demeure bien vivante à nos yeux, comme l'est l'art théâtral.

**2.** Un zoom précis sur une scène emblématique de l'œuvre, pour montrer comment travaillent metteurs en scène et comédiens lorsqu'ils abordent une pièce de théâtre. La partie intitulée « À la table » balaye les questions dramaturgiques fondamentales de la scène choisie. De quoi s'agit-il ? C'est l'équipe qui se réunit autour d'une « table », pour mettre au jour les enjeux du texte, le sens implicite, les dynamiques internes. La deuxième partie intitulée « Au plateau » propose des exemples de notes de mise en scène qui sont l'étape préparatoire pour pouvoir jouer le texte. Ce sont les mêmes indications que celles qu'un metteur en scène pourrait noter après avoir effectué le travail « à la table ». Cela lui sert à diriger les acteurs, à convertir l'écriture, le texte, en paroles, en espaces et en corps. Ces notes sont le point de vue du metteur en scène : à chaque annotation ou interprétation, il prend parti sur le texte et en propose une vision singulière. Ce cahier de mise en scène rappelle qu'un texte de théâtre est avant tout écrit pour être joué, c'est-à-dire pour rencontrer une intention de mise en scène et se déployer sur un plateau.

À vous de jouer !

# I. Molière : tout de suite, là, maintenant !

## Malade, mais pas trop

En 1986, Woody Allen, le célèbre réalisateur américain à qui l'on doit déjà *Annie Hall, Manhattan* ou *La Rose pourpre du Caire*, exorcise, avec *Hannah et ses sœurs*, sa propre tendance à l'hypocondrie : le personnage qu'il s'est composé est en effet paniqué à l'idée d'avoir contracté un cancer de la peau lorsqu'il relève sur sa chemise une tache noire qui ne s'avère être... qu'une éclaboussure d'encre ! Woody Allen rend ici compte de ce qui caractérise précisément les personnes atteintes de cette terreur obsessionnelle qui les conduit à se croire malades en permanence : le délire interprétatif. Rien ne peut venir le tempérer, pas même la parole des médecins, et c'est bien tout le problème ! Une égratignure insignifiante est ainsi perçue comme une blessure préoccupante, une douleur légère devient immédiatement le symptôme d'une tumeur incurable, et tout rhume précède une pneumonie foudroyante ! À partir d'un constat, aussi minime soit-il, concernant son corps ou son état général, l'imaginaire de l'hypocondriaque échafaude mille scénarios catastrophiques et disproportionnés entérinant le pire.

Car c'est bien un rapport paranoïaque qui s'instaure entre corps et esprit : le premier se signale par la douleur ou l'anomalie ; le second s'empare de cette manifestation et invente une fiction calamiteuse pour lui donner un sens. S'exprime donc, dans cette angoisse, une hantise de la perte de contrôle aussi bien qu'une peur panique de la mort.

## « ... Je n'ai pas seulement le loisir de songer à ma maladie. »

Les circonstances de la mort de Molière ne sont, il faut le dire, pas là pour rassurer l'hypocondriaque. C'est en effet pendant les représentations du *Malade imaginaire*, en février 1673, que Molière succombe. Comme Woody Allen, il s'était créé un personnage sur mesure avec Argan, et l'ironie du sort a voulu qu'il soit justement terrassé en jouant cet homme maladivement obsédé par la mort, comme si l'anxiété de l'hypocondriaque trouvait avec cette anecdote une justification et un prétexte pour se déchaîner davantage.

Chez Argan, la maladie est un mode de vie. Perpétuellement malade, consultant un médecin quotidiennement, et tout entier occupé par le tri et l'inventaire maniaque de ses médicaments, Argan trouve un sens à son existence en combattant son propre déclin. La complainte est son langage, c'est avec cette forme qu'il s'exprime, et, pour le fond, il ne parle pratiquement que de ce qui a trait à sa santé – terme qu'il n'aime d'ailleurs pas ! Car ce que redoute le plus celui qui se persuade qu'il est malade, c'est qu'on apporte des dénégations à sa croyance. Plus on tente de le rassurer, ou de le raisonner, plus il se radicalise : il connaît son corps et sait bien qu'on lui ment ; c'est d'ailleurs pour cette raison que la parole médicale est systématiquement mise en doute. L'attention des médecins et les protocoles proposés ne sont jamais à la hauteur du péril ressenti par le soi-disant malade. La confiance est vacillante et, on le voit avec Argan, patient pourtant docile, aucune guérison n'est jamais possible tout simplement parce que la jouissance de l'hypocondriaque repose sur le désir qu'il forme sans cesse pour la maladie : c'est pour lui une quête infinie et éperdue.

## Le souci de soi

Cette traque de la maladie se solde nécessairement par un examen permanent de son propre corps. Il est en effet inévitable qu'un être obsédé par l'altération de sa santé en écoute constamment les manifestations potentielles. « S'écouter », être scrupuleusement à l'écoute de son corps, devient dès lors un impératif indépassable. Dans une moindre mesure, il existe aujourd'hui une forme d'institutionnalisation de cette injonction : notre société, largement médicalisée, nous encourage en effet à nous préoccuper de nos corps, dans une perspective tant esthétique et érotique, que sanitaire. Le souci de soi est ainsi l'un des mots d'ordre du monde occidental contemporain.

Il importe aujourd'hui de cultiver son corps et de l'entretenir comme un patrimoine précieux. L'obsession de la dégradation du corps, c'est-à-dire de la vieillesse, pousse un certain nombre d'entre nous à le soigner avec zèle pour ralentir sa dégénérescence, comme si nous avions l'espoir fou de gagner ainsi l'immortalité. En chosifiant notre corps, en le considérant désormais comme un bien qu'il faut conserver, nous manifestons notre refus du temps qui passe, nous contestons le caractère périssable de notre nature. C'est peut-être au fond cela qu'éprouve un hypocondriaque invétéré, à un degré certes plus élevé que tout un chacun : la haine de la fugacité.

### On ne vit que deux fois

Notre corps glisse inexorablement vers sa fin, et de ce constat naît souvent un refus. C'est précisément ce refus qui anime Argan : il n'accepte pas la perspective de disparaître au monde et a en horreur tout ce qui passe, tout ce qui se dissipe. Son corps est une permanence, un repère essentiel pour lui, et l'entretien de ce corps qu'il estime assailli sans repos par la maladie, loin de le préserver, nécessite de sa part un combat qui l'aliène. Prisonnier de cette obsession, littéralement enfermé dans le souci de son corps, il est incapable de voir avec justesse le monde qui l'entoure. Il s'aveugle en effet complètement sur sa seconde femme Béline qui ne souhaite que sa mort, et sur l'amour que lui portent ses filles qu'il malmène abusivement. Entièrement mobilisé par la lutte qu'il mène contre l'affaiblissement de son corps, donc contre le passage du temps, il n'a de la réalité qu'une image déformée par son narcissisme.

Car n'est-ce pas parce qu'il se préfère en toutes circonstances qu'Argan se méprend sur son entourage ? Il juge plus important de s'analyser constamment que d'observer et d'écouter ses proches. Molière, qui a puisé en lui-même, on l'a dit, pour composer Argan, ne nous raconte-t-il pas ici, au soir de sa vie, les échecs possibles d'une existence ? À force de s'enfermer dans un système de vie qui ne consiste qu'à prendre soin de soi-même, à travailler à sa propre pérennité, ne risque-t-on pas de finir seul et malade pour de bon ? Il faudra qu'Argan simule la mort pour comprendre son erreur : mais combien sommes-nous à avoir cette chance de « mourir deux fois » ?

## II. La scène à jouer

**Acte III, scène x (Toinette, *en médecin* ; Argan, Béralde)**

**À la table**

### Qui

Trois protagonistes sont présents dans cette scène. Argan, tout d'abord, personnage principal de la pièce, vieil homme hypocondriaque et obsédé par sa santé. Son frère Béralde, ensuite, quasiment muet dans cette scène, et plus sage qu'Argan qu'il tente régulièrement de raisonner sans grand succès. Enfin, Toinette, servante de la maison d'Argan, femme truculente et impertinente qui n'hésite pas à défier son maître quand elle estime qu'il a tort ou bien qu'il exagère. Ici, elle est déguisée en médecin : apparaissent ainsi son goût pour la tromperie et son tempérament moqueur. Prompte à railler Argan, elle ne recule devant aucune ruse.

### Quand

Argan est au désespoir : son médecin attitré, Monsieur Purgon, vient de lui signifier qu'il refusait désormais de le soigner. Alors qu'il s'en afflige auprès de son frère Béralde, Argan est averti par Toinette qu'un nouveau médecin, justement de passage, désire l'examiner. C'est en réalité un stratagème imaginé par Toinette pour qu'Argan accepte enfin de marier sa fille Angélique avec Cléante : persuadé par Monsieur Purgon qu'il lui fallait être constamment sous surveillance médicale, Argan préfère ainsi, pour son confort personnel, que sa fille épouse un médecin plutôt que celui qu'elle aime vraiment. Toinette espère, par cette ruse, dénigrer Monsieur Purgon aux yeux d'Argan. Pour éviter d'être reconnue, elle feint la surprise de se trouver une ressemblance troublante avec ledit médecin de passage, ce qu'Argan ne manque pas de remarquer également, sans pour autant parvenir à la démasquer. Béralde est ici plus qu'un observateur amusé de la supercherie de Toinette : il est son complice.

## Quoi

La scène est donc une parodie de consultation médicale. Examinant Argan selon un protocole tout à fait fantaisiste, Toinette manifeste une verve sans pareil pour ridiculiser la « caste » des médecins tout autant que leurs patients crédules. Contradictoire, sévère, catégorique, Toinette joue le rôle d'un effroyable médecin qui plaque son savoir sur une situation qui n'a rien à voir et que l'examen médical pourrait même contredire. Ce faisant, Toinette critique l'incapacité qu'ont certains médecins à mettre de côté leurs prétendues compétences au profit de l'observation. Vaniteux, ils préfèrent prescrire d'ineptes remèdes conformes à leurs connaissances encyclopédiques plutôt que de s'adapter à l'observation des phénomènes, qui est la base de toute science sérieuse. Captifs de leur panique, les patients, pour leur part, se laissent berner et perdent toute capacité de jugement : ils n'osent mettre en doute la parole du médecin, considérée comme sacrée. C'est donc une relation abusive que critique ici Toinette : les médecins exerceraient, en quelque sorte, un chantage terroriste contre leurs patients, en jouant sur leur peur de la maladie.

## Comment

La stratégie de Toinette est simple : il s'agit de faire prendre conscience à Argan de cette manipulation opérée par certains médecins sur leurs patients, en se montrant incohérente, discordante et excessive. On glisse en effet peu à peu dans un registre résolument burlesque où l'ordre est renversé : pour conserver la santé, Argan est sommé de se goinfrer, de s'enivrer, de se crever l'œil et de se couper le bras ! Cette prescription, pour le moins surprenante, joue de l'outrance et du paradoxe : c'est un tour grossier pour tenter de réveiller Argan, dont l'obsession sanitaire est, on l'a vu, plus que tenace. Mais il faut ce qu'il faut : pour rouvrir les yeux d'un aveuglé, tous les moyens sont bons !

## Au plateau : à vous de jouer !

TOINETTE, *en médecin*. – Monsieur, je vous demande pardon de tout mon cœur.

ARGAN. – <u>Cela est admirable !</u> (ARGAN REPREND VIE : LE HASARD LUI PORTE UN MÉDECIN EN REMPLACEMENT DE MONSIEUR PURGON. LA CONSULTATION EST L'UN DE SES MOMENTS FAVORIS ; ON DOIT SENTIR SON EXCITATION ET LE PLAISIR QU'IL A À ENVISAGER L'EXAMEN MÉDICAL.)

TOINETTE. – Vous ne trouverez pas mauvaise, s'il vous plaît, la curiosité que j'ai eue de voir <u>un illustre malade comme vous êtes, et votre réputation, qui s'étend partout,</u> peut excuser la liberté que j'ai prise. (FORMULATION COCASSE QUI TOURNE ARGAN EN RIDICULE SANS QU'IL EN AIT ÉVIDEMMENT CONSCIENCE. TOINETTE ÉPINGLE ICI LA VANITÉ DE SON MAÎTRE : SON HYPOCONDRIE EST TELLE QU'IL EN EST DEVENU CÉLÈBRE, ET C'EST PEUT-ÊTRE AU FOND CE QU'IL DÉSIRAIT, ÊTRE UN OBJET DE FASCINATION POUR LES MÉDECINS, ÊTRE UN « CAS » FAMEUX !)

ARGAN. – Monsieur, je suis votre serviteur.

TOINETTE. – <u>Je vois, Monsieur, que vous me regardez fixement. Quel âge croyez-vous bien que j'ai ?</u> (TOINETTE ESQUIVE : ELLE SENT PEUT-ÊTRE QU'ARGAN EST EN PASSE DE LA RECONNAÎTRE, IL LUI FAUT DONC RAPIDEMENT DÉTOURNER SON ATTENTION. EN DIRIGEANT LA CONVERSATION SUR L'ÂGE, TOINETTE EST CERTAINE D'INTÉRESSER ARGAN, PUISQU'ELLE ABORDE AINSI LES THÈMES DE LA SANTÉ ET DE LA CONSERVATION QUI CORRESPONDENT EXACTEMENT À L'OBSESSION DE SON MAÎTRE.)

ARGAN. – Je crois que tout au plus vous pouvez avoir vingt-six, ou vingt-sept ans.

TOINETTE. – <u>Ah, ah, ah, ah, ah ! j'en ai quatre-vingt-dix.</u> (SUBTERFUGE PEU CRÉDIBLE MAIS EFFICACE AVEC ARGAN ; TOINETTE FAIT ICI COUP DOUBLE : D'UNE PART, ELLE ÉLOIGNE LES SOUPÇONS D'ARGAN QUI VOIT SANS DOUTE EN ELLE, À JUSTE TITRE, LE DOUBLE DE SA JEUNE SERVANTE, D'AUTRE PART, ELLE AMORCE SA CONSULTATION EN RENDANT LE MÉDECIN QU'ELLE INCARNE DIGNE D'INTÉRÊT, CAR CAPABLE DE RETENIR LA JEUNESSE !)

ARGAN. – Quatre-vingt-dix ?

TOINETTE. – Oui. Vous voyez un effet des secrets de mon art, de me conserver ainsi frais et vigoureux. (EN DONNANT LES RAISONS DE SA « BONNE » CONSERVATION, TOINETTE ACHÈVE DE RENDRE SON PERSONNAGE EXCEPTIONNEL...)

ARGAN. – Par ma foi ! voilà un beau jeune vieillard pour quatre-vingt-dix ans. (L'EMPLOI DE L'OXYMORE PEUT MANIFESTER OU BIEN L'INCRÉDULITÉ D'ARGAN, OU BIEN SON ADMIRATION.)

TOINETTE. – Je suis médecin passager, qui vais de ville en ville, de province en province, de royaume en royaume, pour chercher d'illustres matières à ma capacité, pour trouver des malades dignes de m'occuper, capables d'exercer les grands et beaux secrets que j'ai trouvés dans la médecine. Je dédaigne de m'amuser à ce menu fatras de maladies ordinaires, à ces bagatelles de rhumatismes et de fluxions, à ces fiévrottes, à ces vapeurs, et à ces migraines. Je veux des maladies d'importance : de bonnes fièvres continues avec des transports au cerveau, de bonnes fièvres pourprées, de bonnes pestes, de bonnes hydropisies formées, de bonnes pleurésies avec des inflammations de poitrine : c'est là que je me plais, c'est là que je triomphe. Et je voudrais, Monsieur, que vous eussiez toutes les maladies que je viens de dire, que vous fussiez abandonné de tous les médecins, désespéré, à l'agonie, pour vous montrer l'excellence de mes remèdes, et l'envie que j'aurais de vous rendre service. (CETTE PRISE DE PAROLE EST EMBLÉMATIQUE DU TON PARADOXAL AVEC LEQUEL TOINETTE S'EXPRIME. EN SE PEIGNANT COMME UN MÉDECIN INTÉRESSÉ PAR LES CAS LES PLUS GRAVES ET LES PLUS DÉSESPÉRÉS, TOINETTE ESPÈRE VALORISER ARGAN ET JOUER SUR SA VANITÉ : CELUI-CI SOUHAITE EN EFFET SE DISTINGUER PAR SES PATHOLOGIES. L'ANAPHORE OXYMORIQUE DE L'ADJECTIF « BONNE » AMPLIFIE DE PLUS LE COMIQUE DU PASSAGE EN DONNANT AUX PIRES MALADIES UN CARACTÈRE POSITIF DU POINT DE VUE DU MÉDECIN, PARCE QU'À MÊME DE LUI DONNER L'OCCASION D'EXERCER SA SCIENCE. UNE FORME DE CYNISME SE MANIFESTE ICI, ET C'EST BIEN CET EFFET QUE SOUHAITE PRODUIRE TOINETTE DANS CE DOUBLE DISCOURS.)

ARGAN. – Je vous suis obligé, Monsieur, des bontés que vous avez pour moi. (ARGAN RÉPOND SUR LE MÊME REGISTRE DU PARADOXE. DEUX OPTIONS SONT POSSIBLES : SOIT ARGAN EST IRONIQUE ET SE COMPORTE AINSI COMME TOUT UN CHACUN QUI SERAIT HORRIFIÉ PAR LES VŒUX DE TOINETTE ; SOIT IL EST SINCÈRE, CE QUI SEMBLE PLUS CONFORME À SA PERSONNALITÉ : IL AIME LA MALADIE, IL LA

RECHERCHE, ET IL EST FLATTÉ D'ÊTRE SOIGNÉ. ON JOUERA ICI DONC, SELON LES CAS, SUR DEUX FORMES DIFFÉRENTES DU COMIQUE.)

TOINETTE. – Donnez-moi votre pouls. (DÉBUT DE L'EXAMEN MÉDICAL : LE COMIQUE DE LA SCÈNE REPOSE SUR LE FAIT QUE LE PUBLIC, AVERTI DE L'IMPOSTURE, ATTEND, NON SANS JUBILATION, DE VOIR COMMENT TOINETTE VA S'EN SORTIR ET QUELLES ABSURDITÉS ELLE S'APPRÊTE À IMAGINER...) Allons donc, que l'on batte comme il faut. Ahy ! je vous ferai bien aller comme vous devez. (EXPRESSION TAUTOLOGIQUE QUI PARODIE LA PUISSANCE DES MÉDECINS.) Hoy ! ce pouls-là fait l'impertinent ; je vois bien que vous ne me connaissez pas encore. Qui est votre médecin ?

ARGAN. – Monsieur Purgon.

TOINETTE. – Cet homme-là n'est point écrit sur mes tablettes entre les grands médecins. (DÉBUT DE L'ENTREPRISE DE DÉMOLITION DE PURGON PAR TOINETTE.) De quoi dit-il que vous êtes malade ? (JOUER LE MÉPRIS DE TOINETTE : IL FAUT QU'ELLE SOIT CINGLANTE DÈS QU'ELLE PARLE DE PURGON.)

ARGAN. – Il dit que c'est du foie, et d'autres disent que c'est de la rate.

TOINETTE. – Ce sont tous des ignorants. C'est du poumon que vous êtes malade. (TOUR DE FORCE DE TOINETTE : EN CONTREDISANT LESDITS SPÉCIALISTES, DE MANIÈRE PROMPTE, ET ÉVIDEMMENT TOUT À FAIT FANTAISISTE, ELLE ASSOIT SON AUTORITÉ ET CONGÉDIE D'UN REVERS DE MAIN TOUS LES AUTRES MÉDECINS. PREMIÈRE OCCURRENCE D'UN TERME FONDAMENTAL DANS LA SCÈNE, ON LE VERRA : « IGNORANT » JOUERA UN RÔLE CAPITAL DANS L'EMBALLEMENT COMIQUE.)

ARGAN. – Du poumon ?

TOINETTE. – Oui. Que sentez-vous ?

ARGAN. – Je sens de temps en temps des douleurs de tête. (LA LISTE DES SYMPTÔMES D'ARGAN DOIT RENDRE COMPTE D'UNE CERTAINE BANALITÉ : NOUS ÉPROUVONS TOUS, DE TEMPS À AUTRE, LES DOULEURS ET LES SENSATIONS QU'IL ÉVOQUE. C'EST SUR CELA QUE REPOSE L'HYPOCONDRIE : LE REFUS DE CONSIDÉRER QUE L'ON PEUT ÊTRE SUJET À DES MAUX ORDINAIRES. CE PASSAGE OUVRE UNE SÉQUENCE REPOSANT SUR L'EFFET COMIQUE DE L'ANAPHORE « LE POUMON » : EN POSANT LE MÊME DIAGNOSTIC QUEL QUE SOIT LE SYMPTÔME AVANCÉ PAR ARGAN,

Toinette. – Justement, le poumon.

Argan. – Il me semble parfois que j'ai un voile devant les yeux.

Toinette. – Le poumon.

Argan. – J'ai quelquefois des maux de cœur.

Toinette. – Le poumon.

Argan. – Je sens parfois des lassitudes par tous les membres.

Toinette. – Le poumon.

Argan. – Et quelquefois il me prend des douleurs dans le ventre, comme si c'était des coliques.

Toinette. – Le poumon. Vous avez appétit à ce que vous mangez ?

Argan. – <u>Oui, Monsieur.</u>

Toinette. – Le poumon. Vous aimez à boire un peu de vin ?

Argan. – <u>Oui, Monsieur.</u>

Toinette. – Le poumon. Il vous prend un petit sommeil après le repas, et vous êtes bien aise de dormir ?

Argan. – <u>Oui, Monsieur.</u> (En somme, Argan est en excellente santé, c'est bien ce qu'on peut déduire de ses trois réponses successives !)

Toinette. – Le poumon, le poumon, vous dis-je. <u>Que vous ordonne votre médecin pour votre nourriture ?</u> (De nouveau, Toinette s'acharne contre Monsieur Purgon : elle veut le mettre définitivement hors jeu en mon-

TRANT QUE SES PRESCRIPTIONS SONT MAUVAISES ET QU'IL PRATIQUE LA MÉDECINE COMME UN SOT ! NOUVELLE SÉQUENCE COMIQUE REPOSANT SUR L'ANAPHORE DE L'INSULTE QUI EST PROFÉRÉE À SIX REPRISES, AVANT SA DÉCLINAISON LATINE.)

ARGAN. – Il m'ordonne du potage.

TOINETTE. – Ignorant.

ARGAN. – De la volaille.

TOINETTE. – Ignorant.

ARGAN. – Du veau.

TOINETTE. – Ignorant.

ARGAN. – Des bouillons.

TOINETTE. – Ignorant.

ARGAN. – Des œufs frais.

TOINETTE. – Ignorant.

ARGAN. – Et le soir de petits pruneaux pour lâcher le ventre.

TOINETTE. – Ignorant.

ARGAN. – Et surtout de boire mon vin fort trempé.

TOINETTE. – *Ignorantus, ignoranta, ignorantum.* Il faut boire votre vin pur ; et pour épaissir votre sang, qui est trop subtil, il faut manger de bon gros bœuf, de bon gros porc, de bon fromage de Hollande, du gruau et du riz, et des marrons et des oublies, pour coller et conglutiner. (LE RÉGIME DE REMPLACEMENT PRESCRIT PAR TOINETTE EST ÉVIDEMMENT DANGEREUX ET NON ADAPTÉ ; EN L'ENCOURAGEANT À MANGER GRAS ET LOURD ET À BOIRE JUSQU'À L'IVRESSE, TOINETTE LUI PRÉPARE, UNE FOIS N'EST PAS COUTUME, UNE VRAIE MALADIE ! NOUVELLE ANAPHORE DE L'ADJECTIF « BON », QUI A LA MÊME

FONCTION QUE CELLE QUI INTERVENAIT POUR LES MALADIES LES PLUS GRAVES ; ICI, L'ADJECTIF QUALIFIE LES ALIMENTS LES PLUS GRAS.) Votre médecin est une bête. (NOUVELLE INJURE AU PASSAGE...) Je veux vous en envoyer un de ma main, et je viendrai vous voir de temps en temps, tandis que je serai en cette ville.

ARGAN. – <u>Vous m'obligez beaucoup.</u> (ARGAN N'A PAS ENCORE MIS EN DOUTE LA SCIENCE DE TOINETTE : IL SEMBLE TOUT DISPOSÉ À SUIVRE LES PRESCRIPTIONS CONTRADICTOIRES QU'ELLE LUI DONNE ; IL VA FALLOIR QUE TOINETTE ENCLENCHE UNE AUTRE ÉTAPE DE LA SATIRE POUR QU'ARGAN COMMENCE À SE MÉFIER DE LA SCIENCE MÉDICALE...)

TOINETTE. – Que diantre faites-vous de ce bras-là ?

ARGAN. – Comment ?

TOINETTE. – <u>Voilà un bras que je me ferais couper tout à l'heure, si j'étais que de vous.</u> (LE CONSEIL QU'ELLE DONNE EST DU MÊME ORDRE QUE TOUS CEUX QU'ELLE A PRODIGUÉS JUSQU'ICI, MAIS EN POUSSANT LA LOGIQUE PLUS LOIN ENCORE, ELLE RADICALISE SON PROPOS DANS L'ESPOIR DE RÉVEILLER ARGAN. ELLE LE MET EN FAIT FACE À SA LOGIQUE : PRÊT À TOUT POUR SE SOIGNER, ALORS QU'IL N'EST PAS MALADE, ET PRÊT À SUIVRE AVEUGLÉMENT LES CONSEILS DES MÉDECINS, IL EST COMME EMBRIGADÉ ; EN SUGGÉRANT UN REMÈDE DE CETTE NATURE, ELLE SOUHAITE VOIR S'IL AURA UN SURSAUT DE JUGEOTE.)

ARGAN. – Et pourquoi ?

TOINETTE. – Ne voyez-vous pas qu'il tire à soi toute la nourriture, et qu'il empêche ce côté-là de profiter ?

ARGAN. – Oui ; mais j'ai besoin de mon bras.

TOINETTE. – Vous avez là aussi un œil droit que je me ferais crever, si j'étais en votre place.

ARGAN. – Crever un œil ?

TOINETTE. – Ne voyez-vous pas qu'il incommode l'autre, et lui dérobe sa nourriture ? Croyez-moi, faites-vous-le crever au plus tôt, vous en verrez plus clair de l'œil gauche.

ARGAN. – <u>Cela n'est pas pressé.</u> (ARGAN SEMBLE ENFIN PRENDRE CONSCIENCE DU CARACTÈRE ABSURDE DES PROPOS DE TOINETTE : IL COMMENCE PEUT-ÊTRE À CONNAÎTRE LE DOUTE QUANT À LA PERTINENCE DES ORDONNANCES MÉDICALES...)

TOINETTE. – Adieu. <u>Je suis fâché de vous quitter si tôt ; mais il faut que je me trouve à une grande consultation qui se doit faire pour un homme qui mourut hier.</u> (TOINETTE ENFONCE UN DERNIER CLOU : ELLE ACHÈVE DE PEINDRE DE LA MÉDECINE UN PORTRAIT PARADOXAL ET CATASTROPHIQUE. IL FAUT ICI JOUER LE CARACTÈRE TOUT À FAIT ÉVIDENT ET NATUREL DE SA LOGIQUE. PLUS ELLE SEMBLERA « NORMALE », PLUS LA SITUATION PARAÎTRA FOLLE !)

ARGAN. – Pour un homme qui mourut hier ?

TOINETTE. – <u>Oui, pour aviser, et voir ce qu'il aurait fallu lui faire pour le guérir.</u> (« TESTAMENT » DE TOINETTE EN MÉDECIN : ELLE DÉNONCE JUSQU'AU BOUT L'IMPUISSANCE ET LE CYNISME DES MÉDECINS, PASSIONNÉS DAVANTAGE PAR LEUR SCIENCE QUE PAR LE SOUCI DE GUÉRIR LEURS PATIENTS.) Jusqu'au revoir.

ARGAN. – Vous savez que les malades ne reconduisent point.

BÉRALDE. – <u>Voilà un médecin vraiment qui paraît fort habile.</u> (BÉRALDE ENTRE DANS LE JEU : IL CONFORTE TOINETTE ET TENTE D'APPUYER SA STRATÉGIE EN MONTRANT QU'IL A ÉTÉ CONVAINCU PAR LA CONSULTATION MÉDICALE À LAQUELLE IL A ASSISTÉ. IL TESTE AINSI LA CRÉDULITÉ D'ARGAN.)

ARGAN. – Oui, mais il va un peu bien vite.

BÉRALDE. – Tous les grands médecins sont comme cela.

ARGAN. – <u>Me couper un bras, et me crever un œil, afin que l'autre se porte mieux ! J'aime bien mieux qu'il ne se porte pas si bien. La belle opération, de me rendre borgne et manchot !</u> (OPÉRATION EN PARTIE RÉUSSIE : ARGAN DOUTE ENFIN DU TALENT DES MÉDECINS ET MANIFESTE QU'IL POSSÈDE ENCORE UN PEU DE BON SENS. TOUT N'EST PAS PERDU POUR ANGÉLIQUE ET CLÉANTE : TOINETTE, PAR SON DÉGUISEMENT, A RENDU POSSIBLE UN RENVERSEMENT DE SITUATION.)

Achevé d'imprimer en Italie par  Grafica Veneta
en mars 2015
Dépôt légal mars 2015
EAN 9782290108864
OTP L21ELLN000677N001

—

Ce texte est composé en Lemonde journal et en Akkurat

—

Conception des principes de mise en page :
mecano, Laurent Batard

—

Composition : PCA

—

ÉDITIONS J'AI LU
87, quai Panhard-et-Levassor, 75013 Paris
Diffusion France et étranger : Flammarion

*Librio*

536

D0666758

# My Word

## Gizelle Bryant

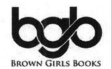

BROWN GIRLS BOOKS

Houston, Texas * Washington, D.C.

*My Word* © 2019 by Gizelle Bryant
Brown Girls Books LLC ~ www.BrownGirlsBooks.com
ISBN: 978-1-944359-79-9 (ebook)
ISBN: 978-1-944359-80-5 (print)

All rights reserved. No part of this book may be reproduced in any form or by any means including electronic, mechanical or photocopying or stored in a retrieval system without permission in writing from the publisher except by a reviewer who may quote brief passages to be included in a review.

First Brown Girls Publishing LLC trade printing Manufactured and Printed in the United States of America

If you purchased this book without a cover, you should be aware that this book is stolen property. It is reported as "unsold and destroyed" to the publisher, and neither the author nor the publisher has received any payment for this "stripped"book.

# Dedication

This book as well as everything else that I do is dedicated to the three people that matter most to me. They have stretched me to be the best version of myself. They have taught me the power and beauty of unconditional love. They have brought my life a sense of purpose and internal peace.

I am forever grateful to be the mother of my three amazing children, Grace, Angel and Adore.

# CHAPTER ONE

*March, 2008*

The doors of the church slammed shut and the sound echoed in my ears. I squirmed a little in my place in the pew.

*What was going on?*

It almost felt like we were being held hostage the way the deacons stood, like soldiers, at the closed doors. All the male armor bearers were poised like they were bearing arms—all aimed at keeping everyone in their place. But for what?

And why had Reverend Lewis, the assistant pastor, just asked all visitors and non-tithing members to leave the sanctuary? Why had the ushers scoured the rows in search of any stragglers who had stayed behind?

The sanctuary was bright with the morning sun that shined through the stained-glass windows, but the members of Pilgrim's Rest Missionary Baptist Church who remained all sat in a stunned silence.

After a few moments, Reverend Ovide Robinson pushed himself up from the huge oak-framed ornate pulpit chair and meandered toward the podium. Just before he got to the pulpit, he reached out his hand, and his wife, First Lady Alberta Robinson, rose from her seat of honor in the first pew. One of the ushers rushed to her and held her elbow as she ascended the four steps up the altar to join her husband.

Reverend Robinson took his wife's hand and then, together, the two stood before the church. Now, there had been many times when I'd sat here in Pilgrim's Rest and every head had been bowed and every eye had been closed, but this was not one of those moments. I didn't have to look to my left nor to my right to know that every eye was on our Senior pastor and his wife.

*What was going on?*

Then in a voice that would have won Reverend Robinson dozens of Stellar Awards if he'd chosen that path, he boomed, "Forgive me, Father, for I have sinned!"

A collective gasp rose through the three-thousand seat sanctuary.

"I have brought shame to my wife, my children and my church family." Reverend Robinson's voice quaked as he spoke.

There were more gasps, but everyone's eyes stayed laser-focused on the Robinsons. My eyes were on our First Lady more than our Reverend. Lady Robinson, as she preferred to be called, stood stoic in her navy St. John's suit, the gold buttons gleaming as if they had just been shined. She looked taller than her normal five feet, five inches. It was the way her shoulders were squared, the way her chin jutted forward. And the four inch stilettos she had on helped, too.

I had to give it to her; while the congregation wore stunned expressions, Lady Robinson's face was a blank slate, the best poker face I'd ever seen. Her glance was straight, focused on the front door of the church, to escape, perhaps? Her lips were pressed into a tight line that to me, made her look like she was holding back a thousand curses.

But those were just small nuances that I saw because I knew her so well. To everyone else, she was a woman who was holding her head high even though she'd just been dealt a low blow.

She was standing in a place where I, as a woman, would never be.

"I have violated my vows to my wife, to this church and to God. I have broken my fellowship with the Lord."

Oh my goodness! I scooted to the edge of the pew as if getting an inch closer would help me to understand this better. What was Reverend Robinson saying? What had he done?

"I will spend the rest of my life atoning for my sins."

*What sins?*

"And with that said, I am sad to announce that I am stepping down."

Now, mumbles accompanied the gasps and for the third time I asked myself what was going on? I couldn't stop asking that question because with every word Reverend Robinson spoke, he gave us a new revelation...and made me ask more questions.

"I don't know how long it will take me to get myself right again, but you, the faithful members of Pilgrim's Rest Missionary Baptist Church deserve better. Thank you and God bless you all."

God bless you all?! God bless you all? Really? My mouth opened wide as Reverend Robinson took his wife's hand, but before he could turn to exit stage right, Mr. Cowell, one of the oldest members of the church, pushed himself up from his seat and held up his hand.

"Reverend Robinson, no disrespect," Mr. Cowell belted out in a volume that belied his eighty (or was it ninety) years. "But you've led us for the last twenty-two years. I think we deserve more of an explanation. We need to know why you're stepping down."

There were mumbles of agreement, though no one else stood up.

Reverend Robinson shook his head, while Lady Robinson turned her eyes away. "The details aren't important," our Reverend told Mr. Cowell.

"The hell they aren't," the lady on the left side of me, mumbled.

At any other time, I may have reminded her, in a sisterly sort of way, that we were sitting in church. But right now, I was feeling her. How could Reverend Robinson drop that piece of news and just leave us sitting in the pews? He'd done something and as the tithing members, we deserved to know exactly what it was.

Reverend Robinson said, "The board will immediately begin a search for my replacement as I go into a cocoon of reflection."

Cocoon of reflection? What the hell? Now all I could think was...this is a MESS.

"My wife has forgiven me," Reverend Robinson said as he dabbed at the perspiration that suddenly moistened his brow. "Now, I need time to seek God's forgiveness and finally, I must have the space to forgive myself." He gave us a nod before he added, "Thank you for understanding." This time, when he took his wife's hand, he didn't stop moving, even as the chatter grew louder, even as more questions followed him through the door.

When he and Lady Robinson disappeared through the side doors that led to the offices in the back of the church, I wanted to jump up, run after him, and ask my question to his face.

Ron, the Minister of Music, stood up and though his face was stiff with shock like the rest of us, he motioned for the small church band to start playing. Pilgrim's Rest was known for a rocking choir but the music wasn't going to calm our spirits today.

I shifted a bit in my seat so that I could look at Jeremy. His eyes were focused on the pulpit, as if Reverend Robinson was still there. I took my best friend's hand, hoping that would pull him from his trance. It wasn't that I didn't understand what Jeremy had to be feeling—if anyone had to be shocked by this news, it was Jeremy. Reverend Robinson was his mentor, the man who'd encouraged him to enter the ministry; he was the reason Jeremy was on staff here as the youth minister.

But most importantly, Reverend Robinson had come into Jeremy's life when he was just a freshman at Dillard, a year before we met. That had been three and a half years ago and Jeremy had told me more than a few times that if it had not been for Reverend Robinson and his encouraging Jeremy to lean on God during his grief over his father's death, he was sure he wouldn't have made it.

And the Robinsons felt the same way about Jeremy. I couldn't count the number of times, Lady Robinson had told me that Jeremy was the child they'd never had.

"So, I guess you were surprised by this, too," I whispered, not sure why I was stating the obvious.

Jeremy didn't move, as if he was frozen in this moment.

"Jeremy?" I shook his leg.

He blinked a couple of times, then muttered, "Huh?" before he shifted his shoulders so that he faced me.

"You were surprised, too," I repeated, wanting to make sure this hadn't been a secret he'd kept from me.

He nodded slowly. "I...I don't. I didn't see this coming."

He was telling the truth. I knew because Jeremy's body had a built-in lie detector—he'd always get this little eyebrow twitch when he was telling a lie, and right now, not a thing moved on my friend. That meant that Jeremy hadn't a clue and if he didn't know, then no one did. The Robinsons would have told the man they called, 'son' first.

"Do you want to go back there and talk to him and Lady Robinson?" I asked.

"And say what?" he replied, over the choir's singing.

*"My help...all of my help cometh from the Lord."*

It was an appropriate song because right now, Pilgrim's Rest needed a whole lot of help that would only come from the Lord. But there didn't seem to be anyone in the congregation who noticed our award winning choir. Everyone was chatting with their pew neighbors as if they were sitting in their dining room spilling tea over Sunday dinner.

"I...I gotta get out of here." Before I could react, Jeremy stood and crossed over the five people to get to the aisle.

Following him, I jumped up and did the same, excusing myself to the faces that were so familiar since this third row was where Jeremy and I sat for every service.

This New Orleans church was the spiritual home for both of us. I was a Senior at Xavier University, a college that was about ten minutes away from Dillard. But no matter how lit our Saturday nights were with my sorority's events or his fraternity's parties, come Sunday morning, we were seated in this third row in church, standing on the Christian foundation that our parents had laid within us.

I rushed behind Jeremy as he dashed toward the doors and for a moment, I wondered if the deacons would let us out. Not that anyone would have been able to stop Jeremy. He barged past like he was a speeding locomotive and the deacon had to jump out of my friend's way.

I was in a full sprint when I passed by the deacon and smiled an apology to him before I stepped from the sanctuary into the lobby.

"Hey," I shouted out as I ran behind Jeremy, catching him before he stepped outside. "Are you all right?"

He shook his head. "Reverend Robinson just stepped down," he said as if I hadn't been sitting next to him. "Do you know what had to happen for him to decide to do this? After what this church means to him? He built this place," Jeremy said, pointing to the stained glass ceiling, just one of the opulent features in the building.

"I know," I said, keeping my voice soft and soothing because Jeremy was so agitated. But he was right. Reverend Robinson had founded Pilgrim's Rest Missionary Baptist Church in the eighties and over the last two decades had grown the membership from a couple of hundred to just under three thousand.

"I just...I just...I just...."

"Okay, Jeremy. Breathe." I rubbed my hand over his back.

He inhaled slowly, then exhaled the same way.

"It's going to be okay," I told him.

"How can it be?" Jeremy shook his head. "The world won't be the same."

I thought that was a little dramatic, but I understood my friend's sentiments. Jeremy and I had been friends since we'd met in Charlotte at MEAC. And for the last two years, everyone called us a couple, though we truly were just friends. True friends who could laugh together and cry together and study together. Best friends who'd visited each other's homes and met each other's families during school breaks. But our real bond came from our love for the Lord. We prayed and read the Bible together. Nothing was more intimate than that to me.

It felt so good to have a guy in my life who wasn't trying to get into my panties. Jeremy never crossed that line; it was like it never occurred to him. I was his sister-in-Christ and that was all that mattered.

The friendship zone was perfect for me because Jeremy wanted to be a pastor and if there was one thing I would never be, it was a pastor's wife.

"Ginger, I don't know...."

I looked around the vestibule to make sure no one was within listening range when I asked, "Do you think he got involved with a man?"

It wasn't that I'd ever heard anything like that concerning Reverend Robinson, but my thoughts were that if he'd just been smashing a woman, it wouldn't be all that serious... unfortunately. If he'd had an affair, he'd apologize to Lady

Robinson, then keep it a secret and keep it moving. He wouldn't have walked away from the church.

Jeremy shrugged. "I have no idea what it is."

"Well," I began, then paused as one of the doors to the sanctuary opened and a matriarch of the church, Mother Madeline Logan wobbled on her cane toward us. Mother Logan always left about five minutes before the service was over, so that meant soon the lobby would be filled with parishioners, all talking about what had gone down in church this morning.

Mother Logan stopped, leaned her cane against the wall, then took Jeremy's hands into her own.

"You all right, Suga?" she asked, cranking her head back so that she could look into Jeremy's eyes.

Jeremy half nodded, half shook his head.

"I know Reverend Robinson is like a father to you," she said. "It's a shame what just happened in there."

Jeremy nodded. "Yes, ma'am. A shame, but I'm fine," he lied.

Mother Logan reached toward his neck, though her reach ended somewhere around Jeremy's chest. Still, she hugged him. "You stay strong. We know all things work together for good to them that love God."

"Yes, ma'am," Jeremy said.

"And to them who are the called according to His purpose."

"Yes, ma'am."

After a pause, she said, "God's purpose, Jeremy. You know they're going to be looking for a new pastor."

I leaned back a little. The way Mother Logan said those words was like she wanted Jeremy to consider the position. What was she thinking?

But then, my friend nodded like that had been something on his mind, too. Now, I wanted to know what *he'd* been thinking?

Mother Logan winked at him before she grabbed her cane and then wobbled her way out of the church.

I waited until she was all the way through the doors before I asked, "What was that about?"

"What do you mean?"

"She winked at you like you two share a secret."

With a sigh, Jeremy took my hand and we walked to his car. But he didn't open the door for me. He leaned against his eleven-year-old Nissan Sentra and I did the same, knowing that move meant he wanted to talk. We didn't have much time—a minute or so and then, the people would be pouring from the church.

Finally Jeremy said, "I've been feeling this calling. A tug, if you will. It's like God has been saying to me 'get ready'."

"Get ready for what?"

He didn't look at me as he shook his head. "I don't know. That's why I hadn't said anything about it to you. But I've been hearing that over and over." He pushed himself from the car, turned and looked straight into my eyes. "But now, I think

He meant get ready for this. I think He meant for me to get ready to take Reverend Robinson's place."

My mouth opened wide. "Jeremy, how can you do that when you're only twenty-one, still in school, and you're not even next in line. Reverend Lewis is the assistant pastor, you're the youth pastor." I felt like he needed all of those reminders.

"Well, we're about to graduate, so I won't be in school any longer and Reverend Lewis doesn't want to lead this church."

"How do you know that?"

"Because in the ministers meetings, he's always talking about going back to Los Angeles. He doesn't like the South."

"Okay, but what about graduate school?" I asked as another reminder. "You've always said you wanted your Masters of Divinity since your Bachelors is going to be in Mass Communications. You've even talked about getting your Doctorate, remember?" I asked because he was acting like he'd knocked every practical thought from his mind.

He shook his head. "There are plenty of pastors in this country who don't have degrees. At least I will have one."

"But you've already been accepted to Howard and Duke."

Now, he shrugged as if my words didn't matter. "And all of that, those are my plans, but God's plans are greater."

There was no way for me to debate God, so I brought it back down to man. "Do you really think the board would consider you for this?"

That question seemed to bring him back to earth. He sighed, then leaned back on the car. "I know."

I breathed, glad that he agreed.

Then, he said, "But I can do this."

I wanted to say more, but he opened the car door, a signal that this part of the conversation was over. I slid inside, and as I watched him walk around the front of his car, I recognized the look in his eyes. It was the determination that he had when an idea was baking inside of him. Or when he was ready to take that cake out the oven and present it to the world.

By the time, Jeremy jumped into the driver's seat, I knew my friend wouldn't rest until he was appointed the new pastor of Pilgrim's Rest Missionary Baptist Church.

# CHAPTER TWO

It was just a kiss. But it was a kiss that had reached to my soul and discombobulated my entire being. I closed my *Marketing in the New Digital Age* textbook, glanced around the library and sighed. A check of the clock on the wall showed that I'd been at this for about an hour. An hour and I hadn't read one full page when this textbook was one from my favorite class.

It was because of that kiss.

With another sigh, I rested my elbow on the table, cupped my chin and remembered last night....

*"I can take you back to your dorm," Jeremy said.*

*His tone held all of his emotions: anxiety, confusion, sadness... and a bit of elation. I knew there was more that Jeremy had to work out, so I said, "If you still want to talk, I still want to listen."*

*He reached across the car and squeezed my hand. Then with a nod, he pushed the gear into drive and pulled the car away from the Riverwalk's parking lot. We'd just taken a Sunday stroll on the*

*Riverwalk, a very touristy thing to do in New Orleans, but after brunch at Willa Jean's, our once-a-month splurge, I knew Jeremy still needed to work out all that was in his head from the service this morning. So I suggested this little walk and talk and that was exactly what Jeremy had done for a couple of hours. It still wasn't enough, but it didn't matter to me. I was here for it and if he needed a few more hours, I'd do that, too.*

*When we stepped into his small two-bedroom apartment, Jeremy did what he always did: he motioned for me to sit on the futon, turned on his CD player, then grabbed two diet Cokes from his fridge. With Keyshia Cole, Jazmine Sullivan and Mary J crooning in the background, it could have been a romantic setting for two college kids.*

*But for me and Jeremy, this was our norm, so I kicked off my shoes, tucked my feet under my butt, and listened as Jeremy continued sorting out his thoughts.*

*"I know I'm young, but I feel this pull."*

*"I know I need to at least get my Masters, but I feel this pull."*

*"I know the board may not see me as a leader yet, but I feel this pull."*

*All I did was nod and listen, letting him get it all out. My goal was to leave him tonight feeling calmer, but hoping that he would realize this was crazy. Even though I felt this was the craziest idea in the history of crazy ideas, I wasn't going to tell him that. He'd have to arrive at that conclusion himself.*

*He said, "There's never been a time in my life when God's voice has been clearer to me."*

*That worried me a bit because I knew Jeremy heard God, just like I did. But still, I played my role—the friend with the listening ear that he'd given to me so many times.*

*The sun had long set, the apartment was dark except for the dim light from an outside street lamp, Keyshia, Jazmine and Mary J. had sang more than a couple of times on repeat, and I'd had about five Diet Cokes before Jeremy took my hands into his. "You have been so wonderful today, Ginger."*

*"What did I do?"*

*"This." He waved his hand in the air. "You listened to me all day, just let me go on and on, repeating the same things."*

*"This is what we do. Isn't that what friends are for? You just needed to talk it out."*

*"I did. I haven't come to any conclusions about what I'm going to do about Pilgrim's Rest, but...." He paused. "I've decided something else."*

*I tilted my head. I didn't know there had been anything else on his mind.*

*He said, "I want this all the time." He stopped and twisted. Even through the darkness, I could see him searching in my eyes.*

*My heart thumped because I knew where this was heading. But to give myself a couple of more seconds, I asked, "What do you mean?"*

*"I want this, I want us. We have such chemistry, Ginger and I don't know what we're waiting for. I don't know who we think we're fooling. I really want to see where this goes with you because I'm thinking we are already more than friends...."*

*I wanted to hold up my hand as a stop signal. I wanted to tell him, 'No, let's not mess up this perfect friendship; plus you want to be a pastor!' But then, he edged toward me. It was three seconds that felt like three lifetimes before his lips touched mine. As Mary J sang one of my favorite songs, we kissed. And every laden emotion that I'd pressed down within me, began to ascend from my toes through my center and settled right there on my heart.*

*When Mary J sang, "Too hard to fake it…" I knew what Jeremy and I had was real. Like the boo Mary J sang about, I didn't want to be without Jeremy. I wanted to stay in this place with our lips connected forever….*

But forever lasted just a couple of seconds because Jeremy's roommate, Aaron, busted into the apartment, talking about it was too dark in there and turning on the bright overhead lights. By the time he realized Jeremy and I were there together, we were on opposite ends of the futon.

When Aaron had asked, "What's up with y'all," I'd looked at Jeremy, he looked at me, and then both of us cracked up. Not sure why, but we had a fit of giggles that wouldn't stop. It didn't bother Aaron; he grabbed a Coke and sat in the living room with us until Jeremy got a call from Reverend Lewis. Of course, he'd wanted to take the call. Of course, he wanted to know if there was news.

"What's got you smiling like that?"

I had to blink a few times to bring myself back from yesterday.

"You're grinning like you just won the lottery," my best girl friend, Dru said as she slid into the chair across the table. Her smile was bright, exactly like it was the first day I'd met her when I'd stepped onto Xavier's campus and found out that she was my roommate. She'd told me that in high school, friends had called her Sunshine and I got it. Because everything about her shined like the sun—from her thousand-watt smile to her sun-kissed complexion, which was almost exactly the color of her hair.

People often said we were twins, which always made us laugh out loud. Yeah, our complexions and our hair coloring were close, but that height thing—Dru had to stand on her tiptoes to measure five feet and I could reach for items on the top shelf of any cabinet.

"So, did we win the lotto or what?" she asked when I didn't respond.

I wanted to tell Dru that I kinda felt like I had won. I wanted to jump up and dance, but all I did was grab my books, stuff them into my bag and say, "Come on. I got something to tell you."

"Ooooh...you don't have to tell me twice." She popped out of her chair and then both of us speed-walked out of the library.

⁓

"So hold up," Dru said. "Are you telling me you're gonna be a First Lady?" Before I could respond, she dumped her backpack onto the ground and danced, doing some kind of shoulder-shimmying two-step in a circle around me. "You're gonna be a First Lady. You're gonna be a First Lady."

I stopped moving because she was making me dizzy.

"Really? So what? Are we in fifth grade now?"

She laughed as she grabbed her bag from the grass and we continued our stroll across campus to our dorm. "I'm just saying." But then as if she had a serious thought, her laughter stopped. "Wait. How are we gonna go to a Kappa party when you're a First Lady?" She frowned as if she was asking me a serious question. Then, she shrugged. "Guess I'll just have to find someone else to roll with."

I shook my head. "And guess I'll have to find a new best friend who won't toss me away so easily."

"I'm not tossing you away, I just got questions. Like can First Ladies strut?" she asked. "Because how you gonna be an AKA and not strut?"

"Are you serious right now?" Before she answered, I continued, "Let me break this down for you. First of all, I'm not interested in being a First Lady since I grew up as a First Daughter. That was enough firsts for me. And besides, I don't know what's happening with me and Jeremy."

"You don't know?" She turned toward me and walked backward. "Who's acting like they're in fifth grade now? Let me break this down for you. You and Jeremy finally kissed. Jeremy told you he wants to take your friendship further. And

I say, 'Hallelujah, it's about time.' You two have been playing footsies-"

"We haven't been playing anything."

"-for too long now," she continued as if I hadn't spoken. "You started with the kiss last night, you might as well let him hit it tonight, then tomorrow, it'll be all official," she said as if she'd just solved all the problems of the world.

"I've already told you, I don't want to be married to a pastor."

"Well first of all, he didn't ask you to marry him, he just kissed you."

"If you weren't my best friend, I'd punch you in the eye right now."

"And second of all, Jeremy Williams is a tall mug of hot chocolate, so whatever hang-ups you have about the church-"

"I'm not hung up about the church."

"-you need to get over it," she continued. "Look, if he wants you on his arm as he becomes the youngest pastor in New Orleans, you need to hop on that gravy train. He's fine and he's gonna be rich? What's there to think about?"

I sighed, but it was only to keep my emotions inside. As much as I hated to admit it, I was excited about the prospect of where our relationship could go from here; but there was so much to think about. First, I didn't want to stay in New Orleans. I had my life mapped out. After graduation in a few weeks, I would start working at Walker-Hughes, one of the largest consumer marketing firms in the country where I'd interned over the past two summers in DC. I was going to work with them for exactly five years before I started my own marketing company. My company was going to be ahead of the curve with this growing digital marketing industry and by 2015, I planned to have offices in the top five markets. For all of this to happen, I'd have to be in a big city on the East or West coast.

So my plans didn't line up with this new desire of Jeremy's. Plus there was the fact that yes, we'd kissed, but I wasn't sure what it meant. Jeremy and I hadn't had a chance to discuss anything at all. Once he got the call from Reverend Lewis, I didn't want to interrupt him in any way, so Aaron brought me back to campus and I hadn't spoken to Jeremy since.

"I've been telling you from the day you met him in Charlotte that he was going to be more than a friend."

"You did say that, but Dru, I don't know." I kicked a rock on the grass, needing to release all of this energy inside of me. "I have my plans and then, I've never wanted to be a First Lady. I guess that's why I've been fighting my feelings for him for so long."

"Wait. Stop. Are we having an honest introspective moment here?"

I shrugged and Dru said, "First, I'm sure there will be a way to line up your plans with his, so that won't be an issue. But that other issue you have, you've got to let go of your hang-ups about First Ladies. What does Jeremy say about it?"

"We've never talked about it because we've never talked about being anything more than friends."

She shook her head. "You always say that, but I'm telling you, I have a hard time believing it."

"Well remember, I was kinda seeing Kenny and he was seeing Daphne when we met. And neither one of us is a hoe."

"And you broke up with Kenny and he broke up with Daphne a year ago. So now you can be hoes together."

"That is not even funny," I said, even though I chuckled. "But by the time everyone was out of the way, Jeremy and I were in such a comfortable friendship space and I didn't want to mess that up. He's the best friend I've ever had."

Dru raised her eyebrows. "Present company excluded, of course."

"Of course."

"But seriously, Ginger, you and Jeremy have all the fixings for a great relationship. You started out as friends and that's what most people miss. When you have that, you've taken care of half of the relationship battle so don't let what he chooses as a profession stop you from having a great love in your life. He's a man first and a pastor second."

I paused. "Who are you now? Doctor Phil? Oprah?"

"Just call me Doctor Phyllis or Oprenah. Seriously, no matter what he decides to do or where you two decide to go, the foundation is there. So go to the edge and jump."

I wanted to take a moment to think about her words, but before I could do that, she hopped in front of me and stopped moving. "Now speaking of shaky foundations...."

I frowned. "I thought you just said Jeremy and I had a good foundation."

"I'm not talking about you. I'm talking about Reverend Robinson. I can't believe I missed church yesterday," she whined.

"Well, that's what happens when you hang out all night Saturday and then Sunday morning rolls around."

"Don't try to change the subject. So what's the scoop with Reverend Robinson? What did Jeremy say?"

"I told you; he doesn't know anything. He tried to call Reverend Robinson when we were at brunch yesterday, but he didn't answer. I don't know if he's spoken to him since last night."

"I should have been there," Dru said as if her presence would have changed things. "If I had been there and had been able to look into Reverend Robinson's eyes, I would have figured it out."

"I don't know how you would have. He didn't say anything except for what I told you."

She nodded, then belted out, "He got a baby on the side," as if that was a fact. "You know that's what happened to that reverend over at Fifth Street Baptist. He got a fifteen-year-old girl, who was a member of their church, pregnant. Word is her daddy pulled a gun on him and told him that if he ever came near her again, he'd be swallowing bullets."

"I know. That was something. But that reverend over there...there'd been rumors about him for years. I heard he may have gotten more than one girl pregnant. But Reverend Robinson? For twenty-two years you've never heard a thing about him. If he was in the streets like that, it would've come out by now."

"Hmph. You just never know what be going on behind church doors," Dru said.

"Well, ever since I've been attending Pilgrim's Rest, Reverend Robinson has been nothing but upstanding."

"Yeah," Dru said. "That's what he wanted us to believe. But you know when the lights go out some of them pastors are the biggest freaks."

"You always say that, but my daddy—God rest his soul— never had any drama. As far as I know, he never had any issues at church. In fact, I've known a lot of pastors while growing up and most of them are men of God...."

"The key word: men. They are still men walking around in the flesh with all of their sexual organs on the outside just dangling around. It has to be hard for a human to operate like that."

I chuckled. "You need to stop, Dru. This is serious. Whatever happened with Reverend Robinson is major."

"It has to be," she said, matching my tone.

"And Lady Robinson is standing by him."

"Hmph. Let that be me. Let my husband shame me like that." She stopped walking, but her neck and her forefinger kept moving. "If that had happened to me, four days later, there would have been a tear-jerking, flower-bringing, homegoing celebration going on. They would've been singing

'Going Up Yonder' and I would've been in the front row, the soprano soloist."

I laughed as Dru went into full-fledged sister girl mode. "Oh no. I am not the one," she said. "I'm not gonna be no stand-by-my-preacher-man-husband like these First Ladies out here."

My laughter stopped, though I still smiled. I didn't want Dru to know that her words had hit a little too close to my home. People always said what they would and wouldn't do, but the truth was no one knew how they'd react in any situation. Dru was judging First Ladies when she didn't know their struggle or their story.

But I'd lived the struggle and the story with my mother. She was one of those women who sat strong at her place in the pews, who stood by her husband, and fulfilled all of her duties as the First Lady of the church—all with a smile on her face, while there was an ache in her heart. The pain didn't come from my father; he was one of the good ones, at least as far as I knew. But it was still tough because of the women. Even though my father lived his love and admiration for his wife in public so everyone could see, women still came at him, right in front of my mother's face. We'd be out at a restaurant and some woman would stop at our table and pass my father her number or ask if he could stop past her house for prayer... and other things. I didn't understand when I was younger, but when I was a teen, there were times when I wanted to jump in these women's faces myself. My sisters, Jada, Lauren and I talked about it all the time—we had no idea how our mom had held back and not beat down or pimped slapped someone through their twenty-six years of marriage.

The little bit of tolerance I had came to an end when we went out for dinner to celebrate my sixteenth birthday and some lady kept rubbing my dad's shoulder while my mom, my sisters and I all sat around the table and watched. While I was giving all kinds of hate-filled glares to the woman, I vowed then that I would never marry any man who had anything to do with any church.

"You know what?" Dru said, interrupting the memory of my vow.

"What?"

"You may be right. I don't think either one of us is built to be a First Lady." She stopped walking. "But um...your chances of becoming one are greater than mine." Then, with her chin, she motioned across the street.

When I followed her glance, there was only one thing I could do—I smiled. There was Jeremy posted up against his old jalopy of a car. Even though we were feet away, I saw his smile that brightened his face and sent tickles to the tips of my toes.

At that point, I could have dropped my bag and ran across the street. But this wasn't a scene out of *Love and Basketball*. This was me and Jeremy. So, I just strolled toward him, casually, the way I'd always had...before our kiss.

"What are you doing here?" I asked as he hugged me. When he leaned back, I could tell that he was 180 degrees from where he'd been yesterday. He was relaxed, happy, not a bit of anxiety oozed from him. And that made me wonder what Reverend Lewis had said to him last night.

He said, "I came to see the most beautiful woman in the world."

"Uh," Dru cleared her throat and my head snapped to look at her. I'd forgotten she was with me. She said, "Thank you, Jeremy, but you came to see Ginger, too, right?

We all laughed.

"Hey, Dru." He leaned in and hugged her. "How you doing?"

"I'll be better when you hook me up with one of your rich friends."

"Well when I get some rich friends, I'll be sure to let you know. And speaking of rich friends," he reached for my hand, "would you mind if I stole yours away?"

"Hold up. She's rich?" Dru leaned to the side. "Nobody told me that."

"Maybe not with money, but she's rich in all the ways that count."

"Awwww...you're so sweet," Dru began, "that I just felt three cavities pop up in my mouth."

"Girl, bye." I laughed.

"Wait, where are you going?"

"It doesn't matter," I said to Dru, but looked at Jeremy as he opened the passenger door for me. "I'll go anywhere Jeremy wants to take me."

"Awww man, the two of you!"

When Jeremy hopped into the car, we waved to Dru, who still stood in the middle of the street pretending to dab away her fake tears.

We laughed at her, then Jeremy turned to me. "Did you mean that. You'll go wherever I'll take you?"

I stared at Jeremy for a long moment and took inventory in my head: we were best friends, he wanted to be a pastor, I didn't want to be a pastors' wife, he had his plans and I had mine.

And then, there was that kiss last night.

I repeated the list a few times, before I nodded.

Then with a smile, he said, "Well then hold on, Ginger Allen. 'Cause if you're rollin' with me, then you're in for a helluva ride."

# Chapter Three

I had no idea where we were going, but I didn't even ask Jeremy. I just went for the ride. When he stopped at a corner shop to pick up two tuna sandwiches and sodas, I grabbed the bag as he paid the cashier and we hopped back into his car.

We stayed silent, each engrossed in our own thoughts that I suspected were much the same. I was glad when Jeremy pulled into City Park and we settled on a bench near the tennis courts.

As the sun ascended in its arch toward the top of the sky and tourists strolled by, this would have been a scene that normally, would have filled me with peace. But it was difficult to feel any kind of harmony with the elephant that squeezed itself on the bench between us.

I pushed my sandwich aside; as much as I loved tuna, today it was tasteless. Jeremy must have felt the same way because he'd only taken two bites before he did the same thing.

He leaned forward, his arms crossed, resting on his knees. His eyes were away from me, when he said, "So are you going to say anything about our kiss last night?" I was trying to figure out what to say, but Jeremy didn't give me a chance. He added, "Because I'm about to kiss you again, Ginger." He sounded breathless and I was so glad my eyes were hidden behind my sunglasses.

He continued, "And when I kiss you, I need to know if you're gonna kiss me back or slap me?"

When I laughed, it felt like the elephant lifted off the bench and ambled away. "You got jokes."

He shrugged. "I'm serious, Ginger. I want to kiss you again. And again. And again. I want to be with you all the time and not just in the way we've been spending our time. I want...more with you."

I inhaled.

"Wait." His forehead creased with lines. "You're not feeling this, you're not feeling me?"

"No," I said quickly. "I'm feeling all of you." When he grinned at my words, I clarified, "I mean, I'm feeling all of what you said."

He nodded. "We've been fooling ourselves; we've been more than friends for a long time. We just haven't added the physical part."

"True, but there must've been a reason why we stayed in that place. Like, aren't you afraid of messing up a good friendship? I mean, Jeremy," I twisted on the bench so that now, my body faced him, "you're truly the best friend I've ever had."

He shifted so that now, he faced me, too. "And that's what makes us so special. Look, I understand your concern because I haven't been able to think about anything else since you kissed me."

"I kissed you?" I leaned away from him.

His double-dimpled grin let me know that he was just trying to get a rise out of me. "My lips weren't there by themselves," he said.

We laughed. And then, we sat letting silent moments pass before I did something that I hadn't expected to do. This time, I was the one who scooted closer, then leaned forward, edging my lips toward him. And when we met, he invited me in for a kiss that again touched me to my soul.

When we pulled back, I was as discombobulated as before. But this time, I'd given Jeremy my answer. We both knew we'd fallen to the other side of friendship.

He palmed my cheek and whispered, "Ginger Allen, take this ride with me. I promise, it'll be worth it."

I had no idea why there were tears in my eyes when I nodded, affirming his words. Maybe it was because I felt so happy, so safe, so secure. And now, I was ready, really ready to take this ride with him.

Fourteen days of bliss; that was the only way for me to describe it. Jeremy and I still did the things we normally did together; we still studied, but now, Jeremy, without looking up from whatever book he was reading, shifted on the futon in his apartment and pulled me back so that I leaned into his chest—and we both kept studying. Or as we strolled across campus and chatted about all the reasons why he still wanted the position of Senior Pastor at Pilgrim's Rest, he'd pause and brush my bangs from my eyes. Or when we went to midweek prayer, as we sat, our shoulders touching because we couldn't get close enough, he held my hand. That was something that he'd always done, but now, he hardly let me go.

It was so different building a relationship on a foundation of friendship. It was as easy as slipping on a new pair of Uggs—they were new, but they felt old, like we'd taken this walk before. It was comfortable already knowing Jeremy, which was why when I slid into his car, and leaned over to kiss him, I knew something was wrong.

"What's up?" I asked as he edged from the parking space in front of my dorm.

He shrugged. "My mind is still all over the place. It's hard for me to get over that I haven't heard from Pastor Robinson in more than two weeks."

"I know." I twisted so that with one hand, I could massage the back of his neck as he drove.

His eyes stayed straight ahead. "It's like they never really cared for me. When they talked about me being the son they never had, they never meant that."

"You know that's not true. Lady Robinson told me so many times how she felt like she'd almost birthed you herself and that always meant a lot to her since she wasn't able to have children. You really were their son."

"That they just abandoned."

This was something that I'd been praying about. I didn't want Jeremy to feel this way, though abandonment was the only feeling that could come out of this situation.

I said, "You know what? Why don't we just go over there?"

"Where?" he asked as he pulled his car to a stop in the parking lot of his apartment building.

"To the Robinsons. We should just go over there. Really, I can't believe you haven't done that already." It was the sound of his silence that made me ask, "Have you?"

"No."

Then his eyebrow twitched and I frowned. Why was he lying to me?

But before I could ask, he changed his response to, "I mean, yeah. In a way. I haven't been to their house. I haven't knocked on the door. But I've driven by. More than a couple of times."

"Why didn't you just go in and talk to them?"

He shrugged. "I don't know. I guess part of me is afraid. For Reverend Robinson to have done this, something horrible had to happen."

"And you don't want to know what it is?" I didn't give him a chance to respond. "Wouldn't talking to Lady and Reverend Robinson help? Wouldn't that give you closure?"

He paused for a moment. "And if I close that door, what will be ahead of me?"

I didn't even let a second pass before I told him, "I don't know, but whatever you have to face, I'm going to be there with you."

He gave me a long glance before he gave me an even longer kiss and then, he churned up the engine of his car.

There were so many things I wanted to tell Jeremy, so many things I wanted him to know so that he'd be prepared for whatever the Robinsons said to us. But I said nothing to him, and just took my prayers to God, asking Him to reveal it all to Jeremy so that he could leave the Robinsons with his questions answered, even if his heart still was not whole when it came to them.

When we pulled up to the Robinson's grand white home with tan shutters, Jeremy turned off the ignition and then, sat in more silence. I knew he had to have so many memories. He'd spent so much time here that he had his own bedroom, even though his apartment was just four miles away. We'd shared just about every Sunday dinner with the Robinsons and many weekday meals, as well.

When his eyes went to the house, I turned to look at the place that had always been so welcoming to me. I'd loved coming over here with Jeremy. The first time, I had to admit, I'd been a bit intimidated when I walked into the massive five-bedroom home. The foyer alone with its marble floor and winding staircase had taken my breath away.

But when Lady Robinson had led us into the gourmet kitchen with its cabinetry that matched the fixtures, I'd felt nothing but love from the reverend and his wife. And I saw and felt the love they had for Jeremy. I had always been so happy coming here to share a meal and great conversation... and to hear the Word of God, which was always part of anything Reverend Robinson had to say.

It was only now that I realized how much I missed this. And if I did, I couldn't imagine how Jeremy felt. When I turned back to him, I saw the deluge of emotions that overwhelmed him. There was a bit of joy in his eyes that I imagined came from the hope of seeing the Robinsons again. But then, the way his lips were set, I saw his fear of what they might say.

Taking his hand, I said, "This is a good thing. I have a feeling that the Robinsons need you, they need their son. You may be able to minister to both of them."

"Then, I'm glad you're here with me." He sealed those words with a kiss before he jumped out of the car. I opened my door, but Jeremy was there before I could get out. He took my hand, pulled me up and into a hug before we turned to the Robinson's house.

As we approached, I wondered if Jeremy had been holding his breath the way I had and then I wondered if this had been such a good idea. If Jeremy walked away from this more hurt, it would be my fault.

Before he rang the doorbell, I had the urge to pull him back. I wanted us to cut and run. Head back to Xavier or Dillard, it didn't matter. Either place would be safer than this. But I stood steadfast as he rang the bell. And we waited. Then, he rang again. And again. And then again.

There were no lights on inside, but the day was just beginning its darkening to night, so no lights meant nothing. But what was clear, was that no one was going to answer.

"Maybe they're not home right now." That was the only explanation I could give.

Jeremy nodded, but it still took him a few seconds to turn around. This time, I was the one who held him and inside, I berated myself. Why had I suggested this? Now, Jeremy felt worse and he still had no answers.

As we got to the end of the walkway, a woman shouted out, "Hey!"

We both looked toward the voice and saw a woman, waving from a dark blue SUV—a BMW, I thought. Jeremy and I paused as the woman, about thirty years old, slid out of the car and sauntered toward us.

"They ain't home. They haven't been home," she said, as if she were some kind of neighborhood watcher. But then, she explained, "I've been here every day for the past three days and they ain't been here. Do you know where they are?"

She looked at me like she fully expected me to answer her question. And I looked at her, wearing a sequined jacket with matching pants like she was heading to a New Year's Eve party—in the middle of April.

Jeremy and I exchanged glances, then he said, "And you would be?"

She did a little gangsta lean back and asked, "Who are you?" as if she'd been offended by Jeremy's question.

I put up my hand to stop Jeremy and took a step forward. "You approached us," I said, keeping the attitude that I felt out of my voice. "So before we divulge anything, it would be nice if you introduced yourself."

She folded her arms as if she had no intention of doing that. But then, she huffed as if she knew she had no other choice. A slow smile crept up on her face. "I'm Shaniqua."

"Shaniqua," I repeated her name as a way for her to explain further.

She said, "Ovide's wife."

"What?" Jeremy and I said together.

"I didn't stutter." She pointed to the SUV where four sets of eyes peered back at us. "And those kids are Ovide's kids."

If I hadn't been stunned into silence, I would have turned to Jeremy to ask who was this fool?

"Look," Jeremy began, "I don't know what kind of game you're trying to run-"

"It ain't a game, it's the truth." She held out her hand as if she were giving us proof. Her ring finger rocked a huge stone—cubic zirconia. "This is my wedding ring."

"Really?" Jeremy said. "So, we're supposed to believe that Reverend Robinson is married to you because of that? That ring means nothing."

"This ring means everything to us."

"You're lying," I jumped in. "Reverend Robinson is married. He can't be married to you when he already has a wife that he's had for almost forty years."

"No, correction: he has two wives," she said, like that was a normal thing. "He has the one who lives here and then, he has his family, that would be us, in Natchez, Mississippi. He has a whole house there." She glanced over my shoulder. "I mean, it's a nice enough house, but not as nice as this one."

My heart pounded in rhythm to the thumping in my head. Could this woman be telling the truth? No way. There was no possible way. But Natchez was only three hours away. Was that where Reverend Robinson went just about every Saturday when he said he was in Mississippi preaching at a youth center? My brain was exploding.

"Look, you don't have to believe me, but I got all kinds of proof. I got our marriage license, I got the deed to our house, which I was smart enough to make Ovide put my name on it, too, and," she pointed toward her car, "I have four little babies, who if we have to take a DNA test, will prove that I ain't lying."

"Oh, my God," Jeremy whispered my sentiments.

"Look, I ain't trying to start no trouble, but I told Ovide that I was getting tired of him coming home just once a week and I promised him I was going to move here 'cause these kids need their daddy. And my mama told me to come on up here and get what's mine." Looking at the Robinson's home again, she said, "And I'm glad I did 'cause even though he got me a nice car and a nice house, he been holding out on me."

"I just don't understand," I said.

Jeremy added, "Neither do I. You knew Reverend Robinson was married?"

"Yeah, I knew, but what's that got to do with me? He said he loved me more than he loved his first wife and he explained how man was not meant to be monogamous. He showed me all the places in the Bible with all of those men like David and Solomon. I told Ovide I didn't want to be one of fifty, but I didn't mind being one of two, long as he took care of me and mine. The problem is now, I can't find him."

"You don't know where he is?" I asked.

Shaniqua looked at me and then, she slowed down her cadence as she said, "I. Told. You. I. Can't. Find. Him."

If I hadn't been so upset, I would have gone for her. But all I did was stand there and try to make sense of this nonsense.

She said, "So, can y'all help me? I need to know 'cause the money in the bank is gonna run out soon and somebody's gonna have to feed these kids. Ovide needs to answer my calls."

Jeremy and I glanced at each other before he said, "We can't help you. I'm sorry, but we don't know where the Robinsons are either."

She hunched her shoulders and we turned away from her. Then, she said, "Guess I'll just show up to the church on Sunday and tell the congregation what's been going on."

The way Jeremy and I spun back around, it was like our movement had been choreographed. "Uh," Jeremy stuttered before he pulled a card from his pocket. "Here, call this number and ask to speak to Reverend Lewis. Maybe he can help you. But do me two favors."

Shaniqua asked her question by just tilting her head.

Jeremy said, "Call him before you show up to the church and don't tell him I gave you his number."

Then, he took my hand and we almost ran back to his car.

# CHAPTER FOUR

It had taken us days, no weeks, to get over meeting Shaniqua. I still wasn't able to add a last name to her first one because Robinson didn't fit. It didn't fit for so many reasons. It didn't fit because it was UNBELIEVABLE.

But it seemed that it was true, or at least that was what Jeremy and I believed. No one had come to talk to us, but the signs were in the little things that were happening. Like how Reverend Robinson's name had suddenly been removed (as the founder) from the church's letterhead, from the assigned parking space sign, and from his office. Then, Jeremy had called the Robinson's (like he'd done so often) and their phone had been disconnected. And finally, Shaniqua never did show up at the church, though neither one of us had any doubt that she would have if she didn't get what she'd wanted. Something was going on, someone had been paid off, though Jeremy and I hadn't been privy to anything that was going on. But we didn't need to be, we'd met Shaniqua. We knew the truth.

None of that was my concern, though. All I cared about was Jeremy and how all of this was affecting him. He'd been crushed, but he hadn't been deterred. If I'd bet that the truth about Reverend Robinson would have changed Jeremy's mind about being the Senior Pastor at Pilgrim's Rest, I would've lost a million dollars.

In fact, my man was even more on fire about getting that chair on the altar. It was like he wanted to step in for his father figure. Maybe make things right because Reverend Robinson had done so much wrong.

But it wasn't going to happen. Not that I had any doubts in my man's abilities, but there was a guest pastor bouncing around the altar right now, who had just lit a flame to this sanctuary.

Now, Reverend Robinson knew how to drop the word, too. Many a Sundays he had members shouting out their hallelujahs and waving their hands in the air. But I couldn't remember a time when everyone in the two thousand seats or so that were filled, were on their feet, shouting and swaying, dancing and praising. I wanted to shout and sway and dance and praise myself, but all I did was press my hands together and rock a little. I contained myself because of Jeremy.

From the corner of my eye, I took a peek at him. He was doing well, at least he was standing. Jeremy's lips were pursed and his arms were straight at his side, though his eyes were on the pulpit, as if he were engrossed in the Reverend Derrick Harwood's teaching. It was an act, albeit not a good one, but

Jeremy was getting better. He looked more engaged than he had in the past three Sundays.

This was the fourth guest pastor in as many weeks since Reverend Robinson had stepped down. And in those four weeks, even though Jeremy still participated in the ministers meetings, even though he still met with the teens in the church, not once had Jeremy been asked to take Reverend Robinson's place in the pulpit. In fairness to the board, Reverend Lewis hadn't been asked either; everyone who'd preached on Sundays were visiting pastors. But that was little solace for Jeremy.

"Saints," Reverend Harwood shouted out. "The Word of God is clear, it is consistent, it is correct and it is our decree."

"Hallelujah," so many sang.

"Amen," others joined them.

I closed my eyes and tucked my chin to my chest. "Lord," I began my prayer in a whisper, "let Jeremy hear Your word. Let him have peace that this is Your will that Reverend Harwood is here today. Guide his steps from this point, taking Jeremy to the best place for him, the place you want him to be." I paused, then added, "And guide my steps, too, Lord. Amen."

When I opened my eyes, Reverend Harwood was already taking his seat and Jeremy followed. I sat, too, but it took minutes for the fire that the reverend had set in the sanctuary to be extinguished and for everyone to settle in their seats.

I covered Jeremy's hand with mine, then intertwined our fingers. He inhaled, then exhaled, a sign that I'd calmed him.

Now, my next goal...I squeezed his hand and turned to him. When he glanced at me, I smiled. He didn't. He just turned his eyes back to the altar. This time, I was the one who took a deep breath in, then breathed out. I had to be patient; preaching at Pilgrim's Rest meant so much to him and the thought of that made me hold onto Jeremy's hand tighter.

But he kept his eyes staring straight ahead, his gaze hard on the altar, his lips pressed together. And his leg quivered like he was in the middle of an earthquake. When he took in a deep breath but didn't release it, I squeezed his hand.

I kept my eyes on the altar, too, not wanting to keep staring at Jeremy. But also, it wasn't too hard to look at Reverend Harwood. If Dr. Martin Luther King, Jr. had a twin who was born fifty years later, this man was it. Everything about him was mesmerizing, from his manner to his looks to his deep baritone that reminded me of Reverend Robinson, this man had it all together in the pulpit. Even though he was now sitting down, I imagined that few eyes were on Reverend Lewis, who now stood at the pulpit. All of us—men and women alike—were staring at the guest pastor.

After the offering, Reverend Harwood returned to the pulpit and he asked everyone to stand for the benediction.

I continued to hold on to Jeremy as Reverend Harwood raised his hand and belted out in song, "May the Lord watch between me and thee, while we are absent, one from another. Amen."

"Amen," the congregants said.

Then, everyone did something I hadn't seen before. The members applauded. Even though Reverend Haywood's sermon had ended minutes before, people stood, not moving from their seats and clapped.

I could feel the heat rising within Jeremy.

When Reverend Harwood waved, then turned toward the back doors, I breathed. Usually, the guest pastors personally greeted the members, but we'd been told at the beginning of the service, that he had to catch a plane to New York right after our service. So there would be no meet and greet.

But then, I guess, Jeremy had a different idea. He didn't say a word when he hopped out of the pew faster than I could follow and by the time I caught up to him, he was standing at the back door (where Reverend Robinson or our guest pastors normally stood) and he began holding his own meet and greet as the first members exited the church.

I sighed. He was not giving up. He'd been lobbying, calling each of the twelve members of the board, letting them know of his interest. Many had the same questions that I had for Jeremy: What about school? Wasn't he too young? Was he ready for that kind of leadership when he hadn't held an assistant's position?

I stepped to the side and people shuffled through the aisles, pressing to get to the front door. From my vantage point, I watched Jeremy in the vestibule, his countenance much different now. He was full of smiles and warm handshakes. He even kissed a couple of babies. He was a pastor on a political campaign. I guess it was all the same.

Dru tapped my shoulder. "You okay?"

"Oh, I didn't know you were here."

"Yeah, girl. I was in my normal seat in the back with my mom."

"Oh, she's here?" I said, looking over at the section where Dru and her mom normally sat. "I wanna say hello."

"She's gone now. You know she sneaks out before the benediction. She said she only came to church today to see me since I never come home."

I laughed. It was kind of funny that Dru stayed on campus since she'd grown up less than a half hour away. But her mother's loss was my gain because we'd been roommates all four years at Xavier.

"But whatever," Dru continued. "She can come and see me here every week from now on 'cause I'm not gonna miss another Sunday service. Not until someone finally steps into the pulpit, and tells the truth and shames the devil about Reverend Robinson."

I shifted and looked away from Dru, feeling bad for a moment that I hadn't told my best friend about Reverend Robinson's second family. Even though we believed Shaniqua, we still didn't know for sure if it were true. And neither Jeremy nor I wanted to spread any rumors about anyone. That was not how we rolled, we didn't gossip. And we weren't going to start doing that now.

I finally said, "That's not going to happen, Dru."

She shrugged. "You never know. Someone may step up. So what are you and Jeremy going to get into?"

I turned my glance back to him and sighed. "I don't know. I'll hang out with him for a little while at least. He misses Reverend Robinson so much."

"Yeah, well." Then, she leaned closer to me and whispered, "Baby! He had a baby," but before she noticed the shocked look on my face, she scooted up the aisle laughing all the way to the door. I couldn't imagine what she would do if she were to ever find out that she'd been right, but she needed to make baby plural.

Turning back to Jeremy, I yearned to be by his side just in case he needed me. But he was in full-fledge campaign mode and standing beside him wouldn't have been appropriate. I was not his wife. So I turned, maneuvered to the left, then, dipped into the ladies' room.

Moving to the lounge part of the area, I pulled out my cosmetic bag, rested it on the counter and just as I began to powder my face, First Lady Eunice Blake pushed open the door and sauntered in.

I'd always said that if she hadn't been a First Lady, she would've been a heck of a full-figured model because not only did she have the features, she had the style...and then, she had that strut.

"Ginger." She also had a Boston accent that I loved. "It is so good to see you."

"It's good to see you, too, First Lady Blake."

I'd shared several meals with her at the Robinson's home, especially after her husband, Reverend Evander Blake passed away about a year and a half ago. He'd been the pastor of First United Missionary Baptist, our sister church. But First Lady Blake had left the church that her husband had pastored for over twenty years after their board elevated Reverend Blake's arch rival (one of the deacons who'd been trying to bring the Blakes down) into the role of Senior Pastor. She'd been an unofficial member of Pilgrim's Rest ever since.

"I'm glad we're going to have a few moments here." She glanced around the lounge. "Are we here alone?"

I shrugged. "I don't know, I think so."

She moved to the space outside of the lounge that held three stalls, checked it out, then returned to where I was standing. "It's just us."

As she leaned toward me, my heart began to pound. Suppose she wanted to talk to me about the Robinsons? Suppose she knew about Shaniqua? No! I didn't want to talk about anything or anyone.

Even though she knew we were alone, First Lady Blake still lowered her voice. "What's the deal with you and Jeremy?"

Her question made me blink, made me lean back a little. "Oh!" I paused and tried to rewind my thoughts. "Well...uh... I'm not sure what you mean. We're really good friends."

She dismissed my words with a wave of her hand. "Oh, I know that. Everyone knows that. What I want to know is what's going on now? Are you going to stay friends or are you ready to take the next step?"

I wondered why she was asking me this. "Well, we're still in school. I mean, we're graduating in a few weeks, but there's still...."

Again, she waved her hand. "Ginger, you know what I'm talking about," she said with a bit of impatience in her tone. "Now, Jeremy told me you were his girlfriend and I just want to make sure the two of you are on the same page because I don't want him to be hurt."

"He said I was his girlfriend?" When I heard my voice, I shook my head to snap out of it. I sounded like a little girl with her first crush.

"Yes. I spoke to him the other night about his desire to lead this church and one of the things I told him was that it's important to have a wife already by his side, no matter where he ended up pastoring."

My lips parted in surprise.

First Lady Blake said, "And he told me he didn't have a wife, but he had a girlfriend who he hoped would be his wife one day. Since you're the only woman I've ever seen him with, I'm thinking that girlfriend is you."

When I'd decided to give up my fears and gave into my feelings for Jeremy, I'd gone in all the way. Hearing that he was calling me his girlfriend really did make me feel grade-school giddy.

"So?" First Lady Blake folded her arms.

"Well, yes, I guess you can say that."

"Say what?" She didn't give me time to respond before she said, "You need to be clear about this, young lady. Because Jeremy Williams is a young man on the move. Whether or not he gets the position in this church, he's going to get it somewhere. And there will be plenty of women who will be willing to stand by his side."

Her words made my eyebrows rise, but her tone, made me say, "I understand. I just wasn't trying to put our business out there like that."

"Well, what you need to do is put it all the way out there because there are wolves who need to know that Jeremy Williams is involved with Ginger Allen."

The bathroom door opened and First Lady Blake stood up straight as a tall leggy woman in a spandex dress that left little to the imagination and rose to her mid-thigh as she moved, sauntered in. She paused, then scowled, her lips pinched like she'd just sucked a lemon as her eyes journeyed up, then down my body.

"Hello, Sharonne," the First Lady said, even though she hadn't acknowledged her.

The transformation was instant when the woman turned her attention away from me. Her scowl flipped to a grin. "First Lady Blake. How are you today?"

"I'm well." She nodded and then with her hand, motioned toward me. "But I'm not the only one standing here."

The woman—Sharonne—turned back to me. "Hi."

I frowned, wondering where all the hate was coming from. "Hello."

The woman moved to the other side of First Lady Blake, leaned over, getting her face closer to the mirror, checked her reflection, then fluffed her stylish bob before she spun and sashayed toward the door. "You have a great day, First Lady," she said over her shoulder.

We were silent until the door closed behind her. Then First Lady Blake said, "And that right there—that's what I was just talking about. She's one of those wolves who wants what you have."

I pressed my hand against my chest. "What I have?"

"Yes. You have Jeremy and that's who she wants. So you better stake your claim and then get ready because these women out here, when it comes to pastors...."

She left her words there but she didn't have to say much more. I knew what she was talking about. I'd lived the struggle, I knew the story.

But I guess I hadn't really been paying attention to the women who had shown interest in Jeremy. I mean, yeah, I'd noticed lots of them always taking long looks at him, but that wasn't any kind of surprise. Jeremy Williams was everything that a young woman would want in a man—he was fine and he had a future.

"Don't worry," First Lady Blake said as if she were reading my mind. "Jeremy has no interest in anyone else, especially not someone like Sharonne, who thinks it's attractive to show all her goodies. A man like Jeremy will choose his forever companion carefully and while Sharonne would be good for a roll in bed, she'd never be the woman who'd stand next to him at the altar. But women like Sharonne don't go away peacefully. So you have to stake your claim." She tapped my shoulder. "Jeremy has the talent to go far. But there is more to this journey than just having talent. And you have what it takes to help Jeremy rise to the next level. You hear me?"

I nodded. "I do." I'd heard her for sure, loud and clear.

"Good." She patted my hand. "I'll be praying for you and Jeremy. "You just take care of your business."

Again, I nodded, then stayed in place as First Lady Blake checked her reflection before she did her own runway strut out of the bathroom. When the door closed, I turned toward the mirror, rested my hands on the counter and let out a long breath.

That little encounter with Sharonne had reminded me of the vow I'd made just six years ago. Was I sure about this? Did I want to move forward to see where this would lead with Jeremy when there were so many wolves preying on pastors out there?

But then, I looked up at the mirror and I thought about Jeremy and how I loved being with him. I loved sitting with him and talking and laughing. I loved studying with him and how he always knew the right answer when I was stuck on a problem with statistics. I loved reading the Bible with him and our discussions of the living God in our lives.

I loved him. I loved Jeremy Williams.

It was too late. My vow had been broken and now I was all in with this man. My only prayer now, was that I hoped he was just like my daddy.

# CHAPTER FIVE

Jeremy and I sat in his car, both of us stiff with surprise. The lights of his Nissan were on, beaming on the theatre that we'd just left. If I thought *Slumdog Millionaire*, the movie we'd just seen had drama, it didn't compare to the phone call Jeremy just received.

He was holding his Blackberry away from his ear so that I could hear Reverend Lewis.

"I didn't want you to come to church tomorrow without knowing the announcement the board would be making."

As soon as he said that, I knew what Reverend Lewis's next words would be.

"A new pastor has been selected to lead Pilgrim's Rest and I think you'll be pleased with the board's...."

"Wait, hold up. Someone has been selected already?"

Even though I knew that was what Reverend Lewis was going to say, I had the same surprise as Jeremy. It had only been two months since Reverend Robinson had left. When

I was growing up, and around pastors with my father, it took churches at least a year to find a new leader between all of the interviews, the guest speakers who were tested out, and the background and financial checks. So how had Pilgrim's Rest done this so quickly? Unless...this had something to do with Shaniqua. Had someone found out about her before Reverend Robinson had even stepped forward? Had someone pushed Reverend Robinson out? That was the only explanation I had for the church being able to move this quickly.

"Yes, Jeremy. We've asked Reverend Derrick Harwood to be the Senior Pastor of Pilgrim's Rest and he's accepted. He'll be introduced officially to the congregation tomorrow."

With the way everyone had reacted to Reverend Harwood a month ago, I was sure there would be no problems from the membership.

Glancing at my boyfriend, his heartbreak was etched all over his face and without closing my eyes, I said a prayer for him.

"Everyone at Pilgrim's Rest loves you, Jeremy, but this was just not your time. Give yourself another ten years or so. Go to school, get on our staff full-time. And the next time there's an opening...."

Jeremy interrupted him, "Thanks for letting me know, Archie," then he clicked off his phone.

If I didn't know how upset Jeremy was before, I certainly knew now. First, he never called Reverend Lewis by his first name; that was just basic respect to Jeremy. And second, he'd practically hung up in *Archie's* face.

"Can you believe that?" Jeremy finally said.

"I'm surprised," was my answer because I could believe it. But what I couldn't say to Jeremy was that as fast and as shocking as the board's decision was, I agreed with them. People were still talking about Reverend Harwood. He was going to be a good leader for Pilgrim's Rest and I had a feeling he was just what the church needed right now.

Jeremy nodded and when I saw he was cool, I was glad for the way he was taking this. But then a second after I had that thought, he slammed his hand against the steering wheel so hard it made me jump. "That's what's wrong with these old churches. They see my youth as a negative. If anything, it's a positive. It's what we need to grow."

"I agree," I said rubbing his back and keeping my voice soft and soothing. "But Reverend Harwood isn't that old."

"He isn't old compared to Reverend Robinson," Jeremy huffed. "Harwood is about forty, I think. So yeah, he's twenty years younger than Reverend Robinson, and I'm twenty years younger than him. If they want to move forward, they need someone younger, someone who has a vision on how to take the church deep into this millennium."

"Well," I said, trying to measure my words, "they didn't have your vision, but that doesn't mean you can't implement it."

He frowned when he looked at me.

I said, "Reverend Robinson believed in you. I believe in you, and yes, I would like to see you continue to at least getting your Master's because that was all you talked about before Reverend Robinson stepped down. But I believe you would be an amazing pastor. And so maybe you don't have to sit on someone's staff. Maybe you don't have to wait until your turn. Maybe you just go and make it happen. In your own church. One day."

He nodded slowly as if he was pondering my words. But then, a smile came to his face. A smile that was genuine, a smile that rose all the way to his eyes, a smile that I hadn't seen since all of this Pilgrim's Rest drama had started.

"You may be right. I may have been too big and too much for Pilgrim's Rest. I may be too big for any church. I may have to do this myself."

I hadn't said all that, but all I did was nod.

"Yeah, you're right," he continued. "And anyway now may not have been the best time for me to be appointed."

"You think?"

He chuckled. "I know." He paused. "Thank you for believing in me."

"That's what best friends do."

"Best friends who are in love," he said.

I was startled by his words but I didn't show it.

When he continued with, "And anyway, we have other things to think about," I smiled because he'd taken away the pressure of me having to tell him that I loved him, too, and I knew what he meant by us having other things to think about.

"That's right. Graduation. For both of us."

"And the celebration begins tomorrow."

"What's happening tomorrow?" I asked.

"Oh nothing. I just mean it's the beginning of our final week in school."

"Yup. We're about to head into our future."

"You got that right." He pushed the car's gear into 'Drive', then squeezed my hand. "Remember when I told you it was gonna be a hella ride with me?"

"Yeah."

"Buckle up, baby. We're about to take off."

# CHAPTER SIX

"Welcome to Pilgrim's Rest." Jeremy shook Reverend Harwood's hand.

I was so proud that not only had Jeremy decided to come to church, but this morning, we'd sat in the front pew of the church as Pilgrim's Rest welcomed their new pastor.

And at the end of service, Jeremy and I had stood in line with the other parishioners to greet Reverend Harwood and now, finally it was our turn to give him our good wishes.

"You're Jeremy Williams," Pastor Harwood said before he pulled Jeremy into one of those brotherman hugs. "It's nice to meet you. I've heard so much about you and I'd love for us to get together this week, maybe have lunch one day."

"Well, this week may be a little difficult. We're graduating on Saturday." Jeremy turned to me. "This is my girlfriend, Ginger Allen. She's graduating from Xavier and I'll be graduating from Dillard."

All of the Reverend's attention was on me now. "Wow, you're a beautiful young woman. Something about hazel eyes on a woman always makes me smile." He took my hand into his. "I guess, I should say congratulations to both of you."

He held onto my hand as he held my gaze and up close, this man was even finer. It was more than his resemblance to Martin Luther King, Jr. He oozed charisma. This man was going to be good for Pilgrim's Rest, but he was going to be trouble, too.

"Thank you," Jeremy and I said together, then, I gently tugged my hand from his grasp. It was almost like he didn't have any plans to let me go.

Reverend Harwood cleared his throat. "Well, then after you graduate, maybe we can all get together next Sunday. Everyone has told me how valuable you've been here at Pilgrim's Rest and I'm hoping you'll be staying in New Orleans. Our church can use someone youthful and on fire for the Lord as I'm told you are."

"We'll see." Jeremy glanced over his shoulder. "I don't want to hold up the line anymore," he told the pastor.

"Let's connect this week," he said to Jeremy, but he kept his eyes on me.

Jeremy waved without making a commitment and then, he led me away. Holding hands as we entered the parking lot, I kissed Jeremy's cheek.

"I'm so proud of you."

"Why? Because I didn't give him an elbow to the eye for taking my position?"

I laughed. "That's one reason. But I know how you felt about this."

"Key word: felt. What you said last night made a lot of sense. I've moved on. I've got to start thinking about doing my own thing."

I smiled, though my thoughts were that if I'd talked Jeremy into accepting this decision, I just might be able to convince him to choose a different career path altogether. When we slid into the car, I asked, "So, where are we going now?"

"Do you have anything you have to do to prepare for your mom and sisters coming in tomorrow?" he asked as we pulled out of the church's parking lot.

I shook my head. "No, I'll pick them up from the airport tomorrow evening, then take them over to the hotel. Besides, that, I don't have anything else planned for today or tomorrow."

"Well, I need to clean up my apartment a little before my family gets in."

"That's cool. Want me to help?"

"Nah. You're my girlfriend, not my maid."

"I don't mind. Plus, you and Aaron are so neat anyway; how long will it take?"

"Exactly, that's my point. Just let me do this, and then, I'll come back to pick you up. Say...in about an hour? Then, we can hang out and get something to eat."

I shrugged. This was unusual. Since Jeremy and I started going to church together, we'd always did something together right after.

"It'll just be about an hour," Jeremy repeated.

"Okay, cool. It'll give me a chance to change into jeans or something."

"Nah, don't do that."

"Why not?" I frowned. "We're just gonna hang out, right?"

"Yeah, but I love looking at your legs and Sundays are the only time I get to do it."

"Okay," I said as he pulled up in front of my dorm. "So an hour."

He nodded before he leaned over and gave me one of what I'd come to call a soul kiss. When I pulled away, there was so much more that I wanted to do with him. But we hadn't gotten there yet, and I loved the way Jeremy wasn't rushing us. It was like he was allowing our relationship to just simmer.

When I pushed open the door to my room, I half-expected to see Dru. But the room was empty and I wasn't that surprised. She hadn't come to the room last night and I didn't see her in church. I guess she was taking Senior week seriously. My girl was tearing up the streets.

I kicked off my shoes, laid back on the bed and sighed. There were so many reasons for my joy and one that was near the top of the list was how Jeremy had bounced back from his desire to be the Senior Pastor at Pilgrim's Rest. Even now, it just seemed so ridiculous, but I couldn't be mad at his ambition. I was just going to have to help him channel it in the right direction.

I was looking forward to every moment of that. Rolling over, I glanced at the photo that Jeremy and I had taken the day after our first kiss. We'd taken it in one of those mall photo booths, but it was the best picture because we were just being us. I took it from my desk and stared at it, loving the way I was leaning back into him, loving the way his arms were around me.

I didn't know where this was going with me and Jeremy. I was so looking forward to going home and beginning the next chapter of my life. But would that life really include Jeremy? He had to decide this week whether he'd been going to Howard or Duke. Of course, I held hope in my heart that he'd go to the HBCU since it would be close to my home, but what I knew for sure was that he had to go where God led him, not where I wanted him to be.

As I stared at the picture, my phone rang. I was smiling before I said, "Hey, Jeremy. You're on your way?"

"Nah, um, Aaron's gonna join us, is that okay?"

"Sure," I said, a little surprised. His roommate had never done anything more than hang out with us at their apartment. But then after thinking about it for a second, Aaron was going to be returning to Arkansas after graduation. Maybe Jeremy just wanted to spend as much time with him as possible.

"So, while I finish up here, he's gonna pick you up and take you to Restaurant R'evolution."

I shot up straight on the bed. "Really, Jeremy. We can't afford that."

"What do you mean we? Did I ask you for anything?"

"Okay, you can't afford that. And what about Aaron? I know he doesn't have any money."

He laughed. "Ginger Allen, you don't know anything. Can't I take my girl out once for a nice celebration?" He didn't give me room to answer before he added, "And I already told you, just buckle up and enjoy the ride. Aaron will pick you up in about ten minutes." And then, he hung up without even saying goodbye.

Really? Was I even dressed fancy enough for Restaurant R'evolution?

This was so odd. One thing about Jeremy was he wasn't impressed with fancy restaurants or designer clothes. He kept his eleven-year-old car not because he had to—he made enough as a youth pastor to have a newer car. But none of that fazed him.

Then, I smiled. This was spontaneous and it would be fun, so I was going to do what Jeremy said. I was going to buckle up.

⁓

"What's up, Aaron, you got stuck with limousine duty, huh?"

"It's not a big deal. How many times have I taken you back and forth?"

"And I always appreciate it. So," I said when he began to edge his Ford truck from the curb. "We're going to Restaurant R'evolution?"

"Yup."

"Is Tasha gonna join us?" I asked about his girlfriend.

"Nope. She's hanging out with her family. They got here this morning."

"Bummer. She's gonna be sorry she missed this."

"I guess. I'm not into restaurants all that much. As long as there's a McDonald's or Chick Fil A nearby, I'm good."

I laughed; this was the reason why he and Jeremy were friends. Aaron tuned his radio to WDUB, Dillard's radio station and when I heard the notes of that intro, I bobbed my head. Leaning back in the seat, I closed my eyes and jammed.

*"I'm lost without you,"* Robin Thicke sang, but my voice drowned his out. *"Can't help myself."*

"Sing, girl." Aaron laughed, but I didn't care. I kept on singing.

And the words made me lean back, close my eyes, and drift back on a memory to the first time I'd heard this song. About two years ago...the night I laid eyes on Jeremy Williams....

*"Will you come on?" Dru said, as she yanked me into the hotel lobby.*

*I sighed. This didn't make any sense. We'd come to Charlotte for the MEAC, and we'd seen a few basketball games, but at night, Dru dragged me from one hotel lobby to another. It was crazy.*

*These weren't official parties, but the people were hanging out like they were.*

*"Why are you moping around?" Dru asked.*

*"I'm not," I practically screamed back just so she would be able to hear me. "I just don't get this. One hotel lobby looks like another. Why are we hotel hopping?"*

*"Because this is part of the fun of being in Charlotte."*

*"And this is why I probably never came here before."*

*"I'm not going to let you wear your Debbie Downer facade today. This was a great idea to get out of New Orleans. We need to celebrate almost being halfway through college."*

*"And I have no problem with that kind of celebration. But hanging out in hotels is not my idea of celebrating anything."*

*I paused taking in the sight around me. There were dozens and dozens of men and women in the lobby, sectioned off in groups, holding cups in their hands, bobbing their heads, some even dancing to Alicia Keyes singing "No One," her voice flowing through the hotel's speakers. It was like we were truly in the middle of a club. "This looks like Freaknik with just a little more class." Then, I did a slow 360 spin taking in every corner. "Did I say class? Let me take that back."*

*Dru laughed. "I think Freaknik is a great comparison. But if you don't want to freak anyone, that doesn't mean I can't. And as a matter of fact...." She smoothed down her tube top, then said, "You see that honey over there?"*

*I followed Dru's glance to a guy so tall, I wondered if he was one of the players.*

"*Yeah, he's purple and gold,*" *she continued, commenting on the wife beater he wore.* "*I'm gonna go holla at him. Why don't you find a seat over there?*" *She waved her hand in the general vicinity of the lobby's couches and when she went switching off, I sighed again.*

*What I really needed to do was get back to our hotel, but I didn't want to leave Dru out there like that. We'd come together and we were gonna leave together. Those were the rules.*

*There wasn't a free seat in the lobby and I began to think that maybe rules were meant to be broken —- for tonight. But just as I had that thought, two girls stood up. I raced to the sofa, sat down, just as a new song came on over the speaker.*

"I'm lost without you...."

"*Would you mind if I sat here?*"

"Can't help myself...."

*At first, I was mad. This song had caught me and I wanted to listen, uninterrupted. But then, I looked up and into the face of a man who made me take a deep breath. There were so many things that made this guy so fine, starting with the chocolate tone of his skin that was clear, smooth. I loved a black man; his coloring was a beautiful contrast to the cinnamon tint of mine. And then, he had these dimples on full display.*

"*Do you mind?*" *He pointed to the seat next to me. He smiled and I sighed.*

"*I'm sorry, of course,*" *I said.* "*I don't own the sofa.*"

*He chuckled.* "*I kinda knew that. But I'm a gentleman and so what a gentleman does is ask first.*"

*Even if he hadn't told me that, I probably would have been able to testify that he was a gentleman in a court of law. It was everything about him, especially the way he was dressed. While most of these dudes were in jeans and wife beaters, he wore black slacks and a white tailored shirt open at the collar. A very business, but casual look.*

*He sat and then began mimicking me. Not on purpose, of course. He just bobbed his head in rhythm to mine. And then, he opened his mouth:*

"Lost without you, can't help myself."

*I leaned away from him.* "Wow! Impressive."

*He blinked and when he glanced my way, it seemed that he'd forgotten where he was.*

"Thank you. But I'm sorry."

"For what?"

"I think if you're not being paid to sing aloud in public, that means that you shouldn't do it."

*That made me chuckle.* "I disagree. If you can sing like that, then clear your throat and blow."

*He laughed.* "Well, I had to find something to do 'cause this." *He paused, glanced around at the party going on and shook his head.* "I'm not built for this. Just ask my boys. The ones wilding out in the corner over there."

*I followed his glance and asked,* "Why aren't you wilding out with them?"

"Didn't you hear what I said?" *And he gave me that double-dimple smile again.* "I'm too much of a gentleman to be doing all *of that. This ain't my thing. Don't even ask me how I ended up here 'cause I couldn't tell you."*

*"Tell me about it," I said. "I have no idea why I'm here either. I mean, I'm a basketball fan and it sounded like a great idea at the time, but...."*

*"But!" he said and we laughed together again.*

*He held out his hand. "I'm Jeremy. Jeremy Williams."*

*"Ginger Allen."*

*"Like Ginger," he paused and frowned, "from Gilligan's Island?"*

*I rolled my eyes. If I'd had a dollar for every time someone said that, I wouldn't need this Business degree that I was working toward.*

*It must have been my silence, that made him say, "Sorry. Didn't mean to offend you."*

*"No." I held up my hand. "You're fine. I'm just irritated because of all of this." I waved at the people surrounding us.*

*"So this must be your first time."*

*I nodded.*

*"Then, I'm gonna assume that you're not from around here."*

*"Nah, I'm from DC. But I go to school in New Orleans. Xavier."*

*His eyes widened. "Get. Out. I'm at Dillard. What are you? A freshman?"*

*"I'm a sophomore actually."*

*"So am I. Wow." He shook his head. "I can't believe we've never met."*

"Well, I'm not a big partier; I don't get out much."

"If I'd seen you at McDonald's I would have remembered." He paused. "I hope you don't mind me saying this, but you're beautiful."

I lowered my eyes, never feeling quite comfortable with being complimented for the way I looked. I had nothing to do with that—I carried the DNA of my parents.

Again he said, "I'm sorry. Did I say something wrong?"

"Oh, no. It's fine. So what are you studying at Dillard?"

"Mass Communications."

"Oh, you want to be a journalist?"

He paused for a moment before he said, "I want to be a pastor."

It was shocking to hear from a man who'd traveled with turnt up friends to hang out in a hotel lobby in Charlotte, but I knew how to play poker. I kept my smile and nodded.

But then as we kept talking about Dillard and Xavier, about my hometown of DC and his of Houston, about how I hoped to pledge the pink and green while he wanted to make the Alpha line, I realized that we had so much in common.

"Hey, what's up?"

Jeremy and I glanced up at the same time, taking a look at Dru, who held a plastic cup half-filled with some red liquid—like she was in a club.

"And who is this?" she said with nothing but flirtation in her tone.

Jeremy stood and introduced himself.

"Well, hello Jeremy," Dru sang. "Are you over here doing naughty things to my friend?"

*"Dru."* I sighed. *"Please. We're just talking. Jeremy is going to be a pastor."*

*"Oh,"* she said, her tone and stature changing. *"Well...uh... God bless you."* She spun away from us, then sashayed toward another corner.

Jeremy and I watched Dru, then, he said, *"I just wanna know, you got something against pastors?"*

*"No."* I shook my head. *"Absolutely not. My father was a pastor."*

*"Oh,"* he said with a bit of joy in his voice. *"Okay. I just didn't know what you meant when you said that to your friend."*

*"I didn't mean anything by it. She was being rude and I didn't want you to think you even had to answer her question."*

*"So, you said your father was a pastor."*

*"Yes."*

Then as other college students mingled, drank, and partied around us, I told him how my father had been the Senior Pastor of Greater Faith, a large church in DC for almost fifteen years before he passed away a few days after my sixteenth birthday.

And he told me how his father had been a deacon at his hometown church. But his dad had passed away as well.

Another thing that, unfortunately, we had in common.

He asked, *"Have you found a church home in New Orleans?"*

*"I'm embarrassed to say that I haven't. Not that I've really looked."*

*"Well, I attend a wonderful place. Pilgrim's Rest. I was just appointed the youth pastor there."*

*"That's wonderful."*

*"Listen, we probably won't be back in time for Sunday service, but they have a great midweek service. I can pick you up and we could ride over together...."*

*He sounded as if he was a bit hesitant, and so was I. Because while I really liked Jeremy in this hour that we'd spent together, I would need to make him understand that we would never be more than friends. Never....*

"Hello," Aaron said waving his hand in front of me. "Are you still here?"

"Oh," I opened my eyes and wondered when John Legend's voice had changed to Beyoncé's. "I must've drifted off to sleep. I don't know why; I wasn't sleepy."

"I don't know if you were asleep or not, but whatever you were thinking or dreaming about, it sure had you smiling."

My response: I only lowered my eyes, though I kept my smile. How could I not? Reliving those first moments with Jeremy, remembering how I'd said never...and now, two years later, my never had turned into something that I hoped would become a forever.

I shook my head, a little surprised at myself for having that thought. Already, it felt a bit like a whirlwind, from friendship to the L word in just two months. But we were still far from the M word, especially since who knew what would happen after graduation?

The thought of that made me a bit sad, but I pushed it out of my head when the valet opened the door. Happy thoughts, only happy thoughts. This was going to be a week of celebration and I wanted to stay in this mode.

I thanked the valet, then waited for Aaron as he got his ticket from the attendant. As Aaron opened the restaurant's door for me, I said, "I told Jeremy this was place was too expensive. We're college kids."

"For just a few more hours." Aaron grinned. "We're about to enter the real world."

I stepped into the restaurant and if the real world was going to be anything like this, I was all in. Even though it was the middle of the afternoon, it felt much later because the mahogany paneled walls darkened the room. There were plenty of lights, though, from the chandeliers that hung everywhere. Very Crescent City.

Aaron spoke to the hostess.

"Oh yes," she said as if she'd been expecting us. "Right this way."

We followed her through the room that really could have been anyone's living room with the heavy burgundy drapes at the windows and the mismatched cushioned chairs at the tables. All of it was perfect for the ambience. Though the restaurant was Sunday afternoon crowded with tourists and natives alike, the chatter was much softer than say, the McDonald's across town with half the people.

"Right in here," the hostess said.

I was confused when the hostess stopped in front of room and pushed open the door. Why was she taking me to a room?

But I followed her, stepping inside. And my confusion was compounded.

I blinked to make sure I was seeing what I saw. The room was a little dark because of the same wall paneling as out front, and I had fallen asleep in the Aaron's truck, so maybe there was some residual fog in my brain.

But the image in front of me stayed the same. "Mom?"

My mother sat at a long table wearing an expression that I couldn't decipher. She was smiling, but there were tears in her eyes.

I would've asked her what was wrong except I couldn't figure out why she was in New Orleans a day early. And how had she known that I was going to be at this restaurant? And then...what were my sisters, Jada and Lauren doing here? Along with Jeremy's brother, Ralph and his wife, Jean, and Dru, who sat at the far end of the table along with three of my line sisters and their significant others.

It was a table full of people that I didn't expect to see, but the one I expected wasn't even here. At least if Jeremy was here, I could get some answers.

Where was he?

Just as I had that thought, music came through the speakers.

"*Lost without you...*"

But it wasn't Alan Thicke's voice.

"*Can't help myself.*"

Jeremy walked through curtains from the opposite side

of the room. I wanted to ask him what was going on, but I didn't want to stop his serenade. Plus, I was stuck on the way he looked; he'd changed into a suit, the only one he owned. It was a little wrinkled, but he still looked gorgeous to me. That wasn't a word I would normally use for a man, definitely not for Jeremy, but that was all I had to describe my man who stood before me, tall, dark and super fine.

"Jeremy?" I said his name as if I wasn't sure he was really the man before me.

He nodded as if to assure me, and kept singing as he strolled closer. He was still a couple of feet away when the music stopped and after a moment, he began speaking, "We've been friends for a while now. Two years. And during that time, every day you put not only a smile on my face, but a smile in my heart."

I pressed my hand against my chest.

"You've touched me in a special way and my only regret is that it took me so long," he paused as he stopped just inches from me, his gaze glued to mine, "to see what was right in front of my face. We met as this song was playing and I had no idea that night that these words would quickly belong to me when it came to you. Ginger, I'd be so lost without you. So now...."

I gasped as he slowly lowered himself, not stopping until he had eased down onto one knee. Then, he lifted the top of a velvet box that I didn't notice until this moment. And when he slipped the ring from the box, I held my breath. It wasn't because of the diamond; I didn't need a lot of light to know that it wasn't very big. Jeremy just wasn't into that kind of thing and really, neither was I.

I held my breath because of this moment. This moment that, in a way, I had just imagined on the ride over. This moment that I never expected. This moment that I wanted to remember forever.

"I love you so much, Ginger Latrice Allen. And my greatest prayer now is that you will do me the honor of being my forever wife. So, will you? Will you marry me?"

"Yes, she will," my mother spoke her first words and everyone laughed.

Jeremy's eyes were still on me when he said, "Thank you, Mrs. Allen but I kind of want an answer from her."

I struggled to swallow the stone that had settled in my throat. It took a moment because I wanted my voice and my words to be totally clear. "Yes, Jeremy. Yes, I'll marry you."

He slid the ring onto my finger, then kissed my hand before he stood. He kissed me, then held me and as our friends and family applauded, I closed my eyes and thanked God. If I hadn't pushed aside my fear, if I hadn't started moving in my faith, I wouldn't be here right now.

So as my future husband held me and as my family and friends jumped up from the table to congratulate us, I said a heart prayer over and over: "Thank you, Lord. Thank you, God. Thank you, Lord."

# PART TWO
# THE PRESENT

# CHAPTER SEVEN

*August, 2018*

Dru held the hand mirror in front of me. "You good?" she asked.

I glanced at my reflection and turned my head from side to side. Marietta, my makeup artist, had my face beat once again, so I nodded. "Thanks, Dru."

My best friend, who'd held the title of Executive Assistant with me for the last seven years, was much more than that. She was my project manager, my idea generator, and my brain. Dru stepped over me and did the same for Jeremy.

But he held up his hand before she could hold up the mirror. "I'm good."

She nodded, turned back to me, then gave me a smile and a thumbs up before she moved behind the camera.

Jeremy snapped the French cuffs of his tailor-made shirt, then adjusted the gold and onyx cuff links that had his initials engraved in the center, before he turned to me. "You ready for this, baby?"

"I am," I said with the smile that I always wore.

"Okay then." The petite woman, whose short blond bob bounced with every word she spoke, swiveled in the chair and turned facing Jeremy. "We're ready, Pastor Williams."

My husband said, "Then, let's go."

Angela Wiley grinned at my husband, then gave a nod to me and her cameraman. "We're ready."

I wiggled my hips a bit to get settled on our sofa as the producer of the show gave the countdown.

Then Angela began, speaking into the camera. "Hello everyone, and welcome to Abundant Life and Abounding Love. I'm Angela Wiley, your host, bringing you the best in gospel news from across the nation. Today, I'm very excited about our guest, Reverend Jeremy Williams."

I tried my best not to narrow my eyes; I didn't want the camera to pick up on any angry-Black-woman attitude, but was Angela saying she only had one guest?

"Welcome Reverend Williams. It is such a pleasure to have you here."

"Thank you," Jeremy responded. Then, he grabbed my hand. "My wife, First Lady Ginger Williams and I are excited to be here."

"Yes," Angela said with a bit of ice in her voice. "Your wife." A pause and then, "Welcome First Lady."

If the cameras hadn't been running, I would have just stared at her. But I gave her the smile that I'd perfected over the last ten years. The First Lady's smile that I'd learned first from my mother.

It was the right thing to do since Abundant Life and Abounding Love was the number one rated gospel television show in America. And today, they were in the living room of our home in the upscale Kalorama section of DC, introducing us to the whole country. So, I had to remember my purpose, keep my focus, and be unbothered by this little heifer who was making it clear that she had her eyes on my husband.

Angela said, "So, let's get to this. I've been following everything you've been doing at your church, New Kingdom Temple, and I have to say I'm blown away by all you've accomplished."

Jeremy squeezed my hand. "Thank you. My wife and I are humbled by all that God has allowed us to do."

Angela nodded. "Well, you should be proud. You're a young...*couple* doing things churches that have been around for generations haven't been able to do. Let me share some of your accomplishments with our audience." She glanced down at her notes. "You started a school in Southeast DC for low income children where they're provided with everything from their school uniforms, to two full meals, computers, iPads...and you make sure each student has internet services in their homes." She shook her head as if she couldn't believe it. "You built the New Kingdom Towers in Northeast, one and two-bedroom luxury apartments for seniors who are living on fixed incomes and their rent is determined by how much they can afford to pay." She paused as if she wanted to give her audience time to appreciate that information. "And, you've paid off your church's mortgage, which you built on the old District of Columbia College campus, and includes your main sanctuary and two buildings—a learning center and a library." She held up her finger. "And may I add, you've done all of this in ten years."

"Well actually," Jeremy began as he leaned forward, not worrying at all about creasing his suit. He didn't have to be concerned about that—suits that cost thousands never wrinkled. Jeremy continued, "We're coming up on our tenth anniversary this October, so we actually haven't reached that milestone yet."

"That's right, I've been reading about your upcoming celebration."

"Yes, we've been blessed and we want to share our excitement with the community. So we have lots of things planned throughout the city."

"Wow, that's great. So everyone out there knows about New Kingdom Temple and it's charismatic pastor," after a couple of beats, her voice dipped an octave when she added, "and First Lady."

"You're so kind," Jeremy said.

Those weren't the words I would have said, so I just kept my smile in place.

Angela continued, "But for the two people out there in America who may not know about you," she giggled as if what she'd said was funny, "can you share a little bit about how you got started? If I remember correctly, you didn't go to school to be a pastor, did you?"

"Actually, I did not," Jeremy began. "I always wanted to be a pastor, but I went to Dillard because that's the school my father attended. They didn't have a Divinity program, so I majored in Mass Communications and had planned to get my Masters in Divinity."

"Oh, I didn't know that."

"Yes, but just a few weeks after graduation, this opportunity came up."

"Yes," I began, picking up where I always did in these joint interviews. "We'd just gotten engaged," I paused and gave Jeremy our rehearsed loving gaze, "had just graduated, and Jeremy had just accepted the offer to attend Duke University."

"Oh," Angela said, "Impressive."

Jeremy picked up. "But then, I got a call from New Kingdom. It was a relatively new church, small membership, less than one hundred, but they were looking for a new pastor with a new vision."

It was my turn. "The founding pastor, Cecil Donnell, had passed away suddenly. They were so new, they were afraid the church would disband. But one of the members of the church we attended in New Orleans, Mary Logan, had a cousin who attended New Kingdom Temple and it was Mary who brought Jeremy to the New Kingdom's board's attention."

"Wow, that was serendipitous."

Jeremy said, "It was. I was the only minister they interviewed, and one of the pastors from the church I attended in New Orleans, Reverend Archie Lewis, agreed to mentor me. So it seemed like a low risk for the church and it was a complete blessing for me."

I nodded with a smile because that was always the best I could do when Jeremy said that.

He told no lies—New Kingdom Temple had been a complete blessing *for him*. When they'd made the offer and he'd accepted, the church was ecstatic. The b oard, w hich consisted of three members at the time, didn't care what degrees Jeremy held or what he didn't have—he'd come with a high recommendation from Mary Logan and one of the mothers of the church, Beatrice Hayden, told everyone that God had spoken to her and Jeremy Williams was the one.

And Jeremy didn't care that there were only eighty-one people on the membership rolls. The fact that New Kingdom Temple was in DC, where I lived, made Jeremy believe this was all God-ordained.

"*This is G od's s tamp of approval o n o ur lives,*" w as w hat Jeremy told me back then.

Angela said, "It was a blessing to the church, that's for sure. You started with less than one hundred members and now, you have over ten thousand." She shook her head. "You are amazing," she said, looking straight into my husband's eyes.

"No," he responded, though he still wore his double-dimpled smile. "God is. God is the one who's amazing."

"Well, Amen," Angela said with a chuckle.

"Amen," Jeremy said.

*Heifer, if you keep playing me.* That's what I wanted to say, but I kept on my First Lady's smile.

"Well now, let's talk about some of the juicy stuff."

Juicy? Where was she going with this?

Angela scooted to the edge of the chair, bringing herself closer to Jeremy. "Reverend Williams," Angela sang my husband's name. "Tell me," she said like they were about to share a secret. "How have you managed to stay above the drama we often see accompanying megachurch pastors."

My husband's smile faded and he shook his head. "I don't know what you're talking about."

"Oh come on," Angela said. "Megachurches are often rocked with everything from abuse of power, to misappropriation of funds, and then," she paused and looked at me, "the affairs. We've seen and heard it all. But never do we hear Jeremy Williams' name associated with any of that."

"Well, first of all, I'd take offense with you stating that as a fact."

"Oh, I didn't mean...."

"No, I'm actually glad you brought that up. Because so many people have that impression of the church. And yes, there are a small number of pastors who've gotten caught up, that's a fact. But it's no greater number than men, or women, in any profession."

"True."

"One thing people must remember is that pastors are no better than anyone else. We are held to a higher standard because of what we were called to do, but we are still men."

Angela sat back in her chair a bit. "Well, Amen."

"Amen," Jeremy said. "Now, I do have to say that my wife and I," he squeezed my hand, "know that God has given us a gift and it is our job to continue to provide spiritual leadership, guidance, and support to the members that God has given to our care. We would be dishonoring Him," he pointed toward the ceiling, "if we were to do anything other than what He has called me to do."

I nestled in closer to my husband when I said, "And we would never abuse that gift. Neither one of us."

Angela gave me a long stare, then nodded before she glanced down at her pad filled with notes and questions. "So, ten is a special number for you. You will be with New Kingdom for ten years and you will be...married for the same number?"

"Yes!" I said, putting as much strength into my voice as I could. "Jeremy and I didn't have a chance to have a long engagement and we didn't have a big wedding. We got married the Sunday after his installation and we've been on this journey ever since."

"Amazing," Angela said.

Now that was something I could agree on with this woman. This journey had been nothing but amazing...for Jeremy. His calling was obvious with the way he walked right into his gift. His sermons were filled with the hope of youth and the fire that was in his heart for God. He was so relatable that many of the college students from the dozens of universities in the District began to attend.

But it had been work building this church. Reverend Donnell didn't have a staff, so we'd had to hire people, though there wasn't any real money to pay anyone. That meant that I had to jump in. And because of that, I'd never spent one day wearing a two-piece suit and carrying a briefcase into Walker-Hughes. Instead, I was in the church's office, handling the business: answering the phones, setting up the systems, paying the bills, making sure we had supplies...and then, I put on my marketing hat, spreading the word about this new church with this twenty-one-year-old pastor.

Getting the word out was one place where I felt comfortable in the church. This may have been a religious institution, but it was still a consumer product, and I put my degree and my knowledge of digital marketing to work. I went straight to social media and Twitter, which was a new thing back in 2008, but a thing that had enough users, especially celebrities.

I had the idea to direct message celebrities, inviting them to New Kingdom whenever they were in town and even offering a private meeting with Reverend Williams if there was anything they ever wanted to discuss.

When I'd told Jeremy about the idea to use social media, he'd only kissed my forehead as if he was saying—*bless your heart.*

But then I'd blessed his. Two weeks after I'd sent the first invitations, Chris Brown strolled into the Holiday Inn conference room where we held our church services during praise and worship. It was a shock to everyone, though no one behaved that way, and at the end of the service, he was so moved, he tweeted about the young dynamic pastor who sounded just like him when he preached. He helped to put Reverend Williams and New Kingdom Temple on the map.

The rest, as they say, is our history. From managing a growing membership roll that doubled every few years, to finding space to rent (first, the hotel, then a school gymnasium, after that, an old utility building) to house our church as we built a massive twelve thousand seat sanctuary, I managed the business side of New Kingdom Temple so that my husband could live his calling.

Angela said, "Well, now that we know how you stay out of trouble, Reverend," she giggled, "let's talk about your family. You have two lovely children."

This part of our interview wasn't rehearsed. Both of us brightened as we glanced at the photo on the mantel that Angela pointed to.

"Yes, our heartbeats," I said. "Our oldest is seven. Our daughter is five."

Even though I smiled, this was an uncomfortable part of our lives for me. The producers of the show had asked for our children to be on with us, but I had nixed that. I always tried to operate from my faith and push aside fear, but it was difficult when it came to our children because of what Jeremy and I had endured over the years. We'd had women stalking Jeremy constantly and a few guys had gotten too close to me. We'd received hate mail from folks who said we were going to burn in hell because of Jeremy's prosperity preaching and even had people turn up at our door, claiming to be relatives so often, we'd finally moved to this exclusive neighborhood three years ago where gates were around every home and President and Mrs. Obama had moved to last year after their years in the White House.

So, I wasn't excited about my children being around too many people I didn't call friends. Last year, Jeremy had tried to assuage my concerns by hiring bodyguards—one for him, one for me and a part-time one who protected our children when they were out of our sight. Still, I kept our children's faces away from all of the lights-cameras-action that had become Reverend Jeremy William's life.

"Our children are the biggest blessing of all in the last ten years. And we're trying our best to give them a normal life."

"Well," Angela sat back in her chair a bit, "that's going to be difficult because Reverend Williams, word on the street is that you're about to get your own television show," Angela said.

It was shock that made our eyes widen. That was true, but it was a top-secret truth, known only by our closest associates.

Before we could say anything, Angela waved her hand and said, "Don't worry, your secret is safe with me." And then, she laughed.

Did she think this was funny?

She explained, "Clearly, I have my sources, so we won't air this until after the press release is mailed out next week."

Behind the camera, Dru's eyes were as wide as mine and she shook her head. I knew she wasn't denying anything, she didn't have to; Dru was my ride and die. There was nothing but shock all over her face.

Jeremy said, "Wow, so, you even know about the announcement."

"A good reporter is willing to do her homework...and willing to do other things."

Angela was ridiculous, over the top, but I wondered how many times I'd said those same words over the years. Women flirted with my husband right in front of my face, giving him their numbers, asking if he would stop by their homes for prayer, letting their hands linger for too long all over his body. I was living the life of my mother, the life that I'd promised myself I'd never accept. But I'd accepted it, embraced it, while giving up so many of my dreams to make sure Jeremy fulfilled his.

But while Jeremy had walked into his calling, I had to admit that in many ways this felt like my calling, too. Because while I'd given up my career, what I'd been given was the marriage that I'd always prayed for. I'd asked God to make Jeremy's heart just like my dad's and He had answered that prayer.

Never once had Jeremy stepped out on me. I knew that for sure not only because I knew my husband's character (and I'd set up systems where my husband never spoke to a woman alone in his office), but with the way the world was set up these days—someone would have definitely made sure that I found out about any indiscretion.

"Well, since you've brought this up," Jeremy said, "my wife and I are very excited about this deal. We'll have a show on BET and at the same time, we'll be developing faith-based films for Netflix."

"That is awesome," Angela gushed. To me, she said, "You're one lucky little lady."

That was it. I'd had enough. The producers would just have to edit out what I was about to say—if they wanted to. I really didn't care if my putting this woman in her place aired on national TV in high-def.

But before I could say a word, Jeremy gently grasped my forearm. "Mrs. Wiley."

"Oh, it's Angela, and it's Ms. Definitely Ms."

"Well, Ms. Wiley. Please don't ever get it twisted. I'm the blessed one. Everything we have at New Kingdom Temple is because my wife has been right by my side making it happen. What we built here, you need to understand and get it right—we built this all TOGETHER."

I settled back and settled down. He'd put Angela in her place in a way that I would have never been able to do. The same way he did to any woman who came his way. Just like my dad.

With the tips of my fingers, I turned Jeremy's chin toward me and then, I kissed my husband, on national TV.

And when he kissed me back, all I heard was Angela's voice saying, "Cut! Cut! Cut!"

I smiled in satisfaction. My point had been made.

# Chapter Eight

This was something I would never get used to.

I leaned back in the chair and my eyes did a slow stroll around the table of the fifteen women gathered. After four years, I still didn't fit in with the First Ladies Council.

This had been my struggle once I finally accepted First Lady Sonya Douglas' invite after she'd been calling me, semi-annually, for more than five years.

*"You and Reverend Williams are doing great things," First Lady Sonya said when she called me the first time and the second time and the third time. "You must join the First Ladies Council so New Kingdom Temple is represented in the DMV."*

That had been First Lady Sonya, the matriarch of the group's pitch. But in our early years in D.C., my focus was on building our church, and three years after we started that, building our family. There was no room in my life for anything else—not the First Ladies Council, my sorority or even the Links who had also reached out to me.

But four years ago, after Lady Sonya's latest call, I began to give her invitation real consideration. Jasmine was one, Jayden was three and while they still needed me, between Dru and our daytime nanny, Carmen, I could spare a few hours a month. And the church—Jeremy and I both had staff to help us fulfill our New Kingdom responsibilities.

I'd been excited about going to that first working lunch at the Four Seasons, though when I'd shared that with Dru, my best friend hadn't felt the same way.

*"Are you serious? You're going to join a club with all those women? There's a reason why the Lord only wanted two or three to gather in his name. 'Cause fifteen or sixteen will be nothing but a mess. A complete and utter mess."*

I'd laughed at my best friend's spin on that scripture in Matthew, though I told her these First Ladies were far from a mess. If I'd thought Jeremy and I had made waves in the district, the First Ladies Council had caused a tsunami with the dozen or so schools they'd opened, plus the hundreds of college scholarships they'd given away over the years.

*"These women are making real differences in people's lives."*

Dru had looked at me with all kinds of doubt, and it turned out she'd been right.

"And child, I tell you," First Lady Cecily Davis' voice brought me out of my memories. "That p astor j ust h ad n o shame." With her French-tip manicured finger, s he p ushed her diamond-studded red-framed cat-eye glasses up the bridge of her nose. "He was just blatant in his disrespect. That's why his wife made her way right up to that heifer's...."

"Cecily!" First Lady Sonya snapped, from her chair at the head of the table.

Cecily pressed her hand against her chest. "Did I say heifer? I apologize." She turned her head and made eye contact with all the women around the table. With a sincere nod of her head, she added, "I didn't mean to say that. I meant to call her....a trick. That's why his wife showed up to that trick's apartment."

Laughter rang out around the table from everyone except for me. I wasn't trying to be self-righteous, but there was no way I could laugh at anyone else's pain. And gossip? That was something else I didn't do. Never had, never would. But this group—a circle of First Ladies, most in their fifties and sixties—had advanced degrees in gossip.

And while the other women had their Masters, Cecily Davis had two Phd's. She was the provost, for sure, bringing the bad news about some pastor and his wife to these meetings that were meant to be planning sessions for the good work we all said we wanted to do.

But Cecily always derailed us with dirt about every pastor and First Lady in the DMV. That was one reason why that woman and I would never be friends; the other—I had a long memory and what was indelible in my mind was walking into this meeting the first time when First Lady Cecily Davis, wearing the longest false eyelashes, French-tip fake nails and a weave that rolled down her back, greeted me with, "*Really, green contacts? Those are so 1984,*" before she ever said hello.

It had been amazing that I'd found the grace to answer her with a smile and the truth: I told her the hazel in my eyes were not contacts but my DNA, just like my sandy brown hair that everyone swore came off the head of some poor woman from Indonesia. The memory of how I'd had to check her reminded me of how much I didn't like being here. Why were these women all up in somebody else's business? They were First Ladies, for goodness sake. Surely, they wouldn't be happy if the tables had been turned their way.

As I gave Cecily a long glance, I shook my head. This woman could have done so much good. Not only because she and her husband, Pastor Davis, had an eight-thousand member church in Ward 3, the richest section of D.C., but with the most diverse congregation out of all of us, Cecily could have been a real shaker making major moves if so many people didn't like her — because of her mouth. She commanded attention with her still model-curvy frame and the way she strolled around still wearing five-inch stilettos, even though she was in her mid-fifties. She'd traded in her Malaysian twenty-two inch tresses for a cute pixie-cut that was a white as snow, giving her an exotic look. She was sassy, she was always designer-sharp...and she had a hard heart that was always filled with bad news.

After the laughter died down a bit, one of the First Ladies asked, "So did his wife really go to her apartment?"

"Yeah, girl," Cecily said, leaning forward like she had all the tea and was ready to spill more.

I said, "So, about the Dress for Success program, not only have I checked on the inventory of clothes and I want to give a report about that, but I've spoken to several schools."

Cecily's mouth snapped shut in shock as if she couldn't believe I'd interrupt her with some nonsense about the business at hand. And the rest of the First Ladies glared at me as if I'd taken away their toys on Christmas morning. "I just thought you'd want to know," I continued, not moved at all by their expressions, "that several schools are really interested in us bringing the program to them, especially Morton High School."

"Morton!" Cecily pressed both hands against her chest, leaned back and cackled. "This is rich. You know Morton is where their daughter goes to school. She's in the eleventh grade and I heard she was the one who drove her mother to that trick's house."

The women gasped and I sighed. How in the world had Cecily diverted my diversion and taken us right back to the gossip? Now that was a gift that I was glad I didn't have.

"And now," Cecily continued, "everyone in her school is talking about how her mama tried to cut her daddy over at the side piece's house. Lord hammercy."

The room filled with a bunch of side conversations and all I wanted to do was grab my bag and walk out. I'd done that before, which was why Cecily wasn't the only one in this group who didn't like me. When it came to me, the First Ladies Council was split in half: there were those who didn't like me, and those who told me about the ones who didn't like me. If it were not for First Lady Sonya, I would have been voted off this island a long time ago. Though I wasn't worried about that. My concern, at this point, was that I didn't jump off and swim away from the island myself.

For four years, it had been that way. Every time I left, I said I wouldn't be back. But I always returned because of the conversation I'd had with my mom after that first meeting...

*"I can't do it, Mom," I said, pacing in my bedroom as I adjusted my earphones to make sure my mother would hear me through the microphone. This was just another example of how I really needed my mom in D.C. with me. I said, "There is no reason for me to go back there and subject myself to that vitriol."*

*I heard my mother's chuckle and I imagined her sitting at her vanity, putting on her making as she prepared to play bridge with a group of women that she'd met in Dallas.*

*"Sweetheart," my mother began, "you know you sound a little like Jasmine with the way you're whining."*

*"Ugh!" I bounced onto my bed and folded my arms.*

*My mother chuckled again before she said, "Sweetheart, I wouldn't exactly classify being served lunch last as vitriol. It's just nonsense."*

*"Do you know why I was served last? Do you know where they sat me, Mom?"*

*"No, I don't," she said. The evenness of her voice was meant to keep me calm, but I was on fire. "Why don't you tell me?"*

*"It was horrible. I wasn't even at the table with them. It had been set for fourteen, yes, but clearly, they could have moved over and made room for me some kind of way. But no." I deepened the fold of my arms. "I sat at this little side table. Like the kiddy table we used to have at Grandmama's house for Thanksgiving."*

*"I'm sure it wasn't that bad."*

*"It was." This time, I did whine. "This was a First Ladies luncheon and I'm a First Lady. First Lady Sonya invited me. She's been after me to join for all these years. But yet, when I get there, they all took one look at me and then...."*

*I paused.*

*My mom picked up for me. "And then, they treated you like Cheryl Smith."*

*It shouldn't have amazed me, but it did. Even over the miles, my mother could detect my issues. I was thirty-two years old and still the mention of that name made my fingers curl into fists. I guess just about everyone had their bully and Cheryl Smith had been mine. She'd followed me through the hallowed halls of Charles Drew middle school, shouting out to anyone who would listen, "Ginger Allen thinks she's cute."*

*That was what she was saying when she wasn't shoving me against the lockers or sticking out her foot when I passed by, hoping to trip me. For a year, I'd put up with her harassment that was accompanied by sneers and snickers from other kids. My first year in middle school had been miserable until....*

*"But remember what you did to Cheryl?"*

*My eyes widened when my mother interrupted my thoughts with her question. "You think I should take off my earrings and fight those women?"*

*Without waiting a beat, my mother said, "Yes."*

*"Mom!"*

*"But not physically," she clarified. "You have to stay in there and fight with your heart, fight with your mind. You're the First Lady of one of the major churches in Washington, D.C.. They know this and with time, they'll treat you that way."*

*"Ugh!" I groaned. "Why does it feel like I'm always fighting?"*

*"You're not always fighting. You didn't have any issues at Xavier."*

*"No, I didn't." I paused. "Because my best friend would have handled it. She would have shut it all down."*

*Now my mom laughed out loud. "You got that right. That's Dru, true till the end. But this is nothing new, sweetheart. You've always had your distracters; you can handle it."*

*I released another moan. "I don't know how you did it. I don't know how you dealt with this for so long."*

*She paused as if she wanted to give me a thoughtful answer. "Well, for starters, we didn't have all of this co-mingling between churches, so I didn't interact with a lot of First Ladies. I do understand, though, the need for the Council because the way everything is set up now, you ladies need the support of one another. This journey is certainly not for the weak or weary and it becomes very lonely. It'll be good to have women you can talk to who are going through the same kinds of challenges. These women will understand what it means to be married to a pastor and they may be able to give you ideas that I can't even give you.*

*"It's going to be great for you to form a friendship with them because the female members of the church are a different breed." There was just a hint of her tone becoming deeper. "They can be callous and cut-throat and when it comes to the pastor..." Her words trailed off, but she didn't have to say more. I'd seen her struggle, I knew her story. And even as good as my dad had been to her, the disrespect from the women had squeezed my mother's heart until the day my father died.*

*"Anyway, this is what you have to remember." She paused as if she wanted to make sure I heard her words. "Allen blood runs through your veins, honey. And we Allens do not allow anyone to run us off anywhere, especially not women." She stopped again. "You belong there, young lady. You belong in that group because you have too much to offer. Just like the youth that Jeremy brings to New Kingdom, you're going to bring fresh ideas to the First Ladies Council. They are so blessed to have you and by the next meeting, they will all realize this."*

*I smiled. My mother was right. This had been one meeting. Surely, once the First Ladies got to know me, they would come to love me....*

"It's so tacky that she would be fighting the other woman." I turned my attention back to the conversation and Cecily was still dragging on.

I couldn't take it anymore. I knew what I was about to do would add up to another notch against me, but I didn't care. When I walked out that door, they could vote me out. Because when I signed up for the First Ladies Council, this wasn't what I expected, nor was it what I wanted.

I was out!

⌒

I'd waited a few minutes, but then, I really couldn't take it anymore. No one seemed to even notice that I'd stood up. Or maybe it was just that no one cared.

"Yes," Cecily said, "and from what I heard, he's been sleeping at the church. Too scared to sleep at home 'cause you know they're from Forrest City, Arkansas, the same city where Al Green was born. And we all know what happened to Al Green."

A bunch of affirmative hums rolled through the room at the same time that I rolled my eyes. Just as I scooted my chair away from the table, the door to the private conference room busted open and First Lady Rena Bradley stumbled inside.

The other ladies gasped, I froze. It was because of the way Rena looked: Eyes puffy, hair disheveled. And what was that she had on? Not that I was being critical of her wardrobe. It was just that the First Lady of Knotting Hill Missionary Baptist Church was a walking billboard for *Vogue Magazine*. From casual to chic to after-five, Andre Leon Talley should have had her on the payroll.

But today, she wore a cotton shift, the kind that my grandmother used to wear—when she was cleaning her house.

Rena's dress, her eyes, her hair...all together, it almost looked as if she'd been beaten.

I was already half-way standing, but now, every woman in the room joined me. With an agility that surprised me for a sixty-three-year-old woman, First Lady Sonya reached Rena first.

"Sweetie, are you okay?"

Before Rena could respond, Sonya had her arms around the woman. Rena, who was already rail-thin, looked so frail now as Sonya led her to the chair where she'd been sitting.

This had to be bad—Sonya never gave up her seat at the head of the table. As Rena settled in the chair, Sonya knelt next to her while the rest of us stared in disbelief.

Rena's head was lowered, her eyes on the shriveled up Kleenex in her hand. She uttered her first words, "I'm okay."

"No, you're obviously not," Sonya said. She smoothed her hand over Rena's hair, pushing it away from her forehead. "What's going on, baby?"

Rena dabbed at her eyes and took a deep breath before she lifted her head. Her eyes scanned the room as if she was taking attendance. For a moment, her eyes settled on Cecily and I wanted to shout out 'Don't say a word'.

Before I could issue my warning, Cecily spoke up. "We're family, baby. You can tell us anything because what we talk about here stays here."

A chorus of 'Amens' resonated throughout the room and I plopped back down in my chair. I had to press my lips together to stop myself from calling all of them liars.

But Rena must not have remembered how many times Cecily had shared someone else's story with us, because she said, "It's Monty."

When Rena said her husband's name, Cecily scooted to the edge of her seat.

"This was delivered to me this morning." Rena pulled an envelope from her purse and handed it to Sonya.

The First Lady took her own deep breath before she stood, though she didn't move from Rena's side. For a moment, she stared at the envelope as if she knew there was nothing but poison inside. When she opened the envelope's flap, she pulled out what looked to be pictures, and she scanned the first one. Then, the second, and the third.

Now, all of the women were on the edge of their seats, and even I began to wonder what was going? Sonya's expression never changed, even when she stuffed the pictures back into the envelope.

"Nuh-uh." Cecily jumped from her seat and made it around the table to where Sonya stood like a guard over Rena. "You are not going to look at those photos and not tell us what's going on." She reached for the envelope, but Sonya held it out of reach of her grasp.

"Really, Sonya?" Cecily crossed her arms. "What makes you think Rena doesn't want us to know?" She turned her glance from Sonya to the rest of us at the table. And they all nodded as if they were part of her Amen corner. Cecily continued, "Seems to me, she came in here so that we could all see, I mean, so we could all support her, right?"

"Amen," Cecily's Amen corner sang out.

Sonya stood steadfast, though she did turn her glance from Cecily to Rena. Rena's eyes moved between Sonya and Cecily and after a couple of seconds, she nodded.

Not a milli-second after that, Cecily practically snatched the envelope from Sonya's hand. But unlike Sonya who'd tried to protect Rena's privacy, Cecily flipped open the envelope and spread all the pictures across that end of the table.

The gasps, the oh-my-Gods, the lawd-have-mercies were immediate. Even I couldn't stop my eyes from widening and my lips from parting in shock.

The first picture was of a young boy, no more than maybe fourteen or fifteen. He wore an open pink button-down shirt that he'd tied at his waist. The boy's head was tilted to the side and his eyes were rolled back in ecstasy—as Reverend Monty Bradley's lips were against his neck.

I pressed my hand against my chest, unable to turn away, even though I wanted to. But each picture was more risqué than the last, until finally, the last photo was of the boy and Reverend Bradley laid up in the bed—butt-naked.

Closing my eyes, all I could do was shake my head. This was going to be another scandal that would rock the church. We'd had quite a few since Jeremy and I had come to D.C. Affairs, pastors embezzling money, even one who'd been involved in a laundering scheme that had something to do with celebrities and their tithes. The challenge when these kinds of things happened was that Jeremy always had to address it from the pulpit. Because people, especially those not in the church, pointed fingers and lumped all pastors together.

But right now my thoughts weren't on what Jeremy would do. All I wanted to do was stand up and hug Rena. So, I pushed my chair back, moved to the head of the table, crouched down and hugged her. She sobbed into my shoulder.

What surprised me was that no one else moved. Well, maybe not no one because Cecily's lips began flapping.

Cecily said, "You know this boy set this up." She held up the first picture. "Look at these closely. In every one of these pictures, he's posing for the camera."

"Unbelievable."

"Pathetic."

"Someone is always trying to bring down our husbands."

"You're right," Cecily said to the other women. "And what makes this so deplorable," she continued as she stuffed all the pictures back in the envelope and then passed it around the table as if she wanted everyone to get a close up view, "is that these people who do this to our men are only doing this for money. It's all about the Benjamins. Blackmail."

I stood up and glared at the women. What were they talking about? They were blaming the boy? I said, "No one would be able to blackmail anyone if the pastor hadn't been in that bed with that boy."

"I just..." Rena began, speaking for the first time since Cecily had begun her blame-the-victim crusade. Tears trickled down her cheeks. "I just...I mean, he's a boy."

"Who probably told Reverend Bradley that he was eighteen," Cecily countered as if she was Rena's husband's defense attorney. "And that means nothing because we don't know how old that boy is. You know how it is with black folks. Men, women, young or old, you can never tell our age."

"So what are you saying?" I asked, facing Cecily directly. "If that boy is eighteen, are you saying that Reverend Bradley being in bed with him is okay?"

My words made Rena sob and I wished that I could pull them back. But, it was difficult for me to turn to Rena because I wanted to make sure Cecily understood what she was saying.

"Of course it's not okay," Sonya stepped in. Moving closer to Rena, Sonya asked, "Have you talked to your husband about this?"

"No." Rena sniffed. "These came this morning after he left for church. For the last few hours I didn't know what to do; I've just been in bed. I didn't even plan to come here, but...I just didn't know what to do."

"Well you know what you need to do," Cecily said. "You need to take those photos and before you leave this hotel, find someplace, somewhere to burn them."

"That's right," another First Lady shouted out.

"Amen," the corner began again.

"What?" I said, the tone of my voice stopping all chatter. "She should burn them? Without her husband seeing them?" I paused and glanced at each of the women. "So then when she talks to him, what is she going to say happened to the photos?"

Cecily leaned back and gave me a gangsta look—at least as much of a gangsta look as she could wearing those red, diamond-studded glasses. "Who says she should say something to her husband?"

I didn't even have a comeback for her because I couldn't make sense out of her nonsense. This woman had just received photos and she wasn't supposed to say anything?

It must have been the look on my face that made Sonya take over. "Rena, sweetheart, I know these pictures are painful."

"Yes, they are," one of the First Ladies shouted out.

Sonya continued, "Only you can decide what you want to do. Only you know your heart and you have to follow that."

Rena nodded and a tear dripped onto her hand.

"I know you," Sonya kept on. "You're not going to be able to be comfortable keeping this secret."

"That's exactly what she needs to do," Cecily said and her Amen chorus joined her, singing the same tune.

I wanted to ask Cecily why did she want Rena to not say anything? So that she could be the one to tell the world?

Sonya held up her hand and that stopped all the chatter. The First Ladies Council was loose when it came to officers; we all just jumped in and participated in the programs. But if there had been a president, it would have been Sonya.

When the room was completely silent again, Sonya said, "So, you're going to have to confront Reverend Bradley and you two decide where you go from here."

Cecily nodded. "And when you're deciding, you need to remember that what God has brought together let no man put asunder."

"Amen!"

First Lady Sonya turned back to Rena. "A true marriage is tested and this is a test that, when you and Reverend come through it, you'll have your testimony."

"Amen," they all seemed to say this time.

My eyes darted from one woman to another. "Come through it? So what you're saying is that whether her husband is having an affair with a boy…or a man …you're all advocating that she stay with him?"

Cecily looked at me like I was some pitiful newbie who didn't possess a single clue. "Sweetheart," Cecily said in a tone as if she were talking to one of my children. "For most of us in this room, our calling is greater than our marriages."

"That's right," someone shouted out.

"And so the call on our lives means that our vows aren't sacred?"

Cecily waved her hand. "Our calling is greater than all of that. You just don't understand."

I folded my arms. "Then explain it to me."

"All right." Cecily took a step closer to me. "Let me break it down for you like you're a two year old."

My eyes narrowed and I felt the blood draining from my lips with as hard as I pressed them together. My mind went back to my middle school bully.

But Sonya stepped between us before Cecily could say another word. "No, Cecily, I'll explain." Facing me, Sonya said, "There is a lot to be considered."

I inhaled, then exhaled so that I could relax a bit. If there was anyone in this group I respected, it was Sonya Douglas. She never contributed to the gossip, though she never backed away from it either. Still, I wanted to hear what she had to say.

Sonya said, "The Bradley's church is on the cusp of great things happening." She took Rena's hand. "Didn't you just get a five-hundred-thousand dollar grant from the Family First Foundation?"

Rena nodded.

"And what do you think the Family First Foundation would do if this ever became public?" Sonya asked.

Before she could answer, Cecily jumped in, "And let me break it down so that it's clear for all of us. If it ever became public that your husband was in bed with a man."

Sonya shot Cecily a look, but she didn't back down.

Rena sobbed before she muttered, "They'd rescind the grant." Then, she groaned as if this was her first time thinking about this.

"And all the good work that you and your husband had planned for that money will be gone," Cecily said. "And what would happen to Knotting Hill Missionary Baptist then?" She didn't give Rena room to respond. "You'd lose members, probably the whole church, really, and everything the two of you have built will go down in flames. And speaking of flames, I already told you what to do with those pictures."

"Cecily," Sonya said her name as if she were making her weary. "It may not be that simple." Turning back to Rena, she said. "Was there a note or anything with those photos?"

I frowned. That was an interesting question. Not something I would have thought about. Why was First Lady Sonya asking her that?

But then, Rena said, "There was a note."

Gasps filled the space.

She continued, "A note and a demand for fifty-thousand dollars."

And then, there was a collective relief of breath. That made my frown deeper until in the next moment, my eyes widened when Sonya waved her hand. "Pay them. Better yet, make Monty pay it."

"That's right," Cecily said. "Yes, now that you told us that part, keep the pictures, show them to Monty and make him pay!"

"Amen!"

Sonya continued, "And get the transaction on tape," she told her as if this were a business transaction. "Tell whoever is blackmailing you you'll play with them this time, but if they come back for more money or if they go public, you will release the video and have them arrested for extortion."

"That is perfect, First Lady Sonya," Cecily said and the rest of the women nodded and mumbled their agreement. "So it's settled." Cecily clapped her hands together and looked around. "Rena is staying with her husband and what we've heard here today, stays right here."

"Amen!"

I rolled my eyes.

"And Rena," Sonya said, "you make sure you get something out of this. Like didn't you tell me you wanted to go to Dubai?"

"Or what about that mink coat you were looking at last winter?" one of the First Ladies shouted out.

"Or maybe," Sonya said, "you'll get that new Jag SUV."

Everyone and every word was surprising to me. But nothing was more shocking than the words that First Lady Sonya had spoken.

Had they really just tried to convince Rena to stay with her cheating husband? Her *cheating with boys* husband. There was no way she would.

But then, Rena said, "Thank you. Thank you all."

"You're welcome."

"That's what we're here for."

"We're all family."

Rena said, "You were right. There is too much at stake for me to do anything except for what you suggested."

"Exactly," Sonya said. "Just remember—that Jag." When everyone laughed, Rena stood, hugged Sonya and then moved to the chair where she'd sat at every meeting.

"All right now," Sonya said. "If you'll take your seat, Ginger, we can get back to why we're here. Let's get back to the Dress for Success program and what you were telling us about the schools."

I glanced at Rena and for the first time since she'd walked into the room, she had a smile, albeit a meek one. And the other women were looking at Sonya as if the last twenty minutes hadn't transpired.

"Ginger?" First Lady Sonya said, as if I were holding up the meeting.

First, I glanced at where I'd been sitting and then, I turned my eyes to the door, the exit from this room and these women. But then, I returned to the seat where I'd been sitting and I gave my report.

# Chapter Nine

For the past three days, all I'd been thinking about was the First Ladies Council meeting and Rena Bradley. I couldn't imagine what that night had been like for her after she'd left the Four Seasons. Had she waited until Reverend Bradley had come home? Had she sat down at dinner with him and then served him the pictures alongside the pork chops and mashed potatoes? And at what point did she ask for keys to her new car, designer purse and international vacay?

I eased my Benz around the curve of the street, then stopped in front of the valet stand. Smiling as the attendant opened my door, I greeted him, took the ticket, and then as I strolled toward the restaurant, I shook my head, hoping that would release my thoughts. Sometimes I felt like I was consumed with thoughts of what those women had counseled Rena to do and really, it was none of my business. If she agreed with them, who was I to tell her anything different?

That was my last thought as I stepped inside the District Winery. The moment I did, I spotted my sister, standing at one of the tables waving both hands. It looked like the top of her head was glowing, but it was just the way the sun, that burned through the wall of glass, shined on her wild blonde afro.

My smile was instant. Even though I was dozens of feet away, I could tell she was propped up on her toes, making sure I could see her. That made me chuckle. While I had taken after my father with my height, Jada's petiteness had come through our mother. Even her big hair did little to add to her five-foot-two frame.

"Hey, baby sis." I leaned over to embrace her. And just like I thought, she was on her toes.

"What's up?" she asked in a voice that belied her size. Her height, was the only thing small on Jada. As she slid back into her seat, she added, "And when are you going to stop calling me your baby sis?"

"That's what you'll always be to me." I hooked my purse on the back of my chair. "You *and* Lauren."

From the time Lauren and then Jada were born, I embraced the role of big sister as if I were a decade older than both of them. We were much closer in age, only two years between me and Lauren and then two years between Lauren and Jada. But that was enough for me to boss them around when we were younger, though both of my sisters would say I'd carried that trait into my adulthood. Jada would say that, more than Lauren who was protected against my big sister tendencies by the barrier of the miles between D.C. and Dallas where she lived.

Jada rolled her eyes and I laughed. "Whatever," she said. "I'm a grown woman, twenty-eight ... and a half, in case you need to be reminded."

This time, we laughed together and as the waiter came to take our orders, we studied the lunch menu ... and the wine list, of course. The wine was the reason why Jada loved coming to this place whenever she hopped on the Acela for our monthly luncheons. It didn't make sense to me that she would take a three-hour train ride from New York to eat at a restaurant that was right around the corner from where she lived in the city. The Brooklyn Winery, which was less than a mile away from her brownstone, was owned by the same people. But she fancied herself a wine connoisseur and it didn't matter to me where I hung out with my sister. So the District Winery was always it.

I ordered the duck wings, with a side of fried brussels sprouts, while my sister told the waiter to bring her a salmon burger and then, we both ordered a glass of Pinot Noir.

"So, what's been going on?" Jada asked once we were left alone.

I snapped the napkin at my place setting open and laid it across my lap before I sighed.

She said, "Oh, church drama, huh?"

"No, the church is fine, Jeremy is fine and the kids are fine." I paused. "I can't believe you won't get to see them this time. I couldn't even tell them I was meeting up with you because they would have tried everything to get out of going to school just to see you. They love their auntie Jada."

"I love them, too. But I have to be back in New York," she glanced at her watch, "by seven or so. On my next trip, though, I'll come down on the weekend so that I can see the kids and Jeremy. You know who I miss most when I come down here, right?"

I nodded. "Who you telling? Mom moved to Dallas how many years ago? Nine?"

"Yup, right when you came home."

I shook my head. "But I understood her need to get away."

"I did, too, but," Jada pointed her finger toward me, "you think you're slick."

"What did I do?"

"You tried to change the subject. I asked you what's going on because I know something's bothering you. So no matter how much you bring up the folks we love, I'm gonna bring this all back to you."

This wasn't the first time I wondered what kind of discernment gift had been given to my sister. It was uncanny, the way she could sense every emotion I felt, like we were twins or something. Not even the miles could stop us from being in tune. Jada always called right at my first moment of frustration or anger or sadness.

"So tell me what's going on?" she said again.

"It's nothing." I shook my head.

"Oh, come on. Don't make me play twenty questions with you. I don't have much time and I'd rather talk about me." She grinned. "So 'fess up."

I would rather talk about my sister, too, rather than what was on my mind. It wasn't that I didn't want to share with Jada; it was just that I didn't want to carry tales about anyone.

But Jada was feeling my energy; she knew something was bothering me.

"Really, Ginger, your silence is making me concerned."

Looking across the table, the cheer that had been in my sister's hazel eyes had traded places with worry.

"What's wrong?" Her voice was a whisper now. "You're scaring me," she said as she reached for my hand.

"Oh no." I waved her words away. "There's nothing for you to worry about. What's got me so bothered has nothing to do with me. This is all about someone else's drama."

"Who? Is Dru okay?"

Because I was the one who now didn't want to play twenty questions, I closed my eyes and said a quick prayer asking God to forgive me for sharing Rena's business. And then, I began the story of the First Ladies Council meeting.

Through the waiter bringing us our wine and then a few minutes later, our lunch, Jada sat transfixed with her mauve-matte lips parted in surprise. She stared at me, without hardly blinking, hardly moving in any way except for when she raised her glass and took two gulps.

When I finished my story, I sat back. Jada said nothing, at first. She just grabbed her glass and finished off the wine before she held it up, her signal to the waiter.

"So, let me get this straight," Jada said, leaning in on the restaurant's table, "this chick comes in and pours her heart out about her husband's gay affair and the First Ladies don't try to figure out how to bury the pastor's body, hide his watches and burn his clothes?"

I shook my head. And the thing was, Jada meant what she'd said. My sister was that ride-or-I-don't-care-if-I die chick who proved crazy existed in all relationships. The dozen or so women my sister had been involved with since she came out to our family at the beginning of my sophomore year in college (when she was only fifteen), could vouch for my sister's occasional lunacy. Jada was possessive; she loved hard and tolerated no foolishness. Cross her at your own peril, 'cause she would take your crazy and raise you one.

"I'm serious," Jada said. "People would have been looking for that pastor come Sunday morning when he was supposed to be in the pulpit."

"Oh, I have no doubt you're serious, and you really need to use your Obamacare and get that crazy of yours checked out."

Before she could say anything, I bowed my head and blessed our food, but when I looked up, Jada was ready to go in.

"I don't need to get anything checked out," she said with a little bit of an attitude. "Everyone thinks I have anger issues, but what I have are reality issues. Every woman I've ever been involved with knows the rules—don't start none, won't be none," she said. Then, the way she stabbed her burger with her knife, I felt sorry for the salmon. "But again, you tried to change the subject on me and this is all about the pastor. So, really, they didn't help her bury the body?"

I shook my head. "No. They took the opposite approach and gave her the reason why she should stay."

While I bit off a bit of my wings, my sister looked up toward the ceiling like she was trying to figure it out. Then, waving her fork in the air, she said, "Okay, I give up. What could the reason possibly be?"

"They said it was financial, but really Jada, it was like a cult in there. Every woman agreed; they all said the same thing. I had a feeling something like this had happened to one of them before."

"Really? You think another one of their husbands has been freakin' a dude?" She held up her hand. "Not that I have anything against gay people." She grinned. "Hey!" she sang as she rolled her shoulders in a little dance.

That made me chuckle for a moment, but then, I went right back to what happened. "I'm not saying that group experienced the same exact scandal. I just wonder if other things have happened before and staying silent is just what they do."

"Y'all church folks kill me," Jada said, shaking her head as she leaned back and took several more sips of her wine.

"What do you mean y'all? You forgot where you were raised? You forgot about your daddy?"

"No." She shrugged. "But you know it's been years since I've walked into any church. And it's because of things like this. I mean, I've heard of 'for better or for worse.' But what happened to basic respect?"

I took a sip of wine, giving myself time to explain it to Jada. "Their argument is that respect comes second to their calling. Everything at the expense of the church they're building."

"Better to walk away than burn that church down, which is exactly what I'd be doing right now."

I just shook my head, sad that my sister was telling the truth. "I think there's a solution somewhere in between staying silent and burning the church down."

"No in between for me. You guys put up with a lot in the name of religion. Y'all are almost as bad as baller wives and the ish they have to deal with."

As Jada mentioned ballers wives, a leggy woman sauntered by and my eyes widened a bit at just how short her dress was. I mean, she couldn't afford any kind of mistake; if she dropped any money, she'd have to just leave it wherever it fell. The hem of her dress ended at the same place as her Malaysian yacky weave—both right at the end of her butt.

It was her purple form-fitting mini that caught my attention, but that wasn't what held it. When she slipped into the chair at a table across from us, she crossed her legs, leaned back in the chair and looked straight at me as if that had been her purpose all along. She looked...familiar. But then, I shook my head, broke eye contact, and returned my attention to my sister, my duck wings and my brussel sprouts.

"Well more power to that First Lady," Jada said. "That's all I got. Wishing her power."

"I've been praying for Rena...and her husband."

"That's because you're a good Christian," Jada smirked. "So besides the First Ladies Cult...."

"It's the First Ladies Council, not cult."

"Not the way you described it, but besides those women, you good?"

My eyes wandered to the table across from us, only because I could feel the heat of the woman's stare. When I glanced at her, she didn't do what most people did when they were caught—she held my gaze.

Again, I shook my head and turned away from her. "Yeah," I said, finally answering my sister's question. "I am good."

"You don't sound anywhere near good."

"No, I am. I mean, Jeremy and I have some things to work out."

She frowned. "Like what? Y'all having problems?" Before I could answer, she continued, "Please don't tell me that. You two are the perfect couple, second only to Mommy and Daddy."

I pushed my plate aside. "We're not having trouble. It's just that I have to deal with all the things that Mom had to handle as a pastor's wife."

"Ah, the women."

I nodded.

But then, Jada's eyes narrowed. "Hold up. He's not stepping out on you is he?"

Right away, I waved my hand, telling her no. But at the same time, I shifted in my chair a bit, trying to use my sister's big hair to get out of the woman's view since I could still feel her gaze. "No, that's one place where I'm blessed. Jeremy is not carrying on with anyone."

"Good, 'cause I'd hate to have to cut a brother...in-law."

"You don't have to cut anyone, Jada."

She shrugged as if she'd meant her words. "I'm just sayin'."

After a moment, I said, "But there is this woman...."

Jada eased to the edge of her seat, squeezing the knife in her hand. "Who?"

"Calm down. There's nothing going on. There's just a woman who works with Jeremy and she makes me a bit uncomfortable with the way she flirts with him. A lot."

"Who? His assistant?"

"No, his assistant is Lizzy, remember? Mommy's friend."

"Sorry, I forgot. Well, whoever it is, you need to fire her."

How many times had I thought of that? "The problem is, she's good."

"So? There are lots of good people in this world. You can fire her or you can tell me her name and I'll pay her a little visit and I promise you, you'll have no more issues."

I chuckled and shook my head. "It's not that serious. In fact, now that I've said it out loud, I shouldn't have even mentioned it. It's innocent flirting."

"Flirting with a married person or even an involved person is never innocent. But if you tell me to back off, I will. You got my number if you need me."

"I do and I won't. At least not in this capacity."

She shrugged. "So what else is going on? You still thinking about all you've given up for the church?"

I raised my eyebrows in surprise. "I haven't mentioned that in a while."

"You haven't, but that doesn't mean you haven't been thinking about it."

I nodded. "I mean, how can I not help but wonder where I would be if I'd taken that job with Walker-Hughes. You know by now my plan was to...."

"Have your own business with five offices all over the country."

I chuckled. "Did I say it that much?"

"Yup, but it was all good. And so it makes sense that you would wonder."

"I mean, I can't imagine I would have been doing better financially. Once Jeremy and I got our church up and going..."

"Yeah, I see you," Jada said, leaning over to take a peek at my newest designer purse, hooked on the back of my chair. "You have it all now—the house, the cars, the kids, the clothes...."

"But it's more than just the money because we didn't get into ministry for that. We've just been blessed. But I do wonder what my life would look like now."

Jada frowned. "You're not talking about a life without Jeremy?"

I felt it again; the woman's stare and I had to turn her way again. This was getting to be too much. So, I glared back at her. But all she did was raise her wine glass and sip, never turning her eyes away.

"What?" Jada asked and looked over her shoulder at the woman before she turned to me. "You know her?"

I shook my head. "No. I mean, she looked familiar at first. But since she's been in here, she's just been staring at me."

"Maybe she recognizes you or maybe," Jada leaned closer and whispered, "she's looking at me." When she leaned back and nodded slowly, I laughed.

"Don't pay attention to her." Jada waved her hand. "Where were we?"

"I was just saying that it feels silly to dream about what could have been when my life is so good."

"Well, I can tell you what wouldn't have been without you...New Kingdom Temple."

I smiled. "Let's talk about something else."

"Okay. What? Politics?"

"No! Tell me about what's going on at work." I was always fascinated by my sister's job. She was the managing editor for Travel Times, an online magazine and website. She'd started with the magazine straight out of Howard University, when it was nothing more than a good idea. However, last year, Forbes Magazine had ranked Travel Times as one of the top ten websites to visit. It was an upstart no more. "So where's your next trip?"

"I'm heading to Australia."

I moaned with envy; well, not really envy. I was so proud of my baby sister and how she'd taken this job even though our mother had given her a serious side-eye when Jada had told us that she'd have to not only live in New York, but she'd agreed to work for free for the first six months. After all the money she'd spent for our education, she wanted us to at least be able to support ourselves. And for the first few years, Jada hadn't been able to do that.

Fast-forward three years and my sister was not only well into the six-figures, but she traveled around the world, staying in the best hotels, eating at amazing restaurants and getting spoiled in the best spas. I wanted to be Jada Allen when I grew up.

Over the next hour, my sister and I talked and laughed and sipped more wine. By the time the check came, my sister had done for me what she always did—she made me feel like I could conquer.

"Ginger?"

Jada and I glanced up—at the staring woman in the purple mini. I'd almost forgotten that she'd been there.

"Yes?"

"Oh, my goodness, it is you. Ginger Allen, right?"
As I kept my glance on the woman's eyes, my sister sat back and checked her out. Not in any kind of sexual way. My little sister had gone into her don't-start-none-won't-be-none mode; she was checking to see if she needed to get up and handle something for me.

The woman said, "So you don't recognize me? You don't remember me?"

"I'm sorry," I said. I narrowed my eyes and tried to remember. Now that she was standing up close, I knew I'd seen this woman before, but I couldn't place her. Was she a friend from Xavier? A sorority sister? That would be the worst if she was one of my sorors and I didn't remember.

"Oh." The woman laughed, a sultry sound that I imagined had men giving her all of their money. "It's like that now? You're all that, a First Lady of a big church and so you can't remember an old friend?"

"I am so sorry," I said. "You'll have to excuse me, but I meet a lot of people. I do recognize your face; I just can't seem to place your name."

She laughed again, though this time, there was little humor in the sound. "I'm Sharonne," she said as if I was supposed to recognize the name.

When she added nothing else, I said, "Oh...hi...Sharonne." And then, I scoured through my memory bank. There was nothing.

Her sigh was filled with exasperation. "Sharonne from Pilgrim's Rest." Another pause. "Back in New Orleans."

She had taken me back ten years and I was able to conjure up a vague memory. At church...in the bathroom...when I was talking to First Lady Blake. But Sharonne and I were far from friends. She hadn't even spoken to me that day, so now, I was surprised that she even knew my name.

Still, I was always in First Lady mode. So I said, "Oh, yes, Sharonne," even though she and I had never had one pleasant exchange. "How are you?"

"Blessed and highly favored," she said. "What about you?"

"The same." I nodded.

From the corner of my eye, I saw my sister move to the edge of her chair.

"So, do you live in D.C. now?" I asked.

"No," Sharonne replied. "I'm just in town to handle some... personal business." She tossed her hair over her shoulder. "Well, I just wanted to say hello. You take care of yourself now." She paused. "Oh, and tell that fine husband of yours, I said hello." She gave a throaty laugh before she nodded at my sister, then sashayed away, her dress edging even higher up her thighs.

Sharonne was barely out of hearing range before she said, "Really?" Jada said. "You were friends with her?"

Shaking my head, I said, "Not at all. I had one encounter with her and that was enough. Really, I'm a little surprised she remembered me."

"Hmmm...." my sister hummed. "Well, I don't trust her, I don't like her, she's a snake, she's a user and...."

With a laugh, I held up my hand. "You got all that from her standing there?"

Jada didn't crack a smile. "Yes, I did. You know how I am. You know how I can feel people."

Those words took my smile away. Because my sister told the truth.

She said, "Just let me know if you ever need me to roll back down here and take care of anything for you."

"She said she doesn't live here, so I doubt if I'll see her again."

"I hope you don't." And then, she repeated, "'Cause I really don't like her."

I didn't tell my sister that I didn't like her either, even though I couldn't figure out why.

# Chapter Ten

It was hard to believe that only ten hours had passed since I'd awakened this morning at seven. I'd started the day at the storage facility, checking out all the donations we had for the Dress for Success program that we needed for the girls at the job fair next week. Then I'd subbed for Lizzy who was the unofficial leader of our unofficial flower ministry. She always took a bouquet to the sick and shut in. But because this was Mother Hayden, the woman who was one of the reasons why Jeremy was at New Kingdom Temple (because everyone believed her ten years ago when she said she'd heard from God about Jeremy), I'd wanted to take her the flowers myself and spend a little time praying and chatting with her as she recovered from her hip replacement. And now finally, I was leaving the kids' school after having conferences with their teachers.

All I wanted to do right now was to crawl into bed even though the sun hadn't yet begun its descent.

But as I rolled onto the campus of New Kingdom, sleep was still hours away for me. I was meeting Wanda, our business manager, for a finance meeting to go over the budget for our tenth anniversary celebration.

Dru had offered to sit in on this meeting for me after we'd reviewed all the appointments on my calendar this morning, but Jeremy and I had put a couple of systems in place when we opened up New Kingdom Temple that we'd followed for the last ten years. One, was that I would always handle the church's finances. Not a check would be written, not a dime would be spent, not a credit card bill would be paid without my approval. And the second was that Jeremy would never meet with any church members alone—not women, not even men. Those were the two things that got pastors caught up: Money and sex. And Jeremy and I were doing everything we could so there would never even be hints of any improprieties.

I eased my Mercedes next to Jeremy's Jaguar, parking in the designated FIRST LADY space. Then, I paused the way I always did when I pulled into my spot next to Jeremy either here or in our three-car garage at home.

Every time I saw his tricked out black XJ, I shook my head. I still remembered his hoopty in college, and how Jeremy said cars and other material things meant nothing to him. Those days were long gone and the gleaming black sedan next to me was proof of that.

I grabbed my bag, then locked the car with the fob before I trotted up the steps, entering the main building through the side doors that led to the offices. The heels of my pumps clicked along the parquet floors of the hall as I made my way toward my office at the far end. I had to pass Jeremy's office to get to mine, so I figured, I'd just pop in for a quick kiss and then get to work.

But just as I lifted my hand to knock on his half-opened door, I heard a woman giggle. I dropped my hand to the doorknob and pushed the door open.

Jeremy sat at his L-shaped Cherrywood desk, facing his computer and then, there was Dana Washington, our Director of Marketing. The woman who I'd mentioned to my sister.

Dana was perched against the edge of his desk. Her back was to me while her breasts were all in Jeremy's face. I wondered how he could even see the screen.

"Pastor, you're so brilliant." Dana purred and then released that trying-to-sound-sexy giggle again.

It looked like Jeremy was sharing something with Dana on his computer and I folded my arms, just watching, wanting to see how far Dana would go before the beat down began.

She didn't make me wait long. When she leaned over and began massaging Jeremy's shoulder, I pushed the door open so hard it slammed against the wall.

Both of them jumped, though I was sure Jeremy did only because he was startled. But Dana leapt off the desk, landing at least ten feet from my husband, which was where she should have been all along. Her eyes were wide at first, but as Jeremy turned his back to her and crossed the room to greet me, a smirk filled her face.

"Babe, is it five already?" Jeremy kissed me.

I returned his affection, though I kept my gaze on Dana, who now stood with her arms crossed. As if she wanted me to let me know she wasn't the least bit intimidated by my presence.

He said, "I was just in here going over some of the caterer's proposals."

"Really?" I said. "With Dana?"

"Oh," her voice sounded so innocent. "I just offered to help Pastor narrow down the list since you weren't here to do it."

I crossed my arms, matching her stance. "You seem to be offering him lots of you these days."

"What do you mean?" she asked in a saccharine-sweet tone. I just stared at her. "Are you okay?"

"You tell me."

Her left eyebrow rose a little and then with a deep sigh, she moved toward us. "Well uh, on that note, Pastor." She paused as she came within inches of where Jeremy and I stood. "I'll be in my office for another hour or so if you need me."

"He won't," I said. "I'm here now so you can go home."

She sighed, shook her head and I really didn't care. Then, when I faced my husband and his eyebrows were furrowed, I cared even less.

Jeremy closed the door behind Dana. "Really Ginger? What was that about?"

"Are you really asking me that? When you were in here with her hanging all over you? We agreed years ago there would be no solo meetings."

"Are you serious right now? That's for members of the church."

"Dana's a member."

"She works here."

"So. That could lead to some kind of sexual harassment suit."

"Really? Sexual harassment?" He didn't give me a moment to answer. "It seems more like you're jealous and you don't have any reason to be. Plus, it's so not becoming." He marched toward his desk as if he were upset with me.

"Don't turn this around on me. You know I'm not the jealous type, not after all I've had to put up with over these years. What I don't like about Dana is her constant and blatant disrespect. She was fawning all over you."

"She wasn't fawning." Jeremy said.

"She's always flirting with you."

"She's not."

I folded my arms, glared at him, and pressed my lips together so that I wouldn't speak aloud the words that were in my head. Because what I was thinking was completely inappropriate for the church.

Jeremy sighed. "Babe." He maneuvered from around the desk. He tried to embrace me, but my arms across my chest stopped him. "Come on. Maybe Dana was fawning over me, but if she was, I didn't even notice. And do you know why?"

Because answering his question with—because you're a fool—wouldn't have done much to diffuse the situation, I kept my mouth shut.

He said, "Because my eyes are only for you." He uncrossed my arms, then embraced me and kissed my forehead.

As always, his touch took away my resistance.

He said, "So am I forgiven?"

"There's no reason for me to forgive you. You didn't do anything. It's just that you're oblivious to the women who disrespect me on a regular basis. It's bad enough when we're out and can't even enjoy dinner without some woman passing you her number, but now I have to deal with it with the staff?"

He frowned. "You've been talking about this a lot recently."

"It's not recent." I twisted to release myself from his arms. "This has been going on since the beginning. It's just that in the beginning, I tried to ignore it like you, but I can't anymore." I sighed. "I'm tired, Jeremy. Just very tired of it, so I had to start speaking up about it."

"I get it, but I want you to hear me. It doesn't matter what a woman tries to do, the bottom line is this. I'm your husband and that means everything to me."

"Seems like you're the only one who respects that."

"Well the truth is," he said, looking into my eyes, "I'm the only one who needs to respect this. Don't you understand? You are the most beautiful, intelligent, engaging, funny woman I know. It wouldn't matter how many times a woman came after me, it wouldn't matter how many times a woman would try to be all up in my face, I am committed to you. You are the woman that God has chosen for me."

It was difficult for me to have a comeback to those words. Difficult for me to continue the argument about women going after him when he'd made it clear (by his words and actions) that none of that matter. So why was I focused on this? What I'd said was true—I wasn't the jealous type. But my other words were true as well—I was tired; this had become a daily thing. But what could we do? As long as Jeremy and I remained committed to each other, none of it mattered, I guessed.

I sighed. "Then, there's nothing else to say."

"You're right. There isn't anything else. Not once God has spoken."

I said, "I know you love me and I don't want to play the jealous, insecure wife. That is not me. I just don't want to find myself in a situation where I will have to beat a hoe."

He leaned back at first, and then released a howl of laughter that shook the walls. "Did you really just say that?"

"I did." My words made me giggle, too. "And I meant it," I added with attitude. "Don't make the Barry Farm come outta me."

"Barry Farm?" He laughed again. "Please, you grew up in upper Northwest, went to private school and probably never even drove past Barry Farm."

"I'm just saying. Don't let the proper home training fool you."

"Oh, that proper home training has never fooled me. Not the way you are in our bedroom." Pulling me back into his arms, he said, "Now can you do me a favor?" He pressed his lips against my neck and I leaned back giving him access. "Can you...." His tongue tickled my neck and I moaned. "Make your...." Now, his tongue trailed up to my earlobe. "Meeting short? So that we can get home and I can get a little of that proper home lovin'?"

I sighed. I loved this man so much. Moving my lips to his, I answered him with a kiss. One of those kisses that, like from the beginning, reached down into my soul.

Jeremy was right. We were a great example of what God had joined together, no man or woman would be able to put asunder.

And so it was.

# CHAPTER ELEVEN

Tyesha Gray squirmed as I buttoned the three buttons on her camel-colored jacket.

"Mrs. Williams, why I gotta wear this?" she whined.

"Because you're going on a job interview and that," I said, pointing to the mini multi-colored sweater dress she had on when she arrived at my house, "won't do. And the proper way to say that is 'why *do* I have to wear this'. Not why I gotta. Grammar is important, sweetie. Remember what you've learned in the classes." I paused as I stepped back. "Now turn around."

With my hands on her shoulders, I shifted Tyesha to face the mirror. Dru adjusted it against the wall so that Tyesha could see her full figure and the smile that beamed from her was like sunshine at noon.

"What you say this was again?"

"It's Chanel," I replied. "A Chanel jacket. Chanel is a designer."

"The skirt, too?"

"No," Dru jumped in. "Someone donated that from Macy's, but it's really cute. You look amazing."

"Yeah, I do."

Dru and I laughed, but Tyesha didn't. She faced me with wide eyes. "I ain't never had no designer jacket before," she said, her tone sincere as she fingered the tweed.

"It's 'I've never had'," I corrected her again. "And this is just the first of many designer jackets I'm sure you'll own." Taking another step back, I said, "Tyesha, Dru is right; you look amazing. You're going to be one of the stars at the job fair."

Five girls from the Dress for Success program were in my home, choosing outfits from donations that had been made by and to the First Ladies Council. While we worked with high school students, we had a special program for children who were about to age out of the foster care system. States were supposed to assist these children during their transition from foster care to independence, but because oftentimes that assistance was lacking, our goal was to provide these children with hands-on help and connections that would continue for as long as they needed us.

"Tell Jean to give me five then come in," I told Tyesha as I headed back to the rack of skirts, dresses and suits. The girls were hanging out in the family room, watching television and talking as I helped each pick out the outfit she'd wear to the job fair at the convention center tomorrow.

"Okay, I'll tell her. But umm, I have a question."

"What's that, sweetheart?"

She glanced at Dru before she asked me, "How long can I keep this?"

"It's yours, I told you that," I said. "You can keep it until you get tired of wearing it."

"Wow," she exclaimed. She hesitated for a moment, then rushed to me, throwing her arms around my neck. "Thank you so much. I've never had anything this nice. I feel...." When she paused, I wasn't sure if she'd done that because she couldn't think of a word or because she didn't feel worthy to say the word that came to her mind.

I had a feeling it was the latter and that made me sad. Tyesha was a gorgeous girl with large doe eyes, deep dimples and natural curly brown hair that swooped a bit past her shoulders. With her slender, but curvy shape, she could have been modeling for Chanel if she were a couple of inches taller and born into a different zip code.

But a lifetime in the foster care system where she'd been in more than a dozen homes, left Tyesha, like most of the girls I'd met, unattached, unloved, and washed in low self-esteem.

I cupped her cheeks inside the palms of my hands. "This makes you feel beautiful, right?"

Tears sprang to her eyes when she nodded.

From the other side of the room, Dru added, "And gorgeous."

This time, Tyesha nodded with a grin.

"And cuuute," I finished.

Now, she laughed, broke from my embrace and rushed through the living room. "I'll get Jean," she shouted over her shoulder.

When we were alone, Dru sauntered over to the rack and stood beside me. She didn't say a word, only stared.

"What?" I asked her.

"I love watching you with these girls. I know you often say you didn't get to do what you wanted with your career, but Ginger, this right here...this is your calling. The love and care you show these girls." She paused and shook her head. "They've never had anything like this before. Did you hear Tyesha? She didn't even want to say that she looked cute."

"I know." I sighed. "I am glad that I'm here for this. Gosh, so many of them have been through so much and now, if we can work to set them up better in their lives, it will be all worth it. This means so much to me. I love what we do with this program. It's the most important thing I'm doing right now."

Dru and I turned toward the entrance of the living room when squeals rang out from the family room. I couldn't see the girls, but I could imagine Tyesha modeling her new outfit, strutting back and forth in front of the sixty-five inch television screen, like she really was a Chanel model.

"That right there," Dru said, pointing toward the sound, "shows that what you're doing is going to have more of an impact than you'll ever know."

"I hope so," I said. "I have to admit, though, I'm a little nervous about the job fair. I want them to all get a couple of interviews."

"Don't worry; you have them prepared."

"They're prepared and I'll be there right beside them to give them that confidence."

"Hey...."

Dru and I turned toward Jeremy's voice as my husband stood in the entryway to the living room. For a moment, I paused and took in all the fineness of my man. Like wine, age was an asset for my man. Yes, the money helped; the way the suits hung just right on his frame, the way his shoes shined and the diamonds glittered from his watch. All of that was alluring—to other people. I still saw the dude who drove the hoopty. The one who was so idealistic. The one who told me to hang on for the ride of a lifetime.

"Hey honey," I said. "What are you doing here?"

"Well," he began, then tossed his computer bag onto the chair, before he came over and kissed me, "I live here, that's the first thing."

I smirked.

"But uh....I had to come home because there's been a change of plans. What's up, Dru?"

"Nothing. I'm cool."

"So," Jeremy glanced at the two racks loaded down with clothes, "what's going on here?"

"We're dressing the young ladies with Dress for Success who are going to the job fair."

"Oh yeah, you told me about that."

"The girls are really excited and I can't wait to escort them through the fair tomorrow."

"Uh...tomorrow?"

"Yeah," I said, turning back to the racks so that I could find the outfit I'd set aside for Jean. "No worries. I cleared my schedule weeks ago. I'll be fine because this is too important to me. I'll be back at the church on Friday."

"Well uh, I'm sorry about this babe, but Dru's gonna have to cover for you at the job fair because I need you to handle the ministers meeting. I have to go out of town."

I narrowed my eyes as I turned to him and over his shoulder, I saw Dru tiptoeing toward the exit. Good, she'd keep the girls occupied while I set my husband straight.

When we were alone, I said, "The ministers meeting? I never attend those. And you're going out of town? Where?" Before he could respond, I fired another question at him, "And why am I just finding out about this trip?"

"Because I forgot." Jeremy held up his hands. "I have a speaking engagement in Atlanta and Dana just reminded me."

"You're speaking at a conference and...you *forgot*?"

There were two things that bothered me about this as I folded my arms. How did one forget speaking at a conference and why was this happening so much? Maybe 'so much' was an exaggeration, but in the last three or so months, Jeremy had come home telling me about some emergency trip he had to take—because he'd forgotten more than a couple of times.

"Yeah, babe. I forgot." Jeremy lowered his eyes away from mine and rubbed his brow. "Sorry, but I really need you to sit in the meeting for me this time. They're voting on taking the irrigation funding project to the board, and that's not something I want to do. You have to be there to sway the discussion and then make sure they vote my way. I want it nixed."

I shook my head. "No, I can't do that, Jeremy."

He lifted his gaze and now, looked at me with a frown. "What do you mean?"

"I...can't...do...it. I can't drop everything because you have to speak at a conference that you forgot. *You* forgot, Jeremy, not me. So you need to either cancel the board meeting or the conference. Either one, it doesn't matter to me."

"You know that's not possible." He sighed with exasperation. "I can't cancel the ministers meeting. Reverend Lewis is flying in from Los Angeles."

I inhaled. That was true. The man who'd been the assistant pastor at Pilgrim's Rest had turned out to be a valuable resource and mentor to Jeremy as we were building New Kingdom. Right away, Jeremy had asked and Reverend Lewis had agreed to be a part of his ministerial team, even though he didn't live in D.C.. But that hadn't mattered. For the last ten years, Reverend Lewis had mentored Jeremy from afar and flew in once a quarter for these meetings.

"Well, you're right," I said, nonchalantly. "You can't cancel the ministers meeting, so I guess it's the conference that'll have to go."

He squeezed his face into a frown as if he didn't understand my English. "You want me to give up a ten thousand dollar speaking gig? Do you know how ridiculous that sounds?"

"It sounds as ridiculous as you asking me to disappoint all of those girls in there." I pointed toward the family room. "And I'm not going to do that. This job fair is important to them. It's important to ME. It's as important as anything that's on your calendar."

"I'm not asking you to disappoint them. That's why we pay Dru. She can cover for you. What are they going to be doing anyway? Just walking up and down a couple of aisles, surely, you don't have to be there for that."

Those words, his belittling what was so important to me, took me from zero to one hundred in three seconds flat. The only reason I didn't go off was that we had a house full of people and we were still the Pastor and First Lady of New Kingdom Temple.

"Maybe we need to talk about this later," I said before I ignited into a rage.

He shook his head. "No time. That's why I came home. I've got to pack now. I've got about an hour before Dana will be here and...."

"Wait. Hold up. You're leaving now? And you're leaving with Dana?"

He looked at me as if I'd just asked a stupid question. "Yeah, now and yeah, Dana. She's going with me." It must have been my expression that made him hold up his hand. "We're not going to have that conversation," he said. "Before you ask, Dana is going because she arranged this conference for me a year ago."

"That's part of her job description. To get publicity for the church and that includes speaking engagements," I told him as if he'd forgotten. "But what's *not* on her to-do list is to *travel* with you. And this is the second time, Jeremy."

His sigh sounded weary. "This is so bizarre. The way you've recently become so...jealous."

"I am not jealous." I felt like I was in the middle of a temper tantrum. "I don't have anything to be jealous about."

He threw up his hands as if I'd just made his point. "That's what I'm saying."

"It's just that you and I decided a decade ago how we were going to handle our church. And traveling with a woman was not on that list."

"Well things change."

With my eyebrows and my voice raised, I asked, "What changed?"

"I have a reputation already. It's set. People know that I'm not caught up in any affairs, anything that's improper. I'm just taking care of God's business and I thought that's what you signed up for, too."

"What I signed up for first," I held up my left hand and wiggled the five carat ring that now graced my finger, "was to be your wife. And as your wife, I feel all kinds of disrespected right now."

"Well, you need to find a way to get over it because those people are expecting me, Reverend Jeremy Williams, to be in Atlanta to speak tomorrow." He snatched his computer bag and moved toward the steps. "The ministers meeting is at noon, as it always is."

His back was to me when I said, "And like I told you, I have plans."

But Jeremy kept walking as if his word was the last word. When I heard his footsteps trotting up the stairs, all I could do was squeeze my hands into fists.

It had been a long time since I'd been this angry and the challenge was, when I got like this, there was no telling what I would do.

# CHAPTER TWELVE

"You didn't go to the meeting!"

My chest heaved, I was breathing so heavily as I paced the width of our bedroom.

"I can't believe you didn't go to the meeting."

I squeezed my cell phone as if I were trying to break it with my bare hand. But better the cell phone than Jeremy's neck, which was what I would've been breaking if he'd been standing in front of me. He had one more time to shout at me and I would click off this phone, right in the middle of his rant.

"Why didn't you do what I told you to do?"

With those words, I pulled the phone away from my ear and stared at it. Had Jeremy Williams really just asked me that? Was he truly speaking to me like I was Jasmine or Jayden?

"I'm talking to you, Ginger. Do you hear me?" Jeremy shouted.

"The real question is," I said, speaking my first words since I'd answered Jeremy's call, "do you hear yourself? You're talking to me like I'm one of your children and you need to calm yourself if you want me to stay on this phone."

I heard his deep sigh and then after a few moments, he said, "Look, I'm sorry. It's just that Lizzy sent me the minutes from the meeting and I'm blown away because that meeting was so important to me, Ginger."

"I know it was. Just like my plans were important to me. But you know what, Jeremy, even though you'd pissed me off, even though you didn't give any consideration to what I had to do, even though you acted like the world revolved around you, I still went ahead and changed my plans."

"How can you say that? You didn't go to the meeting."

"You're a man of God, so you need to stop lying." I paused, giving him a moment to calm down so that he would hear me. "I changed, not only my schedule, but the girl's schedule, too. I went to the job fair early, didn't stay as long as I would have liked and I made it to the church before the end of the meeting. If you have the minutes from Lizzy, you know that."

"You didn't make it in time. They'd already taken the vote to bring irrigation project to the board and you know that's not what I wanted."

"Well, I'm sorry about that, but this is just one reason why you and I need to get back on the same track. You can't take me for granted the way you've been doing. I have a life, too. I'm trying to make a difference in my own way and you need to understand that or we're gonna have some problems."

There was so much tension in the silence that followed, but I didn't care. I'd always been the stand-by-my-pastor-man chick, but I'd never done that silently and I wasn't going to be quiet about what I was feeling now.

"All right," he acquiesced. "I'm sorry, Ginger. I didn't mean to go off. It's just that vote...never mind. Just know that I'm sorry."

This would have been the moment for me to just accept his apology. And in the past, I would have done that. But Jeremy was beginning to feel a little different to me. Like he was a bit off-kilter, moving away from everything we'd built our relationship on. It was like he'd somehow started to rise above me, as if we weren't equals.

It didn't feel like it was time for me to ring the alarm, but there was definitely a yellow caution sign in my heart.

Finally, I said, "Jeremy, it's fine...."

He breathed.

"But we're really going to have to address this because something's going on."

"What do you mean?"

I flopped onto our bed. "You're different. You're changing in everything and in every way. In our relationship, the way you handle things with the church."

"I'm not changing, at least not any way out of the normal. People change, we grow. We're not different, we're better. Look, I really want to talk to you about this, but uh, I've got to get down to the conference. I'm speaking today."

I frowned. "I thought you were speaking yesterday. I thought that was why you had to miss the meeting."

"Uh, yeah. Yeah, I spoke yesterday, but I'm speaking at...a workshop, this morning."

*Was Jeremy stuttering?*

"Look, I've gotta go, but I promise you we'll talk about this when I get home."

"Okay, I'll see you tonight."

"No, tomorrow morning."

My frown deepened. "I thought you were coming back tonight."

"I never said that. I knew I'd be speaking yesterday and then again today. And I'm going to attend the dinner here tonight."

"Well we have a dinner tomorrow. Did you forget we're having dinner with the Douglases'?"

"Ah, I did forget," he said. "But that's no problem 'cause I'm going to fly out first thing in the morning and I'll be there before you get out of bed. I promise, babe. And I love you. I love you so much."

He hung up before I could tell him the same. Something didn't feel right about that call. Jeremy stuttering and then what was up with his change of plans?

But then, I paused. Had there really been a change of plans? I squinted, trying to remember what Jeremy had told me. But now that I looked back, he hadn't told me anything. I'd been so angry when he'd returned to the living room a little less than an hour after our blowup, I hadn't even acknowledged his presence, not even when he'd kissed my cheek goodbye.

He'd texted when he landed and then texted again to tell me goodnight. I hadn't responded to either and hadn't spoken to him all day yesterday.

So maybe this wasn't a change of plans. Maybe it was just that he hadn't told me—which was a change in itself.

"Stop it," I whispered. I didn't want to be that woman. The one who anticipated the worst. Being away from home and traveling with Dana didn't automatically mean that was trouble. Jeremy wasn't like that and I wasn't going to will him to be. For ten years now, he'd been faithful; it would be crazy for him to change now. Plus, the least attractive woman to a man was a crazy, jealous wife.

Pushing myself up from the bed, I glanced in the leaning mirror and gave myself a nod of assurance. Everything was fine with me and Jeremy. We just had to straighten out some stuff.

And we would do that. When Jeremy got home. Tomorrow.

⌒

Like Jeremy promised, my husband returned home this morning before I'd had a chance to roll over. The sun was just beginning its rise when I did and as my eyes fluttered open, my husband came into focus. He was standing right there as if he'd been waiting for me.

It would have been shocking, if it hadn't been such a pleasant sight. Jeremy stood wearing nothing but his double-dimpled smile. And oh, his body saluted me, a clear indication that he'd missed me.

Without saying a word, Jeremy climbed into our bed, pushing the duvet aside. Then, he held himself in a plank over me and covered my face with the softest of kisses, his apology inside each one.

I parted my lips and my legs, accepting all of him, all that he wanted to say, all that he wanted me to feel. And as we made slow love, every doubt inside my mind faded away. Why had I been concerned? As I became faint with the overwhelming feeling of pleasure, I just couldn't remember. There was no need for me to worry. Jeremy and I were as connected as we'd always been.

Throughout the rest of the day, the memory of this morning had stayed in my thoughts. In my office, I could hardly concentrate, my mind constantly took me back a few hours, especially every time I saw Jeremy. Even as he was standing in the hallway talking to Lizzy, all I could see was that sight of him this morning, naked as the day he'd been born.

More than a few times, Dru had asked me if I were okay. And after Lizzy had called my name a couple of times and I hadn't heard her, she told me that maybe I needed to go home and take a break.

But the best part of the day (after this morning) had been Dana. The woman who daily, sauntered into the church offices as if she owned my world, today wore only a scowl. I'd even caught her once rolling her eyes at Jeremy after he'd asked her for a report and then turned his back.

What happened between them?

Whatever. I now felt at ease.

I sighed.

"You okay, babe?"

Glancing over at my husband behind the wheel, I wanted to tell him I was more than okay. I wanted to tell him to pull over so we could have an encore to this morning in the back seat of this Jag. But all I did was squeeze his hand that held mine as he steered the car with his other. I hummed, "Mmm-hmm," letting him know that I was fine.

"This has been a good day," he said and I agreed. He added, "Does it make up for the other day?"

I gave him a long look before I said, "We're on our way." I still wanted to talk to my husband; I didn't want to ignore all that I'd been feeling.

He nodded. "I agree and I'm going to do everything I can to get us back on track. And we're gonna start with this weekend." He lifted my hand, kissed my palm, then released me as he used two hands to exit I-395.

This weekend. I shivered with a bit of anticipation. Jeremy had asked Dru if the kids could stay with her this weekend and she had readily agreed. Jasmine and Jayden had been excited, too; they cheered so much like they always did, I began to wonder if she fed them ice cream for breakfast.

But with the kids with Dru all weekend, Jeremy and I could spend all of our time not only making love, but talking so that we could fix the cracks that I was beginning to feel.

A few minutes later, he rolled the Jag to a stop in front of the Jefferson condominiums. As an attendant opened Jeremy's door, he grabbed his cell from the console while another one opened the passenger door for me.

"Good evening," the attendant said. "Who are you visiting?"

"Reverend and Mrs. Sonya Douglas," Jeremy answered as he came around to my side. He took my hand and led me through the huge glass doors. As Jeremy checked in with the concierge, my eyes circled the lobby and like the last time I'd visited, I appreciated the marble floors, glossy stark-white walls and the chandelier that hung in the center of the space. A light lavender scent filled my nostrils, making me feel like I was inside a spa.

This was only my second visit to First Lady Sonya and Reverend Douglas' home, but I loved that they'd sold the house where they'd lived for more than thirty years once their son and daughter had graduated from college. Now, they lived in one of the most upscale condos in the area and it gave me something to look forward to when Jasmine and Jayden became adults.

"Okay, Reverend Douglas is expecting you," the concierge said as she handed Jeremy a card that was similar to a hotel key. "You'll need this for the elevator."

"Got ya," he said as he grinned at the young woman, then led me to the elevators.

As we stepped into the chamber, I said, "This is really a beautiful place."

"Nothing's more beautiful than you." He tapped the card against the sensor, and then, before the doors even closed, Jeremy pulled me into his arms and we kissed our way to the 17th floor.

I was breathless when the doors opened and if my husband hadn't held my hand and guided me, I wasn't sure I would've been able to step off the elevator. "Let's finish this when we get home," he said.

"Oh definitely." When he rang the bell to 1701, which was across the hall from the only other apartment on the floor, I added, "And maybe we can leave before dessert."

"I agree. Why have pie when I can have your cookies?"

My eyes widened. "I cannot believe you said that."

We giggled like teenagers and when Reverend Douglas opened the door, we both had to fight to keep our laughter inside.

"Well," the reverend's voice boomed. "If it isn't the Williams. Come in, come in. Welcome to our home."

Sonya was standing right beside her husband and we exchanged greetings and hugs before Sonya took my hand and led me into their all-white (including the carpet), chrome and glass living room.

When I settled onto the sofa, I rested my purse to one side, so that Jeremy would sit next to me. He smiled as I made room for him and laid his cell and the elevator card on the table beside us. Sonya and the reverend sat on the love seat across from us and for the first time, I noticed they looked like twins. Not only because of the way they were dressed (both in black slacks and a light blue blouse for Sonya, while the reverend wore a light blue shirt), but their hair was the same shade of silver, though the reverend's was cut short while Sonya had hers pulled back into a loose bun.

"So, I hear there are amazing things going on over at New Kingdom Temple," Reverend Douglas said.

"Yes, sir. We're just trying to follow your example," my husband said with a little bit of head bow.

The reverend laughed. "Well, we did quite a few things, but it's time for the new generation," he motioned toward us, "to take over."

"Oh, are you thinking of retiring?" I asked.

Before he had a chance to say a word, Sonya laughed and shook her head. "Retire? What's that?" Now her husband laughed with her. "The Lord himself will have to come down and pull my husband from the pulpit."

"Now why you got to go and tell the people that?" the reverend asked, though he smiled and grabbed her hand. To us, he said, "My wife tells no lies. I will continue preaching until the Lord calls me home...or tells me to sit my black butt down."

Now, we all laughed and inside, I released an 'Awww' when the reverend leaned over and gave his wife a kiss.

Sonya blushed a bit when she faced us. "I've had quite a busy day, well a busy week really. So we're having dinner catered. We'll be eating in about an hour, if that's okay."

"Of course," Jeremy and I sang together.

My husband added, "It'll give us time to talk a little."

"Exactly, which is the reason why we're here together," Reverend Douglas said. "But how can we talk without having a drink in our hands?" Looking at me, he asked, "What can we get you to drink?"

"Oh, I'll have some water, please," I said.

He nodded. "What about you, sweetheart?"

"Get me a Perrier."

"Okay; Jeremy would you join me and help me carry these drinks back inside?"

"Of course." My husband sprang to his feet, then reached for my hand and squeezed it before he trotted a bit to catch up with Reverend Douglas.

My eyes followed him and I felt so blessed that after ten years, he was still the love of my life. And in that moment, I knew that he would always be.

"So," the first lady's voice made me turn to her, "I heard the job fair was a success."

"It was." I grinned thinking about how the girls had handed out their resumes, answered questions so professionally, and then had asked their own good questions. "I'm really hoping they will all get a call for a job."

"I'm hoping, too. You've done such a great job with them. I knew you would be an asset to the First Ladies Council."

I kept my smile, though I wondered if this was my moment to talk to Sonya about some of the things that concerned me with the group. Not so much about Rena, but all the gossiping among the ladies. "You know, First Lady," I began, and then, Jeremy's phone vibrated on the table. "Oh, excuse me," I said. "Our kids are with my assistant tonight, so I just want to make sure she's not trying to contact us," I explained as I scooted across the sofa to the table where Jeremy had laid his cell.

Grabbing it, I read the text:

*I've been waiting for you to call. I need more of what you gave me last night. It's always great to make up. When can you get away again?*

I clutched the phone as I struggled to keep breathing. Above the text, I saw the name: K. Brunson.

"Ginger."

I heard my name, but the voice sounded so vague. Like someone was whispering to me across the miles. So instead of responding, I studied the name on Jeremy's phone, then tapped the screen to get to the info. When the number came up, I repeated it a couple of times in my head. I only had to do it once, really. This was a number I'd never forget.

"Ginger, are you all right?"

Now, I glanced up. I hadn't even noticed that Sonya had moved; she'd come across the room and was standing over me. "Yes," I said, though I shook my head as I returned Jeremy's phone to the table.

"Are the children all right?"

"Yes," I said, sounding as if I were talking while holding my breath. Then, I added, "but my assistant. She's babysitting and she's not."

"Oh, my goodness." Sonya pressed her hand against her heart.

"What's wrong, sweetheart?" Reverend Douglas said as he and Jeremy returned to the living room.

"It's their babysitter," Sonya said with urgency.

"What? Dru?" Jeremy's eyes were filled with concern.

I had no idea what he saw when he looked into my eyes. Every emotion I could possibly have ebbed and flowed through me. I was angry enough to slap him, but sad enough to cry. I was confused enough to question him, but too embarrassed to say anything in front of the Douglases.

And I was definitely too upset to stay and break bread. The thought of food....

"We have to go," I said to Jeremy.

"Of course," Sonya said.

I snatched my purse and bounced from the sofa as Jeremy grabbed his cell and the elevator key.

"I just hope everything is all right," the reverend said. "We'll call down and tell them to have your car ready."

At the door, we did what we'd done less than thirty minutes before. We hugged and said our goodbyes. But when Sonya hugged me, she whispered, "Call me if you need me. I'm here for you."

I leaned back and looked into her eyes. What did she know? But then, I shook that thought away. She was just telling me that she was worried about my children.

Jeremy and I rushed through the door and then, into the elevator. Once inside, he asked, "What happened to Dru?" He sounded so worried. "What did she say?"

Turning, I faced my husband. But when I did, bile rose within me. "Oh, my God," I said. "I'm going to be sick."

"What? What's wrong?"

"I can't...." I held my stomach and when the elevator doors parted, Jeremy held me and helped me outside where our car was waiting.

He helped me into the passenger seat and all I could do was lean back and close my eyes. He started the car and as he rounded the driveway, he said, "I'm gonna get Dru on the phone."

"No." The word came out in a whisper. "She's not the one who's sick." I opened my eyes and looked at him. "But I am."

He stared at me for a moment and I wasn't sure what made him not question me anymore. All he said was, "All right. I'm going to get you home as soon as I can. Just lay back and close your eyes."

I did what he told me only because that was what I was going to do anyway. I needed to figure this out. I needed to come up with a plan because confronting him with the text alone was not enough. I was smart enough to know that. I needed to know more. I needed to find out first who was K.

Brunson. All this time I wondered if something was going on with Jeremy and Dana. But it wasn't Dana. It was K. Brunson.

Or maybe it was Dana. Maybe that was some kind of code name.

And then...another thought. Of Rena. And her husband. K. Brunson.

Why was there no first name?

K. Brunson.

Was my husband involved with a man?

"Oh, my God," I moaned.

"What?" Jeremy said. "Ginger, what?" he asked me with some urgency.

"Pull over."

"Why?"

"Just pull over," I screamed.

Looking into the rear view mirror, Jeremy made a quick swerve making the tires scream. Then, on the side of the road, the Jag's tires crunched the gravel below and before the car even came to a full stop, I opened the door—but it wasn't in time. I released all of my emotions in a pool of puke, half of it spilling onto the side of Jeremy's Jaguar.

# CHAPTER THIRTEEN

That text had knocked me stone-cold out. From Friday night, when I'd stopped puking on the side of the road (and the side of the car) Jeremy had finally been able to drive us home, until this moment about sixty hours later, I had been in this bed in our guest room, tucked beneath the covers, rising only to go to the bathroom. I hadn't eaten much, though Jeremy kept bringing me food.

For the last sixty hours I'd done only two things—think and weep. I'd taken myself through a gamut of emotions and a dozen questions that all made my head and my heart ache.

But now, it was time for me to get up. Because depression did me no good. Staying in bed solved no problems. Crying until every tear had been squeezed from me answered no questions.

And that was what I needed most right now—the answer to my questions.

"Babe," I glanced up at the doorway.

"You're up." He grinned as if he were so glad to see me.

My response: a blank stare and no words. I'd been silent this whole weekend, parting my lips only to speak to Jasmine and Jayden when they'd called on Saturday and yesterday.

"Still not feeling well?" He stepped into the bedroom and eased down onto the bed next to me.

I closed my eyes and wondered why I didn't just say something. Why didn't I ask him about the text? Why didn't I just go straight to the source?

Because he was the source and I no longer trusted him. I needed more information before I confronted him. Because if he was having an affair, I was out.

So I needed to know for sure.

"Maybe you should go to the doctor, babe." Jeremy massaged my shoulder and I cringed beneath his fingers.

"You're shivering," he said, mistaking my revulsion toward him for something else. Just like he'd mistaken everything since Friday.

He'd mistaken why I was sleeping in the guest bedroom. He thought I didn't want to infect him with whatever had made me so sick on the side of the road.

He'd mistaken why I hadn't gotten out of bed on Saturday. He thought I had a bad flu bug because of how red and puffy my eyes were.

And then, he'd mistaken why I hadn't gone to church yesterday? He thought it was a combination of the above.

But it was time for me to get up. And time for me to speak my first words to him. "I'm fine. I don't need you to take care of me."

"Are you kidding me? Babe, I'll always take care of you." When he kissed my cheek, I closed my eyes and pressed down the rising bile inside of me. "So you feel well enough to get up and move around? You know you don't have to. Dru took the kids straight to school, but Lizzy can pick them up because Dru's running down to New Orleans for a couple of days, remember?"

"Oh yeah," I mumbled, I said, though I had forgotten. I was usually on top of things like this, but I hadn't been in my right mind for the last sixty hours.

"So Lizzy can pick them up if you want because you know this is the beginning of Carmen's vacation, too. Seems like everyone is out of town."

While he chuckled as if he'd somehow found humor in those words, I shook my head. I'd forgotten about our nanny, too. It really was time for me to get back into the game. I had to take care of my business. "Like I said, I'm fine. I'm going to take a shower and get into the office. I'll pick up the kids."

"Are you sure? You were knocked out this weekend. You sure you've recovered from whatever you had?"

I gave him a hard glare. "I'm not sure if I've recovered, but I know for sure that I will. Soon enough." I paused. "And there are no excuses with my kids. I will pick them up."

He nodded, missing all of my cues. "Well, don't do too much today. I don't want whatever took you out to come back."

"Neither do I."

"And remember, I have to head to Richmond this morning. Remember Reverend Lewis said there's a young pastor down there he wants me to mentor?"

I stared at him, not believing what I was seeing. "What?" I asked him. Not because I hadn't heard him, but because I wanted to see.

He said, "I'm going to Richmond to speak to a young pastor." And again, his eyebrow twitched. His built-in lie detector.

I couldn't breathe. Was he going to meet K. Brunson? I was going to be sick.

He said, "I'll only be down there for a couple of hours. I'll be back before dinner." No twitch.

He blew me a kiss as if he knew it was a good idea to stay out of punching range and then, he left me alone. Where was he going? And who was K. Brunson?

I had so many questions and it was time for me to find out a few answers.

⌒

I was drained of energy. I guess that's what happened once you found out that your husband was a liar...and a cheater. But I had to push through.

Swiveling in my office chair, I wondered what were my options. How was I going to find out who was K. Brunson? There had been a part of me that had thought about following him down to Richmond. But he was long gone by the time I'd gotten dressed.

I would probably have to go through his phone, though I had a feeling Jeremy was too smart to leave those kinds of obvious clues.

It would come down to searching his office. That would be a start and that might give me a lead. I didn't want to do it now, though. Not while Lizzy was here. Although I didn't need a reason to be in my husband's office, I wanted to do a total sweep and that would be best done when I was in this building alone. I wanted to leave no paper, no receipt, no anything unturned.

I sighed. His office was where I would start, but what if I found nothing? I knew myself—I could hold my tongue for a while, but soon, all of this rage was going to explode out of me.

Turning toward the window, I looked out onto the manicured lawn outside of the sanctuary. I closed my eyes and said a prayer, asking God to bring whatever was in the dark to light. I needed to know the TRUTH.

"First Lady?"

Lizzy's voice and the tap on the door made me swing my chair around. She walked toward me, holding a stuffed folder, but her eyes were clouded with her concern. "Are you all right?"

I nodded. "I am. I just had...a rough weekend. A flu bug. But I'm better now."

"Okay," she said, but her tone let me know that she doubted my words. "You know I can hold everything down if you want to go home and rest. You may need to do that."

"No, I'm good," I said. "Did you need me for something?" She shook her head. "No, these are just the receipts for the credit card bills. American Express and Bank of America are in there." She placed the folder on my desk and I nodded.

"Okay, I'll go through them."

She turned toward the door, then stopped and faced me again. "You know I'm here if you need me."

I frowned. Why would she say that? Did she know something about what was going on with Jeremy? When Lizzy left me alone, I blew out a long breath. That text had turned me into something I'd never been before—paranoid. How many times had Lizzy spoken those same words to me over the years? And never before had I questioned what she'd meant.

Shaking my head, I grabbed the folder. The least I could do today was reconcile the credit card statements with the receipts, so that I could give approval for Lizzy to pay the bills. This was easy enough; something I did so often, I could do it in my sleep.

I laid out the receipts and began checking each off on the statements. There were dozens of receipts for supplies, and then, meals out. There were a couple of receipts for purchases at a bookstore and then the flowers that were sent from our unofficial flower ministry.

I paused and then eyed all the receipts again. Could what I be looking for be right here in front of my face? I studied each of the receipts—the supplies. There was nothing there. The restaurants. There were thirteen meals this month, but how could I find out who had been to each of the restaurants with Jeremy? Half of the time, I was with him. Maybe I could go over his calendar with Lizzy. Turning to the receipts from the book store—nothing. The flowers.

I paused. There had been five orders for flowers this month. I'd called in one myself for Mother Hayden. This was a long shot, but I'd start here and then move to the restaurants.

I picked up my cell and searched for the number to the flower shop we always used. When the young man answered, I said, "Hello, this is Ginger Williams from New Kingdom Temple."

"Oh, hey, First Lady," the young man said. "This is Elliott Austin. You probably don't know me with all the people there, but I love you and Reverend Williams."

"Oh, thank you, Elliott. Listen, I'm calling about the flowers we've ordered in the last few weeks. I think there's a discrepancy."

"What? On our end?"

"Oh no, no," I was quick to say. "I just need to reconcile our records. Do you keep receipts for all of the flowers we ordered?"

"Yes ma'am. We keep records back for years now that everything is digital."

"Great. So can you tell me the names of the people we sent flowers to this month?"

"Sure. It's not confidential since you're the ones who sent the flowers." He laughed as if that was the funniest thing he'd ever said. I chuckled only to keep my heart from pounding its way out of my chest.

"Okay, let's see what we have here. It seems you ordered five arrangements this month."

That was what we ordered, but I said, "Five. Are you sure?"

"Yes. To a Tory Blunt."

That was one of the young girls who'd fallen off a swing at school.

He said, "Those were sent to Children's hospital."

"Yes, that's correct."

"Then," he said, "one was sent to Beatrice Hayden."

Mother Hayden. "Yes, I actually picked those up myself and took them to her...." My voice trailed off because this was so stupid. Flowers were too obvious, I needed to start with the restaurants.

"And a bouquet, oh, a big one was sent to Katrina Brunson."

My heart stopped. Or maybe it wasn't my heart. Maybe it was time altogether. Because I felt like I was frozen in the moment.

"K...." I had to pause to inhale more oxygen. "Brunson. That one. That's not familiar," I said, sounding like I was breathing through my nose.

"Really?" I heard his concern. "I'm so sorry, First Lady. Is there anything we can do? You can call up the credit card company and report it as fraud."

"Oh, no, I don't think I'll have to do that," I said, feeling bad I'd told all these lies. "You know what. Can you just give me the address it was delivered to? Then, I can reconcile it with our records and see...."

"Sure," he said and began reading off the number and the street. I jotted down the address on 4th Street in Southeast. "Thank you again, Elliott."

"Wait, do you want the other names?"

"No, I think I'll start here and if I need any more information, I'll let you know."

"Okay, I'll see you Sunday and I hope we get this all worked out."

When I hung up, I had to force myself to breathe. Inhale. Exhale. Repeat.

I had a name. I had a telephone number...and now, I had an address.

Oh, and I had one more thing.

Katrina.

At least, Jeremy wasn't screwing a man.

I exhaled.

# CHAPTER FOURTEEN

I was really sitting here. In my car, in front of this townhouse on 4th Street in Southeast. Sitting here, like I was a common stalker.

Yawning, I closed my eyes for a second, something I'd hardly done last night. It had been difficult to do anything after Elliott had given me this information about Katrina. I'd wanted to run over here as soon as I had her address yesterday, but I'd focused my attention on my children rather than on the woman my husband was screwing. And there was no way I was going to come over here with them in the back seat of my car. As long as I could help it, drama and crazy would not be a part of their lives, even though Jeremy had brought drama and crazy into our home.

Jeremy. He'd returned home last night before dinner, just like he'd said. So that part wasn't his lie.

It was amazing that I hadn't confronted my husband. I hadn't confronted him when he'd sat down with us at dinner,

I hadn't confronted him while he worked in our home office afterwards, and I hadn't shaken him awake and confronted him last night as he snored and I lay awake in the dark wondering about Katrina.

I'd done it, though. I'd made it all the way through to this moment without saying a word. Because I wanted the truth and I trusted this woman to tell me the truth more than I trusted my husband.

That made me shake my head. This was what crazy looked like. But I didn't mind because if there was one thing I'd learned from my mother, it was that I had to get my ducks in a row. I needed to know the answers, then, ask the questions.

Putting my hand on the car handle, I paused. Did I really want to do this? Right now, Jeremy could be in there with her—or not. Katrina could be at work—or not. She could be....

"Stop it, Ginger," I told myself. Either I was going to do this—or not.

But still, I didn't move. I just sat and watched the personification of D.C.'s gentrification all around me. Young people jogging, couples pushing strollers, folks walking dogs— all of this being done by people who would have never driven through this neighborhood, not even with armed guards, ten years ago.

Ten years ago. That was when it all began for me and Jeremy. We'd had so many good years in between then and now, so did I really want to know? Did I really want to rock our marriage?

Before I finished asking myself the question, I already knew the answer. Yes! I wanted to know for me...and for Jasmine and Jayden. Thinking about my children made me swallow hard. Knocking on this door would have implications far beyond me.

I took a deep breath as if there was courage inside of the air's oxygen. It was enough to propel me out of the car and once I did that, I kept it moving, not giving myself a chance to turn back or think this through. At the front door, I knocked, then reminded myself to inhale, exhale, repeat.

There was no answer and I felt...relieved. Maybe I didn't want to know. Or maybe it was best to just get the answers from Jeremy.

Then, the door opened.

My assessment was quick: petite, about five-two, no taller than Jada. Young, about Jada's age. Smooth skin, the color of butterscotch and a figure that belonged to a woman pre any pregnancies. She was more pretty than cute, and she was one other thing—smart. Because a flash of recognition crossed her face, but then, just as quickly, she recovered and asked, "May I help you?" as if I was a stranger.

I was a stranger, but I was a stranger that she knew. She was poised, I had to give her that.

"You tell me, can you help me?"

Her eyes were like a scanner, capturing every inch of me from the sunglasses resting on top of my head to my yellow T-strap sundress, and she ended at my sandals. When her eyes connected with mine again, she smirked. "You came to my door. So please, answer my question. May I help you?"

I hadn't played the tape of this confrontation all the way through because I didn't expect to be having this conversation on anybody's doorstep in full public view. But since it didn't look like I was going to receive an invitation inside, I said, "Yes, you can help me. I'd like some answers."

She raised an eyebrow. "What's your question?"

There was no point in standing on someone's doorstep in the heat of a D.C. August afternoon and playing games. So, I got right to it. "What's going on with you and my husband?"

She didn't miss a beat when she said, "You might need to have that conversation with him."

I noted she asked no question about who was my husband. She just stood there, feisty and bold. She wasn't what I expected, but then what had I been expecting? How could a wife ever be expecting to find out that her husband had a chick on the side? I asked, "So, you do know my husband?"

Now, she rolled her eyes and laughed. Crossing her arms, she leaned against the door frame. "*Everybody* knows your husband."

"Then you know why I'm here," I replied. "I'm trying to figure out what's going on between the two of you."

"And every time you ask that question, I'm going to give you the same answer. That's a conversation you need to have with him."

"I will. But I'd like to start with you."

Suddenly, she sighed as if she'd been entertained, but was tired of the show now. "Look, I'm not gonna get into this with you. I'm not gonna confirm or deny. Just go home and have this conversation with J."

My eyes narrowed. J. She'd just confirmed.

So what was I supposed to do now? On television, on one of those reality shows, if this had happened, this chick would've been snatched out of her home by her hair, then beaten down in the middle of the street, left there to be rolled over by a taxi.

But I wasn't a reality star so I just stared at her, wondering if I should persist. And she stared at me, showing that her plan was to resist. There was no need for this to continue.

Just as I turned away, though, Katrina said, "But I will tell you this; I'm not the one you need to be concerned about."

"Excuse me?" I said.

She sighed, rolled her eyes, then bit her bottom lip as if she was trying to make a decision. "You know what? It seems like the gig is up anyway, since he won't even call me back." She crossed her arms in defiance. "No need for me to protect him when he's treating me like some kind of booty call. He thinks he can just call me, get hooked up, then ignore me for weeks until he needs to get hooked up again. So yeah, I'll tell you." With a nod, she said, "J and I are messing around. I just saw him the other night when he got home from Atlanta. He came here to me instead of going home to you." She smirked.

I wondered what it was—was it me being the daughter of a pastor, or me growing up in Jack and Jill, or the poise

I'd learned as a debutante...or was it my training as a First Lady? I didn't know what it was from my past that gave me the fortitude to stand there without bursting into tears like a toddler or stabbing her in her neck like a serial killer.

Whatever it was that kept me strong, allowed me to absorb her words, even though they felt like bullets breaking deep into my chest.

"But like I said," she continued, "I am not your problem. 'Cause J ain't serious about me. He left here Friday morning and I haven't heard from him since. But I know why. Because of that skank. She's the one you need to be checking for."

"Who?"

She held up her hand. "I'm not giving you anymore, not that I have more to give. You're on your own from here. But all I got to say is she's the real hoe. He's been cheating on me with her the whole time, always talking about breaking it off with her and he never does." Her tone was filled with all kinds of attitude.

*Cheating on her? Ummm...WHAT?* This woman had just admitted to having an affair with my husband and she was pissed about some other woman? My head was spinning with confusion. My husband was cheating with Katrina, but he had another woman, too?

I had only one thought at first: when in the world did Jeremy have time? I shook my head. I had no idea why Katrina would add another woman to the mix. Maybe just to do maximum damage to me and Jeremy.

"So really," she continued, "I would advise you to talk to your husband and check out that other one who's about to bring you a whole bunch of trouble."

And with that, she slammed the door right in my face.

Before I went to college, my mother sat me down and gave me what she called her pearls of wisdom:

"*Never rely on a man for money.*"

"*Never sleep with a man if you're not willing for him to be the father of your children.*"

"*Never make a decision when you're angry.*"

"*Never show your full hand when you're in the middle of a negotiation.*"

It was her last two pearls that rang in my ears now. I was angry, beyond that really. In fact, there wasn't a word to describe all of my emotions. So, I needed to rely on one of those pearls—this was not the time to make a decision.

And I had a full hand. I had the truth and now, I had to determine when and how to use it. It was going to be even more difficult to hold everything inside. How could I not slap the slime out of Jeremy with what I knew?

That was why I was still sitting in the car. Because Jeremy's Jag was in the garage. I had no idea why he was home so early, but I knew I couldn't go inside our home. Not yet. I didn't have the ability to walk into the house and not turn into a wife scorned.

But I couldn't sit in the car until I figured out what to do. So, I slid out and as I walked toward the door, I pressed play on the button that had my mother's words in my memory: *Never show your full hand....*

Before I stepped over the threshold, I took a breath, but the moment I entered, I heard voices. I moved toward the conversation and when they were in my sight, Jeremy glanced up. His lips spread into a wide grin. "Babe!" He jumped up from the sofa where he'd been sitting across from our agent, Clyde and another man I didn't know, but who looked familiar. "I called the church and then, I called your cell," Jeremy said with excitement. "I didn't know where you were!" Pulling me into his arms, he kissed my cheek, then took my hand. "Come in," he said as if he'd forgotten this was my home, too. "I have some good news for you."

This was the first time since I'd seen that text that Jeremy had touched me and I hadn't cringed. I guess because I was just shocked; I hadn't expected to walk into a meeting.

"Hello, everyone," I said, pasting on a smile as Clyde and the other gentleman stood. "What's going on?"

"Babe, this is Lawrence Wright." When the blond-haired man reached his hand toward me, that was when I figured it out. He could have been Richard Gere's twin.

"Nice to meet you, Mr. Wright." I shook his hand, then turned to Clyde. "What's up?"

"Just you," he said, pulling me into an embrace.

"Babe," Jeremy said, "Lawrence is from Amazon Exclusive." It sounded like my husband was about to break out into a song.

"Oh...kay." There was silence as I waited for someone to continue.

"Let's all sit down," Jeremy said, leading me to the sofa where he'd been sitting. When we sat and his leg rubbed against mine, I had to focus to keep my body in place rather than sliding to the other end far away from him.

I was glad when Lawrence distracted me and said, "Mrs. Williams, I came here to talk to you and Reverend Williams about joining our team."

"Oh, is this about the books that Jeremy wants to write?" I asked.

"Well, books would be good." Lawrence chuckled. "What we at Amazon have in mind is much bigger than that. Our team has been watching the two of you for some time. And while we know you have a deal with Netflix, we think we'd be able to offer you a much more lucrative package."

I frowned. "You're talking about a development deal?"

The three men nodded together.

I said, "But I thought the Netflix deal was done, right, Clyde?"

Clyde nodded, but now, his grin was as wide as Jeremy's. "It was done, but they're willing to let us buy out of that deal."

"Babe," Jeremy put his hand on my knee and my eyes looked down at where he touched me. "The plan that Amazon has would turn us into a powerhouse couple."

How was I going to sit here and not push Jeremy away?

"Yes," Lawrence picked up. "We're talking about a package that would make you bigger than Joel and Victoria Olsteen."

Clyde added, "The numbers haven't been worked out yet, but we're talking high seven figures."

That took my attention away from Jeremy's hand on my knee. I inhaled. "What?"

The men nodded, letting me know that I'd heard Clyde correctly.

Jeremy said, "They recognize what you and I have together, babe. They know that as a couple, we're just getting started. And because Amazon does so much, they want us to do everything from writing books, to producing original programming to even developing a full merchandise line."

"Wow," I said.

"Exactly." Jeremy laughed as if he thought I was so impressed with the deal. If only he knew my wow was because this was never going to happen.

The men continued talking, throwing out numbers, concepts, ideas. I just sat there thinking when would be a good moment to tell them that Jeremy was a liar and a cheat.

After a couple of minutes of my silence, Jeremy paused. "Are you okay?"

When he rubbed my arm, I watched Clyde and Lawrence staring at me. This wasn't the time to say all that I wanted to say.

"I'm fine," I managed to squeak out. "I was just thinking about..." I paused, trying to come up with something. "The

Dress for Success program. We're going to be taking it into schools," I said to Clyde and Lawrence, though I had no idea why I was explaining this to them.

"You know it's going to be wonderful with all the time and effort you've put into it," my husband said. Then, he turned to Clyde and explained what I'd been doing with girls in the foster care system and how I was expanding the program into schools. He finished with, "I've never seen anyone more committed to anything."

Lawrence grinned. "It's that commitment that has us confident you two are perfect for the slate of projects we have planned. And to be honest, there is something else that has impressed us." He paused. "We did look at several pastors throughout the country and like I said, we love your commitment to your congregation and the community, but we are just as impressed with your commitment to your family and each other."

When Jeremy wrapped his arms around my shoulders and pulled me close, I had to count from ten backwards to stop myself from jerking away.

"I am committed to my wife," Jeremy said. "Because I know that God blessed me with a jewel and I treat her like the precious woman she is." He kissed my cheek and my smile faded. I couldn't help it. There was no way for me to smile *and* not punch Jeremy in the eye at the same time.

"Well, this is going to be wonderful," Lawrence said as if the deal was done.

"I have a question." I raised my hand like I was in a class. "Why us?"

The matching frowns on their faces would have made me laugh if my heart hadn't been so broken.

"What do you mean, babe?" Jeremy asked. "Lawrence just explained it and really, why not us?"

"No." This time it was Lawrence who held up his hand, stopping Jeremy. "I think I know what your wife means and it is a valid question, Mrs. Williams. Like I said, we are impressed with your commitment, but what we also know about you and your husband is that the two of you know how to build something. You've built this dynamic church, a dynamic ministry. And the thing that's most important in today's times with social media and cell phone cameras everywhere," he hesitated for a beat, "you've built a strong marriage that's scandal free."

"Yeah," Jeremy said. "That's been important to me and my wife." He took my hand into his and I wondered how much longer I'd be able to endure this torture.

Lawrence said, "You wouldn't believe how many pastors we had to cross off our list for having one issue or another. I don't know how you do it."

It's simple, I thought. He keeps his hoes in check.

"It's simple," Jeremy said. "We honor our wedding vows. Both of us do." Squeezing my hand, he added, "My wife is my everything. And the last thing I would ever do is bring scandal to her doorstep."

My mouth opened with all kinds of surprise. Jeremy was taking this too far. I needed to call Spike Lee and tell him about Jeremy's acting abilities, because he was putting on an Oscar-winning performance, giving Denzel a run for his money. I wondered just how far he would go.

So, I said, "Yes, it's like Jeremy said, he's committed to me." I looked directly at my husband. "He would never do anything to bring shame to me or our family."

Those words were meant to be a shot to his heart and I expected Jeremy to turn away from me, unable to look into my eyes. I expected his eyebrow to begin twitching so hard it would give him a headache.

But what he did was look me straight in my face and say, "I sure wouldn't."

Not only was this shocking, but it was so sad to me. Because this proved that my husband had moved from one level to another. He was no longer just an ordinary liar, he was now pathological. And that meant I had no idea how long he'd been lying to me. I'd always used his body language as a sign, and since his eyebrow never twitched, I thought all was well in our world. But now I knew that he'd probably been lying to me for years. Maybe even since the beginning.

I wanted to stand up, scream and tell these people Jeremy wasn't the man he claimed to be. I wanted to blow him, his world and this deal up.

But I didn't. Not yet. Because I needed to know his story, I wanted to hear his side. And until that happened, I wasn't willing to jeopardize everything. So I just sat quietly with the perfect First Lady smile on my face.

But if the truth was what I thought it was, Jeremy could kiss more than just this seven figures deal goodbye.

# Chapter Fifteen

"The Word of God is infallible. Let me break it down for you." Jeremy's voice, from the recording on my phone, boomed through the speakers in my Benz. "That means this right here," I remembered him holding the Bible over his head, "there ain't no lies in here. This right here is all truth. You wanna know what God says about anything, just go straight to the source," Jeremy preached. "You don't need to talk to your mama, your daddy, or even the preacher. You can find out for yourself if you just read the Word. Read the Word so you can know, that you know, that you know!"

The recording ended there, but I remembered the way the congregation had risen to their feet in the small meeting room of the Holiday Inn in downtown D.C. Just about all of the 81 members of the church had been in the room that day, but you would have thought it was a stadium full of people the way Jeremy had made those people hoot and holler. He had rocked it on his very first Sunday.

Even with all that was going on with me and Jeremy right now, remembering that time warmed my heart and gave me goosebumps. On that Sunday morning, in front of his own congregation for the first time, it was no longer my speculation, it was our certainty: my husband was a star. I knew it then. I knew it now. I believed in it then. I believed it had corrupted him now.

*Absolute power corrupts absolutely.*

Those were words my father used to say. Those were words that defined my husband now. My husband, the star. The lying, cheating star.

He was the cheating star who I found out about last week and still hadn't had a chance to confront. What were the chances that right as the meeting with Clyde and Lawrence was wrapping up last Tuesday, Jeremy would get a call that stopped us all. Mother Hayden had passed away from a blood clot that was the result of her hip surgery.

That news sent me and Jeremy to our knees. That night, we prayed together and cried, too. Mother Hayden was one of the major reasons why Jeremy was even where he was.

There'd been no time after that. I didn't want to bring up Katrina as Jeremy packed to accompany Mother Hayden's body to her home in Birmingham. That had been her wish and he'd stayed in Alabama with the family, ministering to them, helping them make final plans for the woman he loved like a mother. He'd called me every day since he'd boarded the plane last Wednesday to keep me posted and to share his grief.

There were moments when I was on the phone with him that I was reminded of the man I'd fallen in love with. And during those times, my heart went out to him and I tried to pass him strength through my prayers.

But then, there were the other times when I just wanted to hang up because the image of him in bed with Katrina was just too much for me to bear.

It was just a bizarre time. Why would Jeremy and I be apart right now? Why would Mother Hayden pass away at this moment? Was God trying to tell me something?

What made it worse was that for the six days since I'd confronted my husband's side-piece, I hadn't told a single person about my discovery. For more than one hundred and forty-four hours, I hadn't been able to bring myself to talk to anyone, not Dru, not Jada, not my mom...not until I could talk to Jeremy. He had to be the first one.

I'd held onto that thought, that belief...until last night. Because that was when Jeremy told me he'd definitely be home tomorrow since the funeral was today. That meant we would be face-to-face in a little more than twelve hours. And now, after waiting for so long, I was afraid. What was I supposed to say to him? And once I said it, what would this all mean?

Those questions were the reasons why I was making this right turn into the parking garage of Dru's building. I maneuvered into one of the visitor's spots, locked my car, then pressed the buzzer to gain entry.

Dru knew I was coming, so she buzzed me right in. And as I stepped into the elevator and then headed up to the ninth floor, I practiced what I wanted to say to my friend. But it didn't take much time for me to figure it out. There were only six words to say: My husband is cheating on me.

Even though my steps were silent in the carpeted hallway, Dru opened her door before I had a chance to ring the bell.

"Hey," she said at the same time that she handed me a glass of white wine.

I grabbed the glass, kicked off my shoes, then headed to her overstuffed, so-soft sofa. Sinking into the microfiber, I tucked my feet beneath my butt, lifted my glass and asked, "How did you know?" before I took two long sips.

"Well," Dru began as she bounced onto the other end of the couch. She faced me as she said, "You never call me at night and say you need to come over. Nights are for the kids. Who's with them?"

"I asked Carmen to stay a few extra hours," I said and then, sighed. "I just needed to get out. I needed to talk."

"I know." She laid her wine atop her glass table in front of us. "I know this is hard for you."

I blinked. Did Dru know? "What?"

"Mother Hayden. The funeral was today, right? I know this has been so hard. You've been so distant all week, but I know how close you all were."

Now, I placed my wine on the table next to hers. "Yeah, the funeral was today and yeah, this has been really hard, but that's not what I want to talk about."

Dru tilted her head as if she were confused. "So, not Mother Hayden? Then...." She stopped and waited for me to fill her in.

"You're not going to believe this." And only because I didn't want to play any games and keep her in suspense, I began my story. Starting with being with the Douglases and seeing the text.

"What?" my best friend exclaimed.

"Sit back, there's more."

From there, I took Dru on the journey with me wondering if K. Brunson was a man....

"Oh, my God!"

I told her how I'd found out that K stood for Katrina and I'd even gotten her address. "I felt a little bit like a super sleuth," I bragged.

"I don't know why," Dru said, deflating my ego a bit. "You went through all of that? If you had told me this when you were supposed to, we could have found out who she was and where she lived on the Internet just by using her phone number."

"Really?"

Dru rolled her eyes. "You don't know anything, but what did you do when you found out her address?" She held up her hand. "Don't tell me that...."

"I went over there."

"No!"

"Yes!"

"Is she alive?"

That made me chuckle just a little. "She was when I left."

"And Jeremy's still alive, too?"

That made me want to cry.

"Dude," Dru said as she picked up her wine again. "I can't believe it." Then she took a sip and shook her head. "You know what? I'm lying."

"Wait." I said that word so slowly, it sounded like it had seven syllables. "Are you saying you knew?"

"No." She waved her hands. "Of course not. Because if I'd found out before you, your husband *would* be dead. No, I just meant that Jeremy's not who he used to be. He's different. He speaks to me differently. Like back in New Orleans, the three of us were friends. But now, he treats me...well, as an employee. I mean, that's what I am, but *you* don't *treat* me that way."

"Because you're my best friend first."

"Exactly. But it's not that way with Jeremy. It was when I first came here to D.C. with y'all. But especially since we've been in the new sanctuary and on that campus, he's really different. I'm surprised you haven't noticed."

I shook my head. "And I'm surprised you've never said anything."

She shrugged. "What was I supposed to say? Your husband's caught up? It was bound to happen. All that money now, all that power. People shout out his name when he walks by. He's in demand as a speaker. He's the right Reverend Jeremy Williams now, you know?"

I filled my cheeks with air, then exhaled slowly.

"So what's the plan? You're the First Lady, so you can't go rolling up on this Katrina chick. Does Jada know?"

"I didn't want to talk to anyone before I talked to Jeremy. But now that all these days have passed and he'll be home tomorrow...."

"Well, Jada and I can roll up on that homewrecker and take care of her tonight."

Even though Dru was trying to lighten the moment, I couldn't find a smile. Shaking my head, I said, "No. She didn't wreck my home," I said with a sigh. "This is on Jeremy, if it's even true."

She frowned. "What do you mean if it's even true? You don't believe her?"

"I did in the beginning because everything fit. But I guess I've had too many days of thinking and stewing and thinking and crying and thinking and...."

She held up her hand. "I get the picture."

"And then on top of that, there's this deal with Amazon." I filled Dru in on what happened at the meeting.

"High. Seven. Figures?" She shook her head. "I cannot believe you kept all of this from me. I just thought you were off because of Mother Hayden."

"And that's another thing. Isn't it weird, Dru, that this happened with Katrina and then, Mother Hayden died."

"Huh?" She squinted as if my words sounded crazy. "You think Katrina had something to do with that?"

"No, of course not. What I mean is that when Mother Hayden died, that stopped everything. I couldn't talk to Jeremy and I had to just sit on this for the last six days."

"Oh, and so you're wondering if...."

"God is trying to tell me something."

She shrugged. "Well, we know God hates divorce."

"Exactly."

"Except in the case of adultery."

"Exactly."

"Yeah," she nodded slowly, "I can see why you're in a dilemma."

"I'm just wondering if I should give it more time before I say something to Jeremy."

"Why? If he's coming back tomorrow, why not talk to him?"

I waited a moment to continue, trying to put together the words to explain what I'd been thinking and feeling, especially in the last few days. "Because bringing it up to him now forces me to take action and I'm not sure what action I need to take."

Dru leaned back, her expression pensive, like she was thinking and then weighing what she wanted to say. Then, she said, "You know what? I think you may be right."

"Really?"

"Yeah, because right now, all you really have is the word of some trick from Southeast."

"I have her word and I have her text. Oh, and I have something else." I paused. "She told me she wasn't the only one that Jeremy's been with."

"Wait. WHAT?"

"Yeah, she went on and on about how he was cheating on her."

Dru's eyes widened. "You've got to be kidding me. These side chicks are real bold these days. But now, I really don't know if I believe her and I'm thinking that you need to hold up for a minute. Because not only does she sound crazy, but if you say anything about her to Jeremy, he's probably going to tell you that she *is* crazy. What else can he do? He's not going to say, 'yeah, I have a crazy jump-off who lives a couple of miles away.' He's going to deny it."

Leaning forward, I held my head in my hands.

"Let's do this." She scooted to the edge of the sofa and rubbed my back. "Let's wait just a few more days. Let me talk to Jeremy."

I sat up straight. "What? No! If anyone is going to talk to him about this, it'll be me."

"No, not about this. I'm just gonna have a chat with him. Not say anything directly. But I don't know, Ginger. Let me talk to him and let us figure this out some more. Because really you're right; you don't have enough yet. You don't have enough to make the decision to walk out the door."

And that right there was my quandary. Was I willing to leave Jeremy and take Jasmine and Jayden from their father over the word of a woman? "But," I had another question, "what about if Katrina has said something to him?"

"Well, if she tells him that she told you, she's a fool. Because she'd have to deal with his wrath. But if she did and he says something to you, *then* you handle it. For now, though, I really do think you're right. You can't say anything. Not yet."

I nodded, then, leaned back against the soft couch and closed my eyes. Dru was right; Jeremy would never admit it. Not with just a text and some woman's word. He would tell me Katrina was lying. He'd remind me of the stalkers he'd had in the past. He'd just say Katrina went further than the others.

I was an action person and I couldn't do anything with what I had now—I needed more.

"Okay," I said. "Talk to him. Let's see what happens."

"All right. And what are you going to do?"

"I'm going to do the only thing I can do at this point; I'm going to pray."

# CHAPTER SIXTEEN

For once, I was glad I had a First Ladies Council meeting, especially since it was just the executive board: me, Sonya, and unfortunately, Cecily.

But today, I needed this. Jeremy had been home for two days. I'd been praying for Jesus to be a zip on my lips and so far, my prayers had been answered; I'd said nothing about meeting Katrina. And he'd said nothing to me.

Keeping the secret had been easier than I thought; since he'd been home, Jeremy had been a bit distracted. I was sure it was because of Mother Hayden. For the two days, he'd gone into the church and done his duties, but he'd left the office both days before five, getting home before me and sending Carmen on her way. He'd been spending as much time with the kids as he could.

Jeremy had done this before—it was as if when he had to deal with death, our children reminded him of life.

Of course, I loved when he spent time with Jasmine and Jayden. That was a good thing—except right now, it gave me and Jeremy too many hours together, during the day at church, and then at home at night. And I was concerned—too many hours might lead to me saying something.

But I'd lasted. Because the bottom line was—I needed more before I could make a decision. I just didn't know when, where or how I would get information to find out one way or the other.

I pushed all those thoughts aside, though, as I strolled from the parking garage and into Georgia Brown's. I certainly didn't want to have this on my mind as I met with Sonya and Cecily, which was why I'd decided to arrive fifteen minutes early. I wanted to give myself time to settle down and have my game face on because I didn't want either of them, especially Sonya, to pick up on any of my distress. The last time Sonya had seen me, I was rushing from her apartment. Today my facade would be cool and ever so collected.

At the hostess stand, I was just about to ask for our reservation, when I saw Sonya and Cecily, already seated at a table by the window. I glanced at my watch; had I mixed up the time?

I pointed to them as I passed the hostess and weaved my way through the tables. Sonya and Cecily hadn't seen me yet; they were too involved in their conversation. Their heads were down, close together as they whispered.

They didn't even notice when I stood at the table. "Hello."

Both of them looked up, startled. "Oh, Ginger," Sonya said. "I didn't see you come in."

She stood to hug me and as I slipped into the chair across from her, I said, "I can tell." Turning to my right, I said, "Cecily." My greeting was curt, I knew that. But I never had much to say to her and the vice versa was true, too.

"What's up, girl?" she said as if we were friends.

I didn't know what that was about, but I said, "I'm good. So you two got here early."

They exchanged a glance before Sonya said, "My mother always told me if you're fifteen minutes early, you're on time."

"Then, I'm right on time," I said. "Because I was trying to get here fifteen minutes early."

"Great," Sonya said. "Well, let's order and then we can get to the business at hand."

Cecily and I nodded together, probably the only thing we would agree on at this meeting. As I perused the menu, on the sly I studied Sonya and Cecily. As always, they were both put together, though Sonya was the much more matronly one with the scooped neck rose-colored dress she wore that fell almost to her calves. Cecily hadn't stood, but I didn't have to see the hem of her spaghetti-strap sundress. Every skirt or dress she wore, barely skimmed her knees and her shoe game was almost as on point as mine.

But even as we browsed through the menus, I could tell there was something going on with these two. I felt this vibe, like Sonya and Cecily were still communicating, though they spoke no words. It was in the way they kept glancing at each other and Sonya kept shaking her head. I'd walked in on something.

After the waitress took our orders, I was ready to get to business. While I was glad to have the reprieve from being around Jeremy, there was an expiration time when it came to spending time with these women.

"So," I started, "I wanted to give you both a run-down on what happened at the job fair and then talk about how we're going to schedule the high school visits. I'd love to set that up today so we can take it to the other First Ladies, get their approval and then, get started."

"Of course," Sonya said. "But before we get into all of that," she waved her hand as if what I had to say wasn't important, "I wanted to ask...." She paused and with her arms resting on the table, she whispered, "How are you?"

The beat of my heart sped up. "I'm...fine...why?"

"Oh, well, the last time I saw you." She glanced at Cecily.

"Ah," I said as nonchalantly as I could, then I turned to Cecily the same way Sonya had done. "Jeremy and I were supposed to have dinner with Sonya and Charles," I explained. "But our babysitter got sick." Returning my glance to Sonya, I said, "But it was just a little cold. She's fine, the kids are fine, all is well."

Sonya and Cecily gave each other a long look and now I was sure...something was going on. But I wasn't going to allow them to take me down their gossipy road. Since the Dress for Success program hadn't gotten them on track, I tried another approach. "Oh, you know what I want to talk to you about," I began, keeping my tone light. "Our anniversary celebration. I know you mentioned, Sonya, that you and the First Ladies Council wanted to make a presentation."

"Yes." She nodded. "We really want to if you can fit us on the program."

"Definitely. This is so nice of you."

"Well, we don't want to do it just to be nice." She glanced at Cecily and she nodded. "We want to make a presentation to New Kingdom Temple, but we also want to do a special tribute to you."

"That's right," Cecily said, peering at me through the black diamond-studded cat-eye glasses that she wore today.

Sonya continued, "We want to recognize what few people do—that there are a lot of responsibilities that go along with being helpmeets for our husbands. And at times, that can be overwhelming."

"At times?" Cecily piped in. "You mean most times."

Now, they nodded together.

"Well, I appreciate that," I said.

"And we appreciate you," Sonya said. "When God blessed me with this idea all those years ago to create this support group, I did it for women just like you."

"Thank you," I said. Feeling a great need to turn the conversation back to business, I added, "So I'll have Jeremy's assistant, Lizzy, get the program over to you."

"It can be so overwhelming being a pastor's wife," Cecily said as if I hadn't said a word.

"I agree," Sonya said. God knows that my forty years of marriage has needed support from time to time. We all need the blessing of being around other women with like minds."

I couldn't stop my eyebrows from rising with those words. Like minds? I had nothing in common with these women and this would have been a good time to bring up some of the issues I had with the Council, especially the gossiping. But again, I tried to steer the conversation to where I wanted it to be. "Well...being part of the Council has been...interesting for me. Especially because of the good work the Council does in D.C."

"And I wouldn't have survived without the Council and their support," Cecily held up her hand as if she was about to testify.

Again, it felt like neither one of them were listening to me.

Cecily continued, "I mean, I haven't had the issues that so many of the wives have, unfortunately, had to go through." She paused and placed her hand on my arm. "I mean, my husband and I have had a good marriage, thank you, Lord. But still, sometimes a woman just needs other women to talk to. That's what we want you to know. That we're here for you."

The way Cecily sat on the edge of her chair—I'd seen that stance before. I'd seen the hungry gaze from her eyes. I sucked in air. They knew about Jeremy and Katrina!

I pushed down the rising stone in my throat. "I'm grateful," I said, "but really, today, I don't want to talk about anyone or anything. I just want us to get to the business that we came here to discuss."

Sonya leaned toward me. "We don't have to talk about any of that today, Ginger. That's not why I wanted us to get together. I knew you needed us without the other women around." Reaching across the table, she patted my hand. "You don't have to put up a front for us."

They knew. Oh, my God. They knew.

I blinked, trying to think of something to say, trying to gain control of this conversation. There was no way I was going to talk to them about Jeremy and Katrina.

"I'm not...putting on any front. But the thing is, I don't want to talk about any personal business."

"It's not really personal when it affects all of us," Sonya said. "Everything that happens in every church affects all of us. You know that."

"Yes," Cecily jumped in. "We're intertwined. We're family, baby."

Those words made the stone fill up my throat. She'd said the same thing to Rena. I wanted to jump up, toss a couple of bills on the table, and get the hades out of here. But I was stuck in my seat. It took me a moment to find my voice. "Look," I began. "I appreciate why you formed this group and while there are some who don't mind discussing their personal situations at the meetings, I'm not one of them. Jeremy and I are private people and...."

I had to stop when Cecily snickered. But what was worse, Sonya did, too.

Cecily said, "Private? If your husband was so private, then his business wouldn't be all over the streets."

I found myself once again in a dilemma. My first thought was to get up, walk out and never return to anything that had to do with the First Ladies Council. But that wouldn't have been smart. They knew something and I needed to know what they knew.

Sonya said, "Cecily, please."

"I'm sorry," she said, not sounding sorry at all. "It's just that, Ginger, you sit in judgment of us so much."

"No, I don't. I've never said anything about anyone in our meetings. I don't participate when you're gossiping and bringing someone down...."

"See, that right there." She pointed her finger at me. "That's what I mean," Cecily said. "You're always sitting back, always acting so self-righteous. We can all see the judgment in your eyes, we can all hear it in your voice. But we're not gossiping, we're simply trying to help each other out because none of us are immune." She stopped and sat back as if she'd just dropped the mic. But then, she added, "Including you."

Really, I just wanted to walk out, but I couldn't without finding out what they knew. Looking straight at Cecily, I said, "If you," then, I turned to Sonya, "or you have something to say, I wish you would just say it rather than going through all of this."

"All right." I guess Sonya was designated to be the spokeswoman because Cecily sat back and nodded. "But first,

I want you to know that what Jeremy has done has nothing to do with you. You don't have anything to be ashamed of."

At this moment, I knew how Katrina felt the day I stood in front of her. I wasn't going to confirm or deny a thing.

It was shocking to hear all of this, though. Jeremy had kept his affair from me, but the women on the First Ladies Council knew?

I'd always hated that cliché—the wife is the last one to know. I never believed it. I always thought that if a wife was in tune with her husband, nothing could be hidden from either of them. I guess I was dead wrong.

I sat waiting with my arms folded and glaring at the both of them.

Sonya continued, "As big as the DMV is, at the same time, it's a small community, so it wasn't surprising when we found out a while back and...."

"Wait!" I held up my hand. "Hold up. A while back and you're just saying something to me now?"

"It wasn't our place to tell you," Sonya said.

"Hmph, I wanted to say something." I glared at Cecily, but that didn't bother her. She continued. "I wanted to have your back and make sure you knew."

"But, like I told Cecily when I'd first heard about Jeremy...."

This was a shocker. Cecily was the one who always carried the tales, not Sonya. That made me shift in my seat. Cecily would talk just to be gossiping, but Sonya...she was different.

"I told her," Sonya kept on, "not to say a word. I knew God would reveal it all because whatever is done in the dark will always come to the light."

"Wow," I said, shaking my head. "So, what changed, Sonya? Why're you telling me now?"

"Once I realized that you'd found out...."

I tilted my head.

"When you were at my place," she said as if that had been obvious. "I could tell when you read the text on Jeremy's phone...the way you reacted, I knew then that you'd found out."

Really? I hadn't said a word and she'd read all of that from my reaction?

As if she were reading my mind, she said, "I've been in enough of these situations. Too many of them, really." She shook her head. "So I knew when I saw the look on your face as you read the text. I knew when you looked into my eyes and held back your tears, but not your shock. I knew by the way you wouldn't look at Jeremy once he came back into the room with Charles."

For a moment, I was taken away from the pain of this revelation and just sat in wonder of Sonya. This woman didn't need to be a First Lady. She needed to be part of the CIA's psychological intelligence division.

"So knowing that you'd found out," Sonya said, "I wanted to make sure you had the support you needed."

I was quiet for a moment, then said the only words that came to my mind. "I feel like such an idiot."

"Why?" Cecily said. "You didn't do anything. And if Jeremy hadn't gotten careless with that call or text or whatever it was, you wouldn't have known."

"And that would've been fine with you? That everyone in DC knew my husband was having an affair, but I was in the dark?"

"Like I said, it was going to come to light. It's happened too many times to too many of us and it always does," Sonya said.

Cecily picked up. "So it wasn't like anyone was judging you or talking about you behind your back before you found out." Before I could accuse her of being a liar, Cecily added, "Plus, I know Sonya believes that these things will always come to light, but I was hoping that you would never find out. Once Jeremy took care of his business and just paid the girl off, I figured she'd get rid of the baby and that slate would be wiped clean."

Her words had made it to my ears, but not to the understanding part of my brain. "Excuse me?" I said, sounding like I was accusing her of something.

"Don't go all Christian on me now," Cecily said. "I'm not saying that he should pay her to have an abortion, I just mean pay her off so that she'd give the baby up for adoption. Or maybe just pay her to take the baby and disappear, like that pastor did over in Arlington. That woman never showed up again. And his wife told me that he was so sorry, he's been nothing but faithful ever since."

"Baby?"

Cecily studied me for a moment, then, her eyes widened. "Oh my, Lord." She lowered her eyes, looking away from me.

Through squinted eyes, Sonya said, "Ginger." She paused. "You didn't know about the baby?"

"What...baby?" I stammered.

Cecily pinched her lips together as if she never planned to speak another word again. So this was the moment she chose to get righteous? "Oh, hell no," I said, my voice raising an octave above the appropriate inside level. It was the heat of stares from patrons around me that made me take a breath and lower my voice, though my temperature continued to rise. "You both started this," I said, my eyes on fire with my fury. "So you better finish it."

Sonya and Cecily exchanged glances as if now, all of a sudden, they weren't sure if they should continue.

"It's too late," I said. And then, because I was desperate, I said, "Please. Tell me what you know about Jeremy and Katrina having a baby."

"Katrina?" Sonya and Cecily said at the same time.

Then, Cecily said, "Who's Katrina?"

I blinked. "But you said...."

"We," Cecily pointed between her and Sonya, "didn't say anything about Katrina. I hadn't heard that rumor."

Oh, my God. I pressed my hand over my mouth as Sonya said, "No, her name wasn't Katrina. It was Sharonne. I remember because I thought her name was so unusual."

Sharonne. My head filled with a monument of moments: In New Orleans: In the bathroom with First Lady Blake. Sharonne waltzing in. First Lady Blake's words, "*She's one of those wolves who wants what you have.*"

Then in DC: At the District Winery. The woman sauntering past me, staring at me, then finally speaking to me. "*I'm just in town to handle some...personal business. Take care of yourself now... Oh, and tell that fine husband of yours, I said hello.*"

"I take it that you recognize that name." I had to shake my head to bring myself back to the present and when I focused, I saw the concern in Sonya's eyes.

Pressing my fingers against my lips, I whispered, "If he has a baby..."

My words trailed off, but Sonya picked up my sentence. "He doesn't have a baby. She's pregnant, and now what you have to do is help him face this head on. I'm not sure how far along she is, but there is still time for you to handle this—one way or another."

Cecily leaned toward me. "That's exactly what you will do. You will make sure that baby situation is taken care of and then, you will continue to walk in your place as the First Lady of New Kingdom Temple. You will walk with your head up, shoulders back as you always have and show every woman that no one can come for you. Jeremy Williams is *your* husband."

"What?" Both of them sounded as if they were talking gibberish. Before they could respond, I said, "If he has gotten another woman pregnant...."

Again, Sonya didn't let me finish. She added, "You will make him pay."

That was exactly what they'd told Rena. It had been ridiculous then, it was beyond ridiculous now.

"I do not want a stupid car or a new coat. And I will not stand by my man." I shook my head. "Not when he's not standing by me." Never!

"What are you talking about?" Sonya frowned. "I've seen you with Jeremy. Your husband adores you."

Cecily piped in. "And, I've only seen you together once, when my husband was speaking at your church and Reverend Williams was singing your praises. I agree with Sonya. Your husband loves you. There is no need to go anywhere just because of this incident."

"This is not an incident. You said he's gotten someone pregnant."

"And besides that," Sonya continued, once again ignoring me, "there is so much at stake. You and Jeremy are poised for great things. From your church, to the TV show, and then, Jeremy called my husband to get his advice on this Amazon deal. The two of you are about to sign a deal for a million dollars or more. You can't throw all of that away. You can't walk away. For a baby?"

"You say that as if it's no big thing," I said incredulously. "I would walk away from all of this if Jeremy were just cheating on me. But to bring a baby into our lives." I shook my head. "It's. Not. Going. To. Happen."

"Here's your lunch," the waitress said at the exact moment when I bounced up from my chair. I grabbed my purse, glared at the women, then stomped out of the restaurant.

It wasn't until I was outside that I realized I hadn't left money for my food. That was okay; I hadn't eaten a thing. And after the way Sonya and Cecily had ambushed me, they could pay for that meal.

Once outside, I slowed my roll, though. A baby? Jeremy was about to have another child? With Sharonne? Was that why she was here in D.C.?

I let those thoughts play through my head a couple of times. No, something didn't feel right to me. But I needed help to figure it out.

Pulling my cell phone from my purse, I tapped on the screen, then dialed. When the call was answered, all I said was, "Can you meet me? This is an emergency."

"A baby?" Dru leaned back on the bench at the edge of the wharf and stared out at the Potomac. "Jeremy is having a baby?"

Her tone was as shocked as mine had been. The truth was, I was still stunned. That was why I'd told Dru to meet me down here. The pedestrian traffic on the wharf was Tuesday afternoon light, which was a blessing. I couldn't deal with any crowds. I couldn't be closed in, not in anyway. I needed the air to breathe, I needed the space to think. I had to make sense out of what Sonya and Cecily were trying to get me to believe.

Dru twisted on the bench, facing me now. "Sonya and Cecily told you this?"

I nodded. "Yeah, can you believe it?"

"I can't. What about you?" She paused as if she hesitated asking me the question. "Do you believe them?"

It took a few moments for all the thoughts I'd had since I'd left Georgia Brown's and driven the three or four miles over here to go through my mind. Finally, I said, "I did believe them." I nodded again. "I believed them at first, but once I had a chance to think about it, now I'm not so sure."

She blew out a long breath as if she was a bit relieved by my words. "What made you change your mind?"

I wasn't looking at Dru when I said, "The woman that Jeremy has allegedly gotten pregnant." I paused. "I know her."

"What?" Dru shrieked as she popped up from the bench as if her hearing had failed her because she was sitting down. "You've GOT TO BE kidding me." She lowered herself back to the bench slowly. "This is getting more bizarre by the moment. You *know* this trick? Do I know her? I better not know her."

"Wait, Dru. Calm down. Let me explain." Both of us took a couple of deep breaths. "I met her years ago at Pilgrim's Rest." And then, I remembered. That was Dru's home church. "Yeah," I said, with a bit more energy. "I met her back when we were there. But here's the thing. I just saw her a few weeks ago."

"Where?"

"Right here. In D.C."

"Shut up, Ginger!" Dru stared at me with wide, stunned eyes as if I were telling her some kind of horror story.

Still, I continued, "Yeah, talk about bizarre that her name would come up now." I paused, thinking about what I'd just said. "Or maybe not. Anyway, she was at the restaurant where Jada and I had lunch and she just walked in. It was crazy, Dru. At first, she didn't say anything to me. I thought she looked familiar, but you know, I meet so many people, so I kept talking to Jada. It was so uncomfortable, though, because she kept staring at me. She was having lunch by herself, but it was like all she did was keep her focus on me. But when she got up to leave, she stopped at our table and spoke to me like we were friends or something."

"Okay, so you know that would be crazy if she were sleeping with your man and she walked over to talk to you."

"I know. But then again, chicks these days..."

"True, but I'm already beginning to doubt Sonya and Cecily. Anyway, what did this chick say?"

I squinted, trying to conjure up her words in my mind. "All I remember is something about how she still lived in New Orleans and she was in D.C. for business, I think." I waved my hand because I couldn't recall.

"And you weren't friends before in New Orleans?"

I shook my head. "No. You couldn't even call us acquaintances," I said. "I'm telling you, I met Sharonne once in the Pilgrim's Rest's bathroom...."

"Stop."

"What?"

"Sharonne?"

I nodded, then my eyes got big. "Don't tell me you know her." I hadn't even thought to ask Dru if she knew her from church. These churches were like small towns, so that was never my first thought.

Dru held out her hands in a motion that let me know she wasn't sure. "Is her name Sharonne Phillips?"

I shrugged. "I don't know her last name. I never asked. I'm telling you, I don't think I've exchanged twenty words in my life with her."

"I went to school with a Sharonne Phillips."

"Really?" Now, it was my turn twist toward Dru. "So does she still live in New Orleans or is she here in D.C.? Do you think she's the one seeing Jeremy and...."

Dru held up her hands like a stop sign. "Wait with the twenty questions. I don't know her like that," she shook her head, "but I know her well enough. We were acquaintances back in high school. We were cheerleaders and hung out a few times."

"Dang." I leaned forward and looked across the Potomac to Virginia. Even though it was about four in the afternoon, there were plenty of people strolling across the edge of the river. Folks playing hooky from government jobs. It was that kind of beautiful day on the outside. But a storm raged inside of me. "What are the chances of this?"

"I know, but let's not get ahead of ourselves. The Sharonne Phillips I know may not be the Sharonne that you're looking for."

"I wish I had a picture or something to show you."

"Well, what does she look like?"

I described the leggy woman with the almond shaped eyes, butterscotch skin and expensive weave that stopped just above her behind.

Dru nodded. "The woman I know is about that complexion, she's tall, like the one you're describing. It's been awhile, though, and when I knew her she had a short haircut, not a weave down her back."

"Yeah," I said feeling a little encouraged. "She had a bob back then. I think it's the same woman, Dru. Now, I have to find out if she's involved with Jeremy and if she's pregnant."

"So, she wasn't pregnant when you saw her?"

I shook my head. "Far from it. If she was pregnant then, she was in her first few weeks."

"So if she's that early in her pregnancy," Dru began, "how did Sonya and Cecily find out so quickly?" She shook her head and continued before I could answer. "I think they got this wrong."

"Unless it's a different Sharonne." The hope I'd felt just seconds ago was beginning to fade fast.

"Look," my best friend scooted closer to me, "I know this is really tough for you and I'm sorry, but don't make any judgments yet. Let's figure this Sharonne twist out first. And I have an idea."

"What?"

"I wanna talk to Sharonne Phillips."

"You think she'll talk to you if you call her?"

"Oh, definitely. But uh...I wasn't talking about calling her. I think I need to check this out face-to-face. So, if I could get my boss to give me some time off from work, I'll fly down to New Orleans, hang out with my mom for a few days and figure out a way to hook up with her."

I sighed. "You just got back from New Orleans."

"So?" She shrugged. "The way my mama cooks, I'd fly in for Sunday dinner every week if I could. That two-hour flight is nothing so the only thing that's in between me and that plane is my boss."

I thought about Dru's offer, but it didn't take long for my lips to spread into a smile. "Open up your United app." I motioned toward her phone with my chin. "Let's buy this ticket now. For tomorrow." Leaning over, I hugged her. "Thank you so much, Dru. Thank you for doing this for me."

When she leaned away, she said, "This is part of the best friends code. To have each other's back no matter what. And no worries, *Chica*. I've got yours."

# CHAPTER SEVENTEEN

"This is an opportunity that few people will ever have. It's not even something most people can dream about." Clyde paused. "Ginger? Are you still with us?"

Our agent's voice snapped me out of my thoughts. "Huh?"

He stood on the other side of the small conference table across from me and Jeremy in Jeremy's office. His grin was as wide as any kid's on Christmas.

"Yeah, yeah, I'm still with you," I said, though I hoped he wouldn't ask me to repeat anything he'd told us.

He'd been going over the paperwork the Amazon executives had sent to him and he'd wanted us to see every line. His voice had been trailing in and out of my consciousness, but I'd certainly caught the gist of his words: Amazon had stayed true to their promise. Their offer was for $8 million. It wasn't Michelle and Barack Obama money, but there were bonuses included that would put us in the outfield of that league.

"You don't seem excited," Clyde said as his smile dimmed.

I turned the ends of my lips up into something that hopefully could fake a little joy. That was the best I could do considering I couldn't focus on the millions in front of me when I wasn't sure about the man who sat beside me.

It had been just two days since I'd taken Dru to the airport to head to New Orleans and she'd given me a kind of pep talk.

*"I don't know what I'm going to find," Dru said, "but I'm going to do my best to find something so you can get out of the constipation that has become your life."*

*I frowned. "Really, Dru?"*

*"I'm just saying."* She held up her hands and I guess that was some sort of an apology—kind of. *"It's just that you're stuck. Nothing's moving. Just think of me as the laxative that's gonna get things going."*

She'd winked before she jumped out of the car and headed into the terminal.

I hadn't heard from her since.

"And you got the Netflix people to give us an out?" Jeremy asked, bringing me all the way back into his office.

Even when Jeremy spoke, I kept my eyes on Clyde. I couldn't look at Jeremy; I hadn't been able to look at him since my lunch with Sonya and Cecily on Tuesday.

Jeremy asked, "I mean, they will really nullify the contract?"

Clyde nodded and the way his chest inflated, I could tell he was proud that he'd brokered this deal. "Yep, because from the beginning, I had a clause in your contract that they'd have to match any offer that doubled their package or they'd have to let you go, so..." From his tone, I half-expected him to pop his collar.

Jeremy shook his head. "I can't believe you worked that."

"That's why you pay me the big bucks." Clyde laughed. "And it works out for me, too, because once we sign this deal and we get the sign-on bonus...."

Jeremy laughed and reached over to give Clyde dap. But after they shared their moment, Clyde once again, turned his attention to me. "Ginger, are you sure you're okay?"

I gave him a one-shoulder shrug and Jeremy released a heavy sigh. There was a long moment of silence as Clyde looked from me to Jeremy, then back to me.

"Look, I don't know what's going on here," he pointed his finger between the two of us, "but you guys have to fix this — whatever this is." He leaned forward on the table and all signs of his Christmas cheer was gone as his voice turned stern. "This deal is huge and Amazon isn't playing. Look how fast they got these contracts together. You never see anything in business move this quickly. These people are serious and we don't need any types of chinks in this armor. So whatever this is about, it's not bigger than this." He patted the contracts in front of him.

"I'm all the way on board," Jeremy said. He flashed an aggravated look at me. "We both are. Just give us the weekend, we'll read this over, work it out and we can all reconvene on Monday."

Clyde nodded his agreement. "Okay. That's all you two need. A night. A weekend. To either kiss and make up or go into that big ole sanctuary down the hall and take your issues to the altar."

If Clyde hadn't been Jeremy's best friend since we'd arrived in D.C., I would have told him to stay out of his business. But he'd been there for every part of our life when, as a member of New Kingdom, Clyde stood by Jeremy's side at our quick wedding because Jeremy knew no one else in D.C. who could stand with him. And Clyde had been by Jeremy's side ever since serving first as one of Jeremy's armor bearers, but very quickly moving to our agent when deals started coming in and we wanted to take advantage of Clyde's law degree.

Clyde grabbed his briefcase. "Let's get this done."

Jeremy stood with Clyde and I didn't budge.

Jeremy said, "Let me walk you out and make sure the door's locked since there's no one else here."

After a pause, Clyde said, "I'll see you later, Ginger."

"Bye," was all I could manage.

The moment Clyde followed Jeremy out, I leapt from the chair and ran into my office. I wished I'd already had my bags together to get out of here; I didn't want to be left alone with Jeremy.

But not even a minute passed before Jeremy was standing in my office's door. Why hadn't I packed up my stuff before?

Jeremy asked, "Do you want to tell me what's going on?"

I rolled my eyes and turned my attention back to sliding the folders I needed to take home with me for the weekend into my tote.

His voice stayed steady as he said, "You've been in a funk since I got back from Alabama. And I don't have any idea why. So do you want to stop acting like the kids and tell me what's going on?"

Raising an eyebrow, I raised my voice, too. "Acting like the kids?"

"Come on, Ginger." He threw his hands in the air. "You know what I'm talking about. Clyde just told us we have a contract that with bonuses could more than triple that eight million and will help secure the future of our grandchildren's grandchildren. Babe, you and I have talked about building generational wealth and a financial legacy. This is it, yet you sat there like you were watching a boring movie. All I'm asking is that you talk to me."

I folded my arms. "So you have no clue what's wrong?"

"How would I know what's wrong with you? If I had a clue, I wouldn't have asked you."

*Never show your full hand. Get your ducks in a row.*

My mother's words rang in my mind, but holding this in, not saying anything had been more than I could take—especially after my meeting with Sonya and Cecily. I'd been on an emotional roller coaster going back and forth, up and down, inside and out, between believing Jeremy had gotten a woman pregnant, then, believing he had not.

*Never show your full hand.*

My mother was right about this, the same way she'd been right with every piece of guidance she'd given to me. But I didn't have it in me to stay silent. My mother was a far better woman than me. So I looked Jeremy straight in his eyes when I asked, "Who is Katrina Brunson?"

And he looked straight into mine when he asked, "Who?" My husband stood there as stiff as a statue. Not a muscle on him twitched, he hardly even blinked.

But I was not about to be fooled. "You know, the woman who lives over in Southeast. The one who's mad at you because not only won't you return her calls, but she says you're treating her like a booty call and now, you're cheating on her."

I hadn't meant to say all of that. I hadn't meant to play that much of my hand.

But he still stood there, cool, beyond collected, not twitching, not blinking. "I don't know what you're talking about."

Slowly, I moved from around my desk, but I didn't dare get too close to him because I truly didn't want to catch a case. "You know what pisses me off the most," I said through clenched teeth. "How many times have you sat next to me on television with a straight face and talked about how God had given us a gift and that we couldn't provide the proper spiritual care if we didn't honor that gift? How many times have you sat next to me on TV while Katrina and her friends were watching and laughing at the joke of our marriage?"

He squinted, then shook his head as if he was confused. "So is this what's been bothering you?"

"Bothered?" I leaned back a little. "You think that's all I am is *bothered* when I hear that you are screwing some miscellaneous chick?"

"That's all you can be is bothered 'cause it's not true. I told you. I don't know any Katrina."

"I can't believe you're standing in God's house in the place where He's blessed you to be and you're telling me this lie."

"And that's one reason why you should realize I'm not lying," he said. "I wouldn't want to dishonor God, I wouldn't dishonor you, I wouldn't dishonor God's house."

Without thinking about it, I took a couple of steps back to get out of the way of the lightning that was about to smite him.

"Seriously, Ginger," he continued, "I wouldn't lie to you."

Now, I busted out laughing. I mean, I laughed so loud and for so long that all Jeremy could do was stand there and wait for me to get it together. It really took me about a minute to gather myself enough to ask him, "So you wouldn't lie to me?" But then, I stopped all laughter when I said, "What's so sad about this is you think I'm stupid." I paused. "I talked to Katrina and she told me everything!"

He paused. And for a moment, there it was. Just a little bit of a twitch of his eyebrow, just a little shift of his feet and in that instant, I was relieved. Maybe Jeremy still did have a soul.

Then, he said, "Wait, what does she look like?"

"Jeremy!" I shouted his name, which was something I never did. My parents had never raised their voices and I had followed their lead. But Jeremy was driving me to places I never thought I'd go. "Do. Not. Even. Try. To. Play. Me."

"Ohhhhh." He snapped his fingers as if he'd had a sudden recall. "I know who you're talking about. I didn't recognize the name Katrina. I call everyone by their last names." Then he paused. "But are you for real? You think there's something going on with me and her? She's someone who came by the church seeking counsel and you can ask Lizzy. She's sat in on every session."

So this woman had been to the church and I hadn't noticed?

"And so, what? You suddenly remember that? Now you know who I'm talking about?"

"Yeah, it took me a minute, but Ginger, you've got to know...." He took a step toward me. "I would never dishonor you...." He got closer. "In that way at all." He reached for me and I frowned, confused. Did this man really think he could hold me and kiss away my fury?

I took a step away from him. "Do not touch me."

He sighed and dropped his hands to his side. "You're being ridiculous. I don't care what she told you; you've been married to me. You know me."

"And I know what she told me, too."

"She's delusional," he said, raising his voice for the first time. "I don't like sharing people's issues, but you've left me no choice." He paused and his face became clouded with sadness, as if he was grieved by what he was about to say. Finally, he spoke, "She's a woman who's struggling with the death of her baby's father."

My eyes narrowed. It wasn't that I believed him, it was that I no longer completely believed Katrina. The truth was, I didn't know what to believe.

He continued, "If she said anything is going on, it's just in her mind. I can assure you of that," he said.

I wasn't sure if it was a straight lie or not, but I said nothing.

"So," a smile crept onto his face, "are we good?"

Again, I gave him nothing.

"Well, at least you're not screaming at me. That's something." His smile was wider now.

I folded my arms.

"Ginger, you've got to know how much I love you."

His tone was soaked with sincerity and these were words I did believe. I just wasn't sure anymore if our definitions of love were the same.

I grabbed my briefcase. "I want to get home to the children. I don't like keeping Carmen late on Fridays." I crossed the room, walking past him, not looking at him, saying nothing.

I'd told him more than I wanted to, but the thing was, I hadn't played my full hand. I'd said nothing about Sharonne, nothing about her pregnancy. My plan was to only go to him when I was locked and loaded. When there was no way he'd be able to deny it.

That is—*if* Sharonne were pregnant.

If what Sonya and Cecily told me turned out to be a lie, that would be a relief. I would still be faced with Katrina, though.

Inside my car, I dialed Dru once again and like these last two days, I got her voicemail. But then, my phone vibrated with a text notification:

*I'm in the middle of something. But I'll be home tomorrow.*

That was it. I picked up the phone to call her, but then I read her text again. Was she with Sharonne?

I couldn't take it, so I texted her that question.

Right away, she responded: *I can't talk. Explain later. Flight is in the morning. Early.*

Leaning back, I closed my eyes and released a howl, trying to rid my center of all the anxiety simmering inside of me. I'd have to wait until morning? What was going on? Why couldn't Dru just tell me?

Turning on the car's ignition, I rolled my car from the spot that said FIRST LADY and I prepared myself for a long night without sleep.

# Chapter Eighteen

When my cell phone rang and I saw Dru's name on the screen, my heart had already started racing before I could tap the 'Accept' button.

"Dru?" I asked as if I wasn't sure she was on the other end.

Her response: "Are you alone?"

"I am, I'm home," I said, her question not making me feel any better. "But Dru, what's going on? You've kept me waiting and I can't take it."

"I'm sorry, I'll explain it all, but I just landed. We're still on the plane, but as soon as I get off, I'll hop in an Uber and be at your place in about thirty."

"No," I said. "I'm alone now, but I don't know for how long. Jeremy took the kids to the driving range and he'll probably take them to get something to eat afterward. But I have no idea and I don't want us discussing this when he and the children come back."

"All right; where do you want to meet?"

"I'll jump in the car and pick you up, but Dru, tell me, is Sharonne pregnant?"

"Ginger, I know it's hard, but I don't want to talk about it over the phone."

"Damn it, Dru," I said, raising my voice once again. Something that had never been part of my life was becoming a habit. "Do you know how long I've been waiting? Just answer that question. Is she pregnant?"

"I'll be outside the United terminal waiting." And then, she clicked off the phone. My best friend had just hung up in my face. What in the world was this about?

I wanted to call her back, but that would just waste too much time. I'd been dressed and waiting, so all I had to do was grab my purse and jet down the steps. I set the house alarm before I trotted into the garage. My plan was to set a speed record with how many minutes I could shave off of this normally twenty-minute ride to Reagan National Airport. I had to get there before my head exploded from all of my anxiety. Why wouldn't Dru tell me whether or not Sharonne was pregnant? There had to be only one reason why she didn't want to tell me over the phone: It was not good news.

Tears were already filling my eyes when I spotted Dru thirteen minutes later standing on the edge of the curb in front of Terminal 2. I eased my car to a stop a few feet away from her.

I held my breath as she strolled to me, searching her face for any signs of what she was about to say. Why wasn't she running to the car? Didn't she realize the damage that had been done to my heart because I hadn't heard from her in these past few days?

"Hey," she said, dropping into the passenger's seat. "I know you're mad that I hung up on you," she started before I could go in on her, "but you'll understand if you give me a chance to explain."

"Is she pregnant, Dru?" I asked, knowing that I wouldn't be able to breathe if she didn't answer my question—one way or the other.

When Dru shook her head and said, "No," all kinds of relief swept over me.

Tears of joy seeped from my eyes. "Thank you, Father," I shouted, but when I reached over to hug Dru, her expression did not match the celebration I wanted to have in this car. "What?"

"She's not pregnant because she already had the baby. Her baby's nine months old."

My victory had been right there in my hands and Drew had just snatched it away. Now, I cried for a different reason.

She said, "That's what I didn't want to tell you over the phone. Sharonne has a baby. A boy."

"Oh, my God." I dropped my head onto the steering wheel. "Is it Jeremy's?"

She shrugged. "I don't know, but let me tell you she sure knows a lot about the two of you."

"Oh, my God."

"That's why I didn't want to talk to you while I was down there. I hooked up with Sharonne pretty quickly. Folks who don't go far from home still hang out in the same places with the same people. So she and I ran into each other by," Dru put her hands and made air quotes, "accident on Thursday when I went to the mall."

"Do I want to hear this story?"

She was washed in sadness when she shook her head. "No, but you have to."

My heart was broken already, I figured. So, I motioned for Dru to wait as I shifted the car back into drive and maneuvered around to the cell phone lot. When Dru started this story, I didn't want to be interrupted by vigilant cops who didn't allow cars to stop for longer than thirty seconds.

I'd barely rolled my car into the last spot before Dru began, "So Sharonne is a manager at the Coach store in the mall and I just happened to wander in there. She recognized me right away, but then she got a little suspicious and asked me if I worked for you."

"What?" I leaned back to get a better view of Dru. "She knew that?"

"Yeah." Dru kind of nodded and then shook her head at the same time. "I don't know if she knew it from our circle or from Jeremy. But when she kinda shut down after I told her that I did work for you, I had to come up with a new game plan. So I told her that I worked for you once, but I no longer worked for you 'cause you were jealous, out of control, and over the top."

When I raised my eyebrows, Dru shrugged. "Look, I had to come up with something. I was trying to be her new best friend, if only for a couple of days. I walked into that store already knowing from a couple of our friends that she'd had a baby and if I wanted to get more information out of her, she was going to have to trust me."

"Because you wanted to see her baby."

"Yup. That's why I made up all kinds of lies about you and she couldn't get enough. We only had a chance to chat for a couple of minutes because she was at work, but I'd given her so much juice about you with promises of more to come that I wasn't surprised when she invited me to come to her place after she got off from work."

There was only one thing on my mind. "Did you see the baby?" I wasn't sure why I asked that question; maybe, just to be sure there was a child. Sonya and Cecily had been wrong—so maybe Dru's friends had been wrong, too.

She nodded. "I did. I pretended I was shocked and told her I didn't know she was married. She told me she wasn't, but her baby's father was."

I groaned. "Jeremy."

"She didn't say." Dru shook her head. "She never said it was Jeremy, and I'm not sure why since she knew that I knew you. I tried my best to get her to talk about him; I even hung out with her all day yesterday since Friday was her day off. I thought she would have said something, but while she talked about how she planned to be with the baby's father and how he was going to leave his wife for her...."

"I can't believe this," I whispered.

"I didn't push," Dru said, "for two reasons. One because I wasn't sure whether or not she was trying to play me and the second is I want to keep this connection to her open, just in case."

"So, that's it?" I closed my eyes. This was not getting any better. "You didn't find out if Jeremy was her kid's father?" I sighed. "Your trip was a total waste."

"No, it wasn't because we know a couple of things now. We know she's not pregnant, we know she already has a child...."

"Who may or may not belong to Jeremy."

"That's true, but we're going to find out."

I shook my head. "I don't think I can take it, Dru. I'm already on the edge. I can't wait until you go back to New Orleans to try to get more information. I just can't."

"You don't have to wait." When she reached into her purse, I frowned. When she pulled out a baggie, my eyes widened. "I got her baby's pacifier and his brush."

"Oh, my goodness," I said, slipping the baggie from her fingers. "How?"

"I told you I hung out with her all day yesterday. Whew." Dru leaned back in the seat like the thought of yesterday exhausted her. "When she'd asked me if I wanted to hang out, I thought she would be taking her son to the park or something. But no, that chick had me in her car all day long as she ran errands. And she got out of the car one too many times leaving me alone with her baby and the diaper bag. That's when I came up with the idea to...."

"Steal the child's pacifier?"

She nodded as if what she'd done was no big deal. "I took the pacifier and the brush because I wasn't sure which would work better for DNA. I've never done this Maury Povich stuff before, but I kinda like it."

"I can't believe you did this," I said, looking down at the bag.

"Look, desperate times call for desperate measures. She wasn't giving up any information about the father and truthfully, even if she'd said it was Jeremy, this is what you'd need. You have to have a DNA test done so that you can know for sure. If he's not the father, this will give you peace. And if he is, you need to go to him with more proof than just Sharonne's word.

"Locked and loaded," I said.

"Yeah, that's one way to put it."

As I sat staring at the baggie, I couldn't believe my life had come to this. First sitting in front of the house of a woman who might have been my husband's jump off and now, I was holding a baggie with DNA stolen from a baby who may or may not belong to Jeremy. I hadn't been raised this way, but I guess that wasn't any kind of insurance policy from having to deal with this kind of reality television drama.

Dru gently took the bag from my hands, as if she knew I was in a fragile state. "We have to do this, Ginger. You need to know definitively one way or the other. You need to know in order to make any decision. Because honestly, if it's just Katrina, then...."

"You think I should stay and work it out," I said before she could finish.

She nodded. "But this, a baby...."

"Changes the game," I interrupted her again.

"It does, though I'm not saying that means you should leave."

"Are you kidding me? My husband fathers a child out of wedlock and I'm supposed to stay? You know who you sound like, right?"

Dru shook her head. "No, I don't sound anything like Sonya, Cecily, or the rest of them biddies. All I'm saying is that I'm not going to be the one to tell you what to do either way. I'll be here to discuss it and pray with you, but...."

"It's all on me."

She nodded, then held up the baggy. "I'm going to drive this over to Silver Spring. I already did the research and there's a lab there that can get results in forty-eight hours. They're open today, but only until one." We both glanced at the clock; we still had a little more than three hours. "But we'll be able to find out if Jeremy is the daddy, okay?"

Her question made my heart ache in all kinds of way. I was Ginger Williams, First Lady of New Kingdom Temple, one of the largest, arguably the most influential predominantly African American churches in the country's Capitol. What in the world was I doing here?

"Ginger?" Dru called my name taking me out of my descent into the abyss. "We just need one more thing."

What was Dru talking about? What else could she possibly need from me when she'd already taken my heart.

She said, "We're going to need Jeremy's DNA," she explained.

Of course, I hadn't thought of that, but I hadn't thought of much. I nodded, then, turned on the car's ignition.

"Okay," I said. "Let's go to my house. Jeremy's DNA is all over the place." That was my attempt at humor, but all I wanted to do was cry. "And then," I continued, "I'll drive you to the clinic."

"No," Dru shook her head. "You don't have to do that. I'll handle this, Ginger. I got you."

"I know you do and I thank you for that. But I want to make sure this gets there myself. I don't have to go inside the clinic with you; it's a better idea that you handle it because I don't want anyone to recognize me. But you and I will deliver this to the clinic and then, you and I will pick it up. Because like you said, when I go to Jeremy, if he is this baby's father, there will be no way for him to deny that it was a mistake, that the envelope was tampered with, that someone got something mixed up; he won't be able to say anything. If we find out that Jeremy Williams is the father, all of us are going to know this for sure."

Dru nodded as if she understood. She laid her hand on my arm, I knew to give me comfort. "It's going to be okay. No matter which way this turns out, I got you, okay?"

I leaned over to hug my friend and then, I prayed that all of this would be as easy as she believed.

When we broke our embrace, I looked into Dru's eyes, wanting to ask her the final question. "What's the baby's name?"

This was something I'd been thinking about. Women like Sharonne had a pattern when it came to naming their children after being impregnated by a man who belonged to someone else. I held my breath because if Sharonne had named her son....

"Andre," Dru said. "Her baby's name is Andre."

I breathed, buckling with a little bit of relief.

"But I don't know what last name she gave to him."

"That's all right." I turned my attention back to the car. His name is *not* Jeremy." And for a reason that I really couldn't explain, that gave me a little bit of hope.

# CHAPTER NINETEEN

"Mommy, Auntie Jada said she's going to do my nails," Jasmine shrieked.

The way my daughter jumped up and down, her pigtails flying in the air, brought a smile to my face. For the first time since this drama began, I'd spent a morning smiling. It was because of Jada. My sister had just popped up in church this morning. Right when the praise and worship team made their way behind the altar, my sister had stepped in front of the pew and stood next to me.

I hadn't seen her at first. Didn't even know she was there until I heard her voice:

*"I have a meeting in Hampton tomorrow, so I figured, I'd spend the day and the night with my favorite pastor and his wife."*

I'd turned to her with a screech and a hug, holding her in an embrace so tight, I sent her intuition into high alert. She'd stepped back from me with a frown on her face and questions in her eyes, but before she could ask one question, the praise and worship team began singing.

I raised my hands to the Lord giving Him praise for so many things in that moment.

Since that time, I hadn't been alone. At least not long enough for Jada to corner, then question me. And really, she hadn't been alone either; Jasmine had been her shadow from the moment she saw her auntie once church was out.

"So Mommy, can Auntie Jada do it? Can she paint my nails?"

I looked up at my sister as she joined me at the kitchen table. "As long as it's a neutral color, it's fine."

"Yay!" Jasmine sang, waving her hands in the air, her pigtails still bouncing. "I want hot pink, Auntie Jada."

"All right. Let me see what I have in my bag."

"Wait." I held up my hand, looking at Jasmine first, and then turning to Jada. "Hot pink is not neutral."

"Ugh!" Jada groaned and then turned to Jasmine. "Your mother is so 1960."

My five-year-old squeezed her face into a frown. "What does that mean?"

"It means Mom's old," Jayden said as he strolled into the kitchen, opened the refrigerator, and grabbed a small bottle of orange juice.

But before he could make his way out of the kitchen, I stopped him. "Hold up." Jayden spun around. "Since when do you just walk in here and grab something out of the refrigerator without asking me? Did you get a job that I didn't hear about?"

Jasmine giggled. "Mommy, Jayden can't get a job. He's only seven," she told me as if she seriously believed I needed that reminder.

"Well, he needs to start acting like he's seven."

I gave him a little side-eye and Jayden said, "Mom, can I have this juice, please?"

I waited a beat before I nodded. As he ran out of the room, Jada shouted out to him, "Don't go too far, Jayden. I'm gonna do your nails next." That sent Jasmine into a fit of giggles.

Jada set out a little manicure set she carried in her purse, just as I heard the garage door open. This was going to be interesting—interacting with Jeremy while Jada was here.

I was so glad for her presence; she was the distraction I needed to get through one day of my two-day wait for the paternity results. Since today was Sunday, Dru had told me the results would be in on Tuesday. So I truly thanked God for Jada today because waiting tomorrow was going to be brutal.

But while she was a great diversion, she also presented me with a dilemma. How was I going to hide everything from her? I really didn't want to talk to Jada about Jeremy; she loved him. And until I knew everything for sure, there was no need to damage their relationship by telling her about his affair and the possible pregnancy. No, I had to find some way to keep this all from her—for now.

When the door opened, Jasmine slipped from the chair. "Daddy's home," she sang and ran into her father's arms. He scooped her into the air. "Daddy, Auntie Jada is here."

"I know," he said. "I already saw her in church, remember?"

"Oh, yeah," Jasmine said before she climbed back into the chair to prepare for her manicure.

Jeremy kissed my cheek and because Jasmine was sitting inches from me and because my sister's eyes were on me, I didn't slap his face away. Then, he turned to Jada. "So what's up, my favorite sister-in-love?" He pulled her into a one arm hug.

"Just you. But uh...Lauren said you say the same thing to her."

He laughed. "I admit to nothing."

I wondered if he'd said that on purpose or had that truth come from his soul.

Jada playfully pushed his shoulder. "Just like a man," she kidded him without knowing she was speaking his truth. "So, how are things going, Rev?"

He glanced at me and my mouth opened wide when he said, "Not well, but maybe you can talk to your sister about that."

I couldn't believe he was putting our business out there on Front Street like that. He knew I didn't believe him about Katrina; did he really want me talking to my sister about that?

And why would he even say that in front of Jasmine, who was now looking at the three of us with nothing but curiosity in her eyes.

Jada's eyes went from Jeremy to me, then back to my husband. "Uh..."

"He's just kidding," I said with a little laugh to Jada, though those words were for my daughter's ears. "We're fine. You know Jeremy's a jokester."

"Yeah." Jasmine giggled. "Daddy's a jokester."

Jeremy smirked, then walked over, leaned in and kissed my cheek once again. But this time, his kiss had an accompanying message. "We're not fine," he said, his volume revealing that his words were meant for my ears only. "But we will be because I will never give up on you, I'll never give up on us. No matter what I have to do." Standing up straight he said, "So uh, are you taking Jasmine back to the church for the children's choir anniversary rehearsal, or do you want me to do it?"

"Oh!" I tapped the heel of my hand on my forehead. "I'd forgotten all about that," I said, while I wondered about Jeremy's words. I wasn't sure if what he'd said was meant as a promise or a threat.

"Why don't you do it?" Jada said to Jeremy. "It'll give me a chance to have some time with my sister."

Before I could protest, Jeremy said, "That sounds great to me. Come on, Munchkin."

"What about my nails?" Jasmine asked, looking between her father and her aunt.

"We'll do them later," Jada told her. "I promise. You go on with your dad to church so you can sing like the beautiful angel you are."

Jasmine's face brightened. "Mommy said I'm an angel, too."

244 | Gizelle Bryant

Jeremy held out his hand to our daughter. "So let's go get your sneakers and a sweater and then we'll head back to New Kingdom."

With a hop from her chair, Jasmine slid her hand into his. She skipped beside Jeremy, all was well in her world. The sight of my husband with our children had always been one that filled my heart each time with even more love for him. He was a good father, but what was going to happen now? What would our lives look like after Tuesday? Would the children and I even be here for our anniversary?

"All right, it's time to get to talking."

Almost that quickly, I'd forgotten my sister was here. And when I turned around, by her stare I knew I was in for quite an interrogation. But because I had hopes of stalling and maybe even changing the conversation altogether, I said, "Talking about what?"

She wagged her finger in front of my face. "Don't what me," she said. "Jeremy can fake the funk, even though this time, he didn't even try. But you? You can't fake a thing. First of all, if I wasn't here, I'm sure a slap may have been the answer to his kiss."

"You're so violent," I said.

"And next, you never forget anything on your children's schedule. How would you forget Jasmine had practice unless there is something seriously on your mind? So talk." Then, after a pause, she said, "Wait. Is this about those First Ladies? Are they still getting to you?"

I shook my head. "I wish to God they were my problem."
Just as I said that, Jasmine skipped back into the room.
She gave me a hug and then, while she went to hug Jada,
Jeremy ambushed me with another kiss, this time on my lips.
It was a gentle kiss, filled with his kind of love.

When both of us were sure Jasmine and Jeremy were out
of the house, Jada asked, "So what is your problem with that
fine man? I mean, I'm not even attracted to dudes, but anyone
with eyes can see Jeremy Williams got it going on in all kinds
of ways."

Her tone sounded like she thought whatever the problem
was, it was my fault. She needed to know the truth, so I said,
"I just have one little problem with him—he's cheating on
me."

Jada's lips snapped shut. Then, a moment later, she
whispered, "No. Way."

I nodded and matched her volume, not wanting Jayden
to overhear anything, though that was hardly possible with
the way he blasted his TV in his room. I said, "I confronted
the woman."

"Get out."

It wasn't a story that I wanted to repeat, but as Jada sat
on the edge of the chair, I told her about Katrina Brunson.
"But it gets worse," I said, when I got to the end of that story.

Jada must've heard the tears in my voice because she
scooted her chair closer, held my hand and I continued, "I
think he may have gotten someone pregnant."

"What?" she screamed.

"Keep your voice down. Remember, Jayden."

"No f'ing way," she whispered. "Who? Where she at?"

"Someone you know."

Her mouth was as wide as her eyes.

"Not directly," I said and then reminded her of our lunch and the mystery of that staring woman. I told her everything, from the pregnancy story that came from Sonya and Cecily to the baby reality that Dru had uncovered. "But I haven't said a word to Jeremy about this part."

"Why not?" And before I answered, she held up her hand and said, "Wait. Mom and her pearls of wisdom."

I nodded. "Mom was right about this one. I'm glad I still have cards that Jeremy hasn't seen. I don't want to give him time to concoct a story. I just want the truth so that I can do what I have to do. And it's not going to be an easy decision to make."

"I know." She released my hand and leaned back in her chair. "Ten years of marriage, two amazing children...."

"And eight million dollars on the table."

"Wait! What?" she whispered as if she didn't understand.

I filled her in on the Amazon deal and all she did was shake her head. "So there is so much at stake," I told her.

"This is crazy," Jada said. "So what're you going to do? What're you going to do if it's true? If he really is Andre's father?"

"That, my dear sister, is the ten years, two children, eight million dollar question."

"Do you think you can walk away from all of that?"

I shook my head. "It would be hard, but here's the thing. I know that everything I do is not just about me. My children are watching. And what would me staying say to Jasmine?"

Jada shook her head as if she vehemently disagreed with me. "No, Jasmine is too young to understand. You don't have to worry about her."

"That's not true. I believe children are always watching. Did you notice Jasmine when Jeremy came in here and told you that things were not well?"

The way my sister frowned, I reminded her how Jasmine had watched and heard every word we'd said, and then had even repeated that Jeremy was a jokester.

"She doesn't even know what a jokester is," I said. "But she watches our words, she watches our body language and I don't want my children to grow up in a tense home." I shook my head. "Besides, one day Jasmine will grow up and if Jeremy is Andre's father, she'll ask me why I stayed. I'd better have a good reason for her if I decide to do that."

Jada nodded. "And you'll have to have an equally good reason for leaving."

"I agree," I said and then, I nodded, wanting my sister to know that I understood her point. "So, a lot of my decision will be about my children. I'm raising them consciously, knowing that every word I speak, every decision I make, every reaction I have impacts them, even now, as young as they are. But this is what I know also—breaking vows and *disrespecting* me is *not* okay. True or not, Jeremy hasn't said one word to me about this. All I get are lies on top of lies on top of lies and that speaks to his character. So that is part of my decision, too."

She nodded. "That is so true." A beat and then, "You're really a good mother."

"Thanks."

"And you know what? Jeremy is a good father." She paused, then with a sideward glance, she said, "And he's a good man."

My eyebrows stretched to the top of my forehead. "Wow, I didn't expect this."

She shrugged.

"One of the reasons why I didn't want to tell you what was going on was because I didn't want to affect your relationship with Jeremy."

She waved her hand. "I've been involved in enough relationships to understand their dysfunction. And this is what I know—no one is as bad as the worst thing they've ever done. If Jeremy is the father, that will be the worst thing. But on the ledger of his life," she paused, "he's done so many good things. That's the problem with people sometimes. Folks allow one bad thing to wipe out a slate that covers ten thousand good things."

Resting my elbows on the glass table, I folded my hands and rested my chin on them. My sister had said more than a mouthful.

She added, "I feel sorry for pastors."

"Why?" I asked.

"Because they're held to a higher standard."

"Well," I shrugged, "that's biblical."

"I know. But it seems like those men walk around with a target on their backs. I remember how it was for Daddy. Man, every Sunday temptation was being thrown his way. Every time we went out, there was some woman willing to do something for Mommy's man. It was just crazy."

My sisters and I didn't talk about that time of our lives very much, but it did surprise me how observant Jada was even at that age. I said, "Yeah, but Daddy said no to all of that. He didn't fall."

"We don't know that for sure, Ginger." She shook her head slowly.

I squinted at her implication.

She held up her hands as if she was trying to hold off the attack that she knew was coming. "I'm not saying he did, I'm just saying we don't know. And let's say he didn't fall to that kind of sexual temptation; we do know he fell to something. That's biblical. Because every single one of us sins and falls short."

I let her words settle before I asked, "So are you saying...if Jeremy's the father of Sharonne's son, I should forgive him?"

"Well, you're gonna have to forgive him no matter what. Daddy taught us that. The whole Christian doctrine is built on forgiveness, so I don't understand folks who go to church every Sunday talking about, 'you gonna have to give me time to speak to him again after what he did to me'." Jada sucked her teeth. "I just don't understand it. Look." The legs of her chair scraped against the tiles on the kitchen's floor as she turned her chair to face me. Taking both of my hands into hers, she said, "I just want you to remember that Jeremy is a man who is preaching the word of God. So Satan's job is to bring Jeremy Williams down. Satan's job is to kill and destroy this man of God."

I sighed. "You know, I hate when people bring up Satan. It feels like an excuse. Satan didn't cheat, Jeremy did."

"I know that, but hear me out. Now, Jeremy may have allowed the devil in and Jeremy may have cheated, but I just want you to consider this is not just about a man who cheated on his wife. This is about a man of God who is being targeted for destruction."

I stared at my sister for a moment. We'd all gone through so much being a pastor's kids. But Jada had gone through the most. Our father had already passed away when Jada came out, but all of us still worshipped at New Faith Missionary Baptist Church, the church that my father had built. But once news of her being gay spread within the church, men and women who'd worked with our parents, men and women who'd watched us grow up, men and women who'd given us hugs every Sunday, gifts at Christmas, and sincere condolences when our father died, shunned Jada. The hate was enough to drive our mother out of D.C. and Jada out of the church forever.

"What?" Jada asked. "Why are you looking at me like that?"

I shrugged. "It's just that...."

"You're surprised that I'm dropping all this Christian wisdom?" She grinned.

And I laughed, grateful for the weight she'd taken off this conversation. "Yeah, I'm a little surprised."

"Listen, I know how to separate God's word from God's people. 'Cause God's word is always right, but His people... not so much. My not wanting to go to church is about not wanting to be around people. But God...I thank Him that He's everywhere."

"Whew!" I held up my right hand. "I feel like I just got a Sunday sermon."

"You already had a pretty good one with that man you married."

I hesitated—the man I married. "Yeah," I said, and even I could hear the sadness in my voice.

Jada leaned over and hugged me. "I'm so sorry you're going through this, but I know one thing, you're a strong woman and no matter what you decide, you won't be broken."

# Chapter Twenty

This morning, when I got out of bed, I weighed my options. How did I want to spend this day of waiting? I could have easily stayed home, but I'd only end up pacing the halls and watching the clock. I'd even thought about booking the day at the spa, but that would be a waste of a good hot stone massage.

So after Carmen got the kids off to camp and after a leisurely breakfast of toast and coffee with Jada, I'd hugged my sister goodbye, listened to her admonishment that I should not worry, then watched her drive off before I'd made my way here, to New Kingdom, where it would take me less than a minute to walk the few hundred feet from my office to the altar.

But as I sat at my desk, these minutes were ticking by exactly the way I feared—so slowly. And with each tick of the clock, another thought tried to take over me, making me question my future even more.

Swiveling my chair toward the window, I gazed out at my view of the front of our church. It was Monday morning, so there were no cars, just mine. Mondays were our Saturdays; not even Jeremy came to the church. This morning, my husband had risen before the sun even breeched the horizon, on his way to his weekly golf foursome with three other pastors. That was how he spent this free day in the spring and summer. In the winter, he'd play chess, all of it his way of decompressing from the blessing of his spiritual responsibilities and the curse that was the weight that came with all of that.

So I was alone, though I expected Lizzy to show up at any time; she used these days to catch up on paperwork without interruptions from the phone or staff. Dru also sometimes came in on these light days, but when she'd called this morning to review my calendar, she'd told me she had a few errands to catch up on.

So what was I going to do? How was I supposed to spend this time as I waited for still another twenty-four hours for the results that would tell me what I knew my husband never would—the truth.

"Oh, God," I whispered as I lowered my head. I needed to pray, needed to ask God for patience and peace as I waited. But just as I rose to take my cares into the sanctuary, the bell rang from the side door that led to our offices.

That made me frown. The only person I was expecting was Lizzy and she had her key. Moving from my office to the hallway and to the security panel right beside the door, I hit the button to turn on the outside camera. Our church was in a changing neighborhood, near R and 13th Streets in the Northwest section of the district. Still, we were a church, as vulnerable as anyone with the way the world and guns were set up today.

As the camera scanned the area and settled on the heads of the two women, I sighed. My first instinct was to pretend no one was home. But when she heard the whir of the camera, Sonya looked up and wiggled her fingers in a wave. Plus, the two would've walked past my car to get to the door. I was stuck.

So I hit the buzzer, and watched the door open before Sonya and Cecily stepped inside.

"Good morning, First Lady Ginger," they said in unison as if their greeting had been rehearsed.

My eyes narrowed. What was this about? They'd never addressed me this way. "Good morning," I said, making no move to invite them further into the church. "I wasn't expecting you ladies."

"Oh, we know that," Sonya said. "But Cecily and I were talking last night and we wanted to check on you."

"Okay...I'm fine. Check complete." I stopped there, wanting them to get the hint, knowing they wouldn't.

"Ginger, honey, would you mind if we had a word with you in your office?" Sonya asked.

There were only two reasons why this wish would be granted. One was because it was Sonya, and not Cecily asking.

And the second—I'd been raised by Valencia and Theodore Allen. I'd been raised right.

So, with a smile I didn't feel, I pivoted and led them down the hall, the sound of their footsteps marching on the parquet floor behind me. Inside my office, I glanced first at the loveseat and two chairs on the far end of the room, the place where I often had meetings. But I kept moving, offering instead, the less comfortable chairs in front of my desk to Sonya and Cecily.

Once they were settled, I planted my arms on the desk as if I were preparing to speak at a formal meeting. "So ladies, how can I help you?"

"That's the question we have for you," Cecily said as she peered over her ivy-green diamond studded glasses. Today's eyepiece was the exact shade of the two-piece sleeveless pantsuit Cecily wore. She inched up a bit, from her seat and leaned across the desk, reaching for my hand.

I didn't move and after several moments, Cecily cleared her throat, then dropped her hand to her lap and her butt back in the seat. Still, she said, "I wasn't sure you understood the other day when we told you we were family."

"No, I understood," I said, "I speak perfect English."

Cecily's smile faded, and now, Sonya leaned forward, though she didn't reach for me. "We know it can't be easy for you with Jeremy's baby on the way."

I stayed silent, having no intention of telling them they were just two gossiping biddies with wrong information.

"But here's the thing," Sonya picked up where Cecily left off and I wondered if these two practiced with each other the way Jeremy and I did before an interview.

When Cecily nodded at Sonya, my wonder turned to certainty.

"You'll be fine, Ginger. You won't be the first woman in the middle of something like this and unless Jesus plans to return at this moment, you unfortunately won't be the last. The key is to get on top of it before it gets on top of you. Get ahead of it before it becomes news."

"Isn't it news already?" I asked, matter-of-factly. "I mean, Sonya, you heard it from someone and Cecily, once you heard it, you told it, I'm sure. You're the best news reporter in the business."

Cecily narrowed her eyes, pursed her lips and for the first time since they'd entered my office, I smiled. I'd managed to shut Cecily up, but Sonya would not be deterred.

"We know you're angry, Ginger and we understand that. But truly, we're here to help. You cannot let too much time get past you on this. It's just a matter of how you make it go away."

I raised an eyebrow. "Uh, no. It's a matter of how I go away."

Sonya and Cecily did that exchanging-glance thing again. It was Cecily who said, "Are you serious?" with so much attitude, I wondered why she was taking this so seriously.

"I can't stay with Jeremy if he has a baby outside of our marriage."

Cecily wiggled her hips to the edge of her seat but before she could say anything, Sonya touched her arm and she spoke. "Are you hearing what you're saying, Ginger?"

"Not only am I hearing it, but I thought about it before I said it. I'm sorry, Sonya. I know how you feel about this; I was there when you told Rena she had to stay after she had proof of her husband's infidelity. But if that's what one has to do as a First Lady, then I'm not cut out for the job."

"You're more than cut out for this, Ginger," she said. It was the first time that she'd spoke to me with such sternness. "You helped build this church." Her arm swooped through the air like she was Vanna White. "Even Reverend Williams gives you accolades whenever he speaks. He always says that New Kingdom Temple wouldn't have happened without you."

"And he's right." I nodded. "We built this church together."

"So then explain to me why you would want to leave all that you've built because some woman, and I'm using that term loosely, on the side got pregnant?"

I didn't really need to answer Sonya. Because if she had just repeated the question, she would have had her answer. I said, "You know, Sonya, I really don't feel comfortable talking about my personal business with you." I paused, looking at both of them. "But how you start is how you finish in life and since this all started with what you told me, I have to finish it because this is the last conversation I will have about my husband and my business with you." I paused long enough for the two of them to glance at each other again.

I continued, "I don't know yet what I'm going to do because I haven't yet found out everything that I need to know, but it would be hard for me to see a way where I would stay with Jeremy if I found out that he fathered a child outside of our marriage. And not only because that would be blatantly disrespectful to me, but to our children as well. And what would I say to my daughter one day? How would I tell her that I want her to be with a man who respects her if I stayed with a man who didn't respect me?"

"Jeremy hopping into bed with a woman has nothing to do with respect. Trust me. But what we're saying is that it just doesn't make any sense that you would risk all that you've built...."

"I didn't risk anything." I pressed my hand against my chest. "I never stepped out on my husband. Never have, never would. I took those vows seriously."

"I'm talking about you just walking away from all of this. If you were to leave, it would cause quite a scandal in the DMV."

"And beyond, really," Cecily jumped in as if she'd been itching to get back into this fight. "You know the African American religious community may be spread out over this country, but what happens to one, affects us all. If a pastor steps down under suspicious circumstances, it shines a bad light on all pastors. If a First Lady leaves her husband, again, it shines a bad light on all pastors because obviously, the pastor must have done something wrong." She shook her head. "This is bigger than you, First Lady. There are so many others that you must consider in this situation."

"Nope," I said in a tone that I knew would put them more on edge. But it was because I was so pissed. Who did they think they were to come into my office and make demands on my life? "The only people I'm considering in this matter are me, Jasmine and Jayden. Not even Jeremy counts in this situation. This is all about me and my children."

"And I'm telling you it can't just be about that." Cecily slammed her palm on my desk and I was just a little too happy when she flinched. "That's the most selfish thing I've ever heard."

"I'm sure it's not. I'm sure you've heard other things that are truly selfish." I sighed and shook my head at the same time. "Ladies, I don't know what else to tell you. I don't have another way of saying this." I stood up, but neither Sonya nor Cecily followed. "But I thank you for all of your concern, and now, I have so much work to do."

"And we have work to do, as well," Sonya said. "We are the black church trying to make a difference in this world for our people. On the First Ladies Council, we've done so many things, but much of what we do depends on outside donations and financing."

I folded my arms and tilted my head. "What does that have to do with what's going on with me and Jeremy?"

"This is what you don't understand. It is all intertwined." She clasped her hands together. "We are all connected. If this were to get out, if New Kingdom Temple were to fall because of you...."

Because of me? Me? I did nothing wrong! I held up my hand, stopping her. "I doubt if that would happen." It took everything in me not to roll my eyes.

"Don't underestimate your power or the force of this kind of scandal. There's a church not too far from here who lost seventy percent of their membership behind an embezzlement scandal."

"Exactly!" Cecily said, sounding like she was cheering Sonya on. "And there's a church in Los Angeles that split right in half after their pastor had a scandal similar to this."

Sonya picked up the tag-team. "And both of these examples were rising churches, much like New Kingdom. Your membership roll is ten thousand today, but with all the deals you have on the table...." When I frowned, Sonya added quickly, "Jeremy confides in Charles about a lot. My husband is a sort of mentor to him, you know that. I know what's on the table for you. I know what you'd be walking away from. But the bottom line is, we would all lose because of you. The First Ladies Council has a reputation to uphold and in the 22 years since this council started, only one of us has filed for divorce. And she did it very quietly...."

"And she came to regret it," Cecily said. "Within a month she was asking herself what had she done. She lost everything. Yes, she got some money at first through the divorce, but her husband fought her all the way, leaving her in the end with virtually nothing. All because she couldn't find it in her heart to forgive her husband for a little indiscretion."

*A little indiscretion?* Is that what they thought this was? These women made Stepford wives look like a light-hearted show on the Comedy channel.

Sonya nodded as if she was fine with Cecily's words. "The bottom line is this, Ginger, because of your stature, you leaving Jeremy could ruin everything and just cannot happen."

"With all due respect, First Lady Sonya, you cannot tell me what to do in my marriage or in my life. That's the real bottom line. And that's my final word."

This time, after Sonya and Cecily exchanged glances, Sonya nodded and they both stood. Wordlessly, they grabbed their purses and turned toward my door.

But right before they crossed the threshold, Sonya turned back. "I hope you'll give serious consideration to our words. You cannot even think about getting a divorce. You cannot leave your husband because if you do...I'm afraid you will regret it. And that's not a threat, that's a promise."

My eyes narrowed as I watched them walk through my door and then out of my sight.

Still, I stayed in place for a moment, not believing their audacity. It was all about the pastoral community, something I didn't know until this moment. They had no cares about the wives and how we were affected by all of this.

Shaking my head, I strolled into the hallway, wanting to make sure the door was locked behind the First Ladies. But when I was just a few feet away, the door opened suddenly, shocking me.

"Oh, my God!"

"What?" Dru said.

"You scared me. I was just coming out here to make sure the door was locked."

"Yeah, I just saw those ladies leaving. What did they want?"

"They told me I had to stay married to Jeremy no matter what or else I'd bring down the whole black church religious community." I motioned with my hands to make my point.

"Lies! Did they say that?"

"Practically. Seriously, Dru," I said, turning back to my office. "I just cannot wait for this to be over tomorrow. I don't even know how I'm going to sleep tonight. The wait is killing me when all I want to do is move forward one way or the other."

"Well then," Dru said over my shoulder. "Let's just go ahead and move forward."

It took a moment for me to understand her words, but still when I did, I was confused. Pivoting to face her, I said, "What are you...."

Dru stood behind me, holding up a manila envelope. "One way or the other."

I just stood there staring at the envelope, knowing already what was inside and Dru just stood there staring at me.

It felt like we were having a face-off that had lasted for at least a day. I just couldn't get my feet, or any part of me for that matter, to move. Just couldn't take the few steps to Dru, even though she held her hand out, ready to pass the envelope to me.

Finally, I spoke my truth in this moment. "I'm afraid."

She nodded, she swallowed. "I know you are."

Then, I wondered how had she passed that lump that had been in her throat to me? Still, I was able to squeak out, "Have you looked at the results?"

"Of course not," she said in a tone that made me think I'd asked a stupid question.

"How did you get them?"

"I'd asked for a rush, but I wasn't sure if I would really get them today. I didn't want to get your hopes up...or down depending on what's in here." She waved the envelope.

"So this was the errand you had to run?"

She nodded. "But I don't want to stand here and have small talk with you."

I bit the corner of my lip, almost trying to draw blood. "I'm only doing this because I'm afraid. I know I said that already, but I wanted to make sure you heard me."

"I did and I understand. But this," she waved the envelope again, "is what you need."

Staring at Dru for just a moment more, I turned away from her, and returned to the chair where just a while ago, I'd faced off with the Real First Ladies of D.C. I had to sit so that my heart could start beating again. Dru did the same, sitting across from me. And then, she leaned forward, placing the envelope in the center of my desk.

My eyes stayed on the packet that held not only the truth, but my future.

"What do you think is inside?" I asked.

"The results," Dru said, even though she knew what I meant. "We don't have to guess. We don't have to wait any longer." She paused. "You said you didn't want to wait anymore."

"I don't. But I'm scared."

"Okay," her voice was slow, soothing. She spoke to me in the same tone she used for Jasmine, "so let's do this. Let's talk this out. What are you afraid of?"

That was a good question, but it was difficult to articulate. Because there was so much. But I said, "I'm afraid I'm going to find out that Jeremy is Andre's father."

She nodded. "And if you find that out, what will you do?"

Another great question. "Well, I would do what my mother said, never make a decision when I'm angry."

"You've told me that before. That's good Mama advice."

"Except I won't be angry. If those are the results, I'll be so sad. The saddest I've ever been in my life."

"That's not true." She shook her head. "Nothing was sadder than your dad passing away."

This was why she was my best friend. Dru was helping me put this into perspective.

Leaning onto the desk, Dru said, "Look, when you open this envelope, whatever is inside is between you and me. You can do whatever you want, either way. You know you will never have any judgment from me."

"I know that."

"I just don't want that to play into your decision. I just don't want you to be afraid."

I stared at the envelope. Sitting here like this was ridiculous. I'd tortured myself during the wait and now that what I'd been waiting for was here, I was doing the same.

It was time.

As if she knew the conclusion I'd just come to, Dru picked up the envelope, then handed it to me. I still waited a moment, but then, I took it from Dru and held it only for a second or so before I ripped it open.

It was a single sheet of paper that began with lots of words. Headings that said: Method, Results and then four columns filled with dozens of numbers. But I wasn't interested in any of that. My eyes scanned the paper in search of the bottom line. And that's where I found it. Right at the bottom. I took a breath and read aloud:

"In conclusion, based on our analysis, the alleged father X cannot be excluded as the biological father of the tested child. Based on the analysis of STR listed above, the probability of paternity is...." I paused, swallowed, but the lump stayed stubborn and stayed in place. And I spoke aloud my greatest fear. "The probably of paternity is ninety-nine point nine, nine, nine, nine, nine, nine, nine, nine, nine, nine...."

I couldn't stop. I just kept saying the number nine. Over and over. Dru didn't stop me either. She sat there, and waited for me to run out of nines. And finally, I did. Or maybe I didn't, maybe there had been nines in me, but I was too exhausted to continue.

There was nothing left inside of me except for nines and sorrow. But still, I managed to raise my eyes and look at my best friend. She sat in the same position that she was in when she'd handed me this news. Only one thing had changed—there were tears trekking down her cheeks.

I tilted my head and thought about how my best friend and I were always in sync. Because the tears she had matched mine exactly.

# CHAPTER TWENTY-ONE

With the remote, Dru parted the slow-opening gates, then just as slowly, she rolled up my driveway. She eased the car to a stop, turned off the ignition, then twisted in her seat and faced me.

"Thank you for driving me home," I said.

"This is what we do."

I nodded. Dru was right; I would do anything for her, but she had never had this kind of drama in her life. "I'll pay for the Uber for you to go back to get your car."

"You pay me well enough; I can afford it."

She smiled, or at least she tried to. But it was hard through the tears in her eyes. Again, my best friend and I were in sync.

When I turned my attention to the palatial home where Jeremy and I had lived for the last nine years, I sighed. "I loved this house, I loved this neighborhood."

"You're speaking in past tense. You still love your home," she said. "You still love your neighborhood."

I nodded.

She asked, "So what now?"

I shook my head because the thoughts that came with the answer to that question took my breath away.

"Remember what your mother said about giving yourself time to make the right decision?"

It took a bit of effort, but words finally croaked out of me. "This is not about a decision. Not yet. First, I have to speak to Jeremy. And from there, I'll figure it out."

I was grateful when Dru said nothing and just allowed a few moments of silence to sit between us. That was easiest for me right now. Easier not to have to speak when my head pounded even harder than my heart.

"I'm going to say something you're going to find hard to believe." When Dru said that, I faced her. "Those First Ladies, I know I've called them all kinds of names, and everything I've said about them is true. But the part you told me about what they said, the part about all that you've invested. That's a good question. Are you ready to let it all go for an affair?" There was no judgment in her tone, just sincerity, just concern.

This was an easy question for me to answer. "This isn't an affair. This is a baby. And this is ridiculous." My words gave me strength. "I have to go inside now. I have to talk to Jeremy."

"Are you going to talk to him here? With the kids?"

I half-shrugged. "It's almost eight." I couldn't believe how much time had gone by. Dru and I had just sat in my office after I read the results. We'd just sat there crying and talking, talking and crying, until all of those hours had passed by. "Jasmine's in bed," I said, finishing my thought, "and Jayden is in his room with the TV blasting because he hopes to be deaf by the time he turns fourteen."

She snickered, but then stopped. It was too difficult to laugh through sorrow. "Do you want me to go in with you?"

"No." Now, I was the one who turned to her and tried to smile. "Don't worry; he'll be safe. I really don't want to go to jail."

Any other time, Dru would've laughed. But now, more tears filled her eyes. I leaned in and hugged her.

She whispered, "I love you. And no matter what, I have your back. I got you."

"I know and thank you. Stay in the car until Uber comes. Even this late, it's too hot to be outside."

She nodded, and then pulled me into another embrace, hugging me as if she never wanted to let me go. But then, I broke away, slid out of my car, and walked what felt like the green mile to my front door. I inserted the key and pushed the door open, all in the same motion because I was afraid that if I hesitated for even a second, I would cut and run and no one would ever see me again. I might have done exactly that if Jasmine and Jayden weren't behind these doors. I was coming home for them.

I'd barely stepped over the threshold before I had to face my tragedy.

Jeremy took a stutter-step toward me, raising his arms as if he were going to embrace me. Then, he read the lines on my face and the tears in my eyes and he stepped back, out of striking distance. "Where were you?"

His question surprised me; I thought he'd ask about my tears, first. But then...maybe he was afraid to know. I told him, "I had some things I had to take care of. A report I had to read."

He hesitated for a moment as if he were waiting for me to tell him more. When I didn't add anything, he said, "I tried to call you; Clyde was here with the papers, did you forget?" There was no anger in his tone, even though I knew $8 million meant so much to him.

"I did forget." I left off the part where I would normally apologize. Because in the past, I would have been sorry. Today, I was not.

He couldn't hold back his curiosity any longer. "Are you all right?"

I shook my head.

Again, he stepped toward me as if he thought whatever was bothering me needed his embrace. Before even one of his fingers touched me, I moved out of his reach. "We need to talk."

He searched my eyes for some clues, I guessed. "Oh...kay."

"Where are the kids?"

"I just checked on Jasmine. She's falling asleep and Jayden is playing video games; I told him he had thirty minutes left on his clock."

I nodded. "I want to go someplace where the children won't hear us."

He peered at me as if he was trying to figure it all out and for the first time, I had a thought—did Jeremy know about his son? Had he been taking care of him during these past months? Had he been there for his birth? Had he gone to visit since?

"Oh, God," I moaned.

"Babe?" He sounded like he was on the edge of hysteria. "What's wrong?"

It didn't matter where I talked to Jeremy because our children were going to find out. They would know in the next few hours. So I moved with unsteady steps into the living room. Jeremy followed and I didn't have to turn to him to know that all of his concern was etched on his face.

"Ginger," he whispered my name.

I dropped my bag onto the carpet and sank into our sofa. I held my head in my hands wondering how it had come to this.

Jeremy lowered himself onto the couch next to me and when I finally looked up, the first thing that surprised me was the civility of this. I could have walked into our home, grabbed a couple of plates, glasses and knives and used Jeremy's head as my target. But I had two children upstairs. I always remembered them and I always remembered that I'd been raised by Valencia and Theodore Allen. I'd been raised right and wanted to do the same for my children.

So instead of TV drama, we were going to talk like two adults, though one of us was an adult who lied and cheated.

"I know about the baby," I said, not willing to spend any time going back and forth. I wanted the truth to be out between us.

He didn't even flinch. "What baby?"

If he weren't breaking my heart, I might have been impressed. "I know about the baby you had with Sharonne."

He gave me a long look and then a long sigh. I couldn't believe it. Finally, he was going to tell me the truth.

Then, he said, "You know you're being ridiculous."

I blinked a couple of times because that was not what I expected. "What?"

"You're saying that I had a baby with some chick named Sharonne?" He chuckled, though it was a sound filled with pity—for me!

"So you're saying you don't know anyone by that name?"

"No, that's not what I'm saying. But I am saying that I have two children and they are both," he pointed toward the ceiling, "upstairs in their beds right now. I do not have another child and frankly, Ginger this is getting a bit old."

"Old?" I popped up from the sofa, forgetting about all of that civility. "You know what's old, Jeremy? What's gotten old is First Ladies from other churches coming to me and telling me what's been going on with my husband, what's been going on behind my back."

"Is that what this is about? Gossip from women? You're right that is old. That's as old as time and you need to stop listening to these people. You know everyone is going to be coming for us now. The news is out about this." He reached over to the end table and grabbed papers that I assumed were the Amazon contract. He waved the pages in the air. "We're about to be multi-million dollar stars and folks all over this city will be coming for us, trying to shoot us down."

"Do you think Sonya Douglas, Reverend Douglas's wife is a liar who's trying to shoot us down?" There was a little twitch in his eyebrow. I continued, "Because she's the one who told me. I don't know who told her." I paused. "Maybe her husband? Maybe you confided in him."

Again, a pause. Then, "I don't know where she got what, but what I know is that you know me. You've known me for a long time."

"I thought I did."

"And so, you have to trust me. But even if you don't...."

I leaned back a little. "What's a marriage without trust?"

He shook his head. "At this point, you and I are a team. We're in this together and both of us need to have a single focus. Both of us need to cut out all the noise. We don't need to listen to anyone or anything. Both of us need to ignore it all."

I folded my arms, and looked down at him, still sitting on our sofa. "And is that what you're doing, Jeremy? You're ignoring your son?"

"My son," he pushed himself up, moving slowly and speaking at the same speed, "is upstairs." He said that without a flinch or a blink. He said that looking me dead in my eyes. "And I don't have time right now for you to be coming at me with rumors and lies. Not when there is so much at stake."

I let so many silent seconds pass, that Jeremy began to shift his feet.

"It's amazing," I finally began, "how you think you know someone and you really don't."

He looked into my eyes. "You know me, Ginger." He took a step toward me. "Think about it. Think about where we've come from." Now, only inches separated us.

This time, I would not be moved. This time, I wasn't going to duck from his touch. This time, I was going to stand.

He said, "We've built this together. We have a family, we have a church, we have a ministry that is growing and about to explode." He sounded like he was acting as his own defense attorney. "And one other thing that we have; we have love." When he rested his hands on my shoulders, I didn't flinch. "I have never loved a woman the way I've loved you."

He leaned forward, his lips aimed toward mine. He was tentative, though, as if he wasn't sure if I would move or maybe slap him away.

I didn't.

His lips covered mine and still I didn't move. My hands stayed by my side, my lips did not invite him in. But for some reason when he leaned back, there was a smile on his face. As if he had no clue that was our final kiss.

"So we're good?" he said, and that made me ask myself— did Jeremy really think I was that pathetic?

My response: I stepped away from him, but only to reach for my bag and I pulled out the envelope.

When I faced him, Jeremy was already trembling. His eyes were on what I held and he was already afraid. His hands shook when I handed him the manila envelope. Did he somehow know what was inside?

Still, he asked, "What is this?"

I said nothing, just watched him pull out the paper that I'd read hours before. And then, I watched his eyes buck. That broke me again, because he was filled with horror, but not surprise.

"So, I guess our two children are not your only ones." He was still staring at the paper. "Congratulations, you're a daddy again."

I wasn't sure if his silence was because of his shock or his story—the one he was trying to come up with for me.

Finally, he stuttered, "Wh-How...?"

"Are you asking how did I find out?" He didn't move, just kept staring at the paper he held in his trembling hand. "I told you. First Lady Sonya came to me, but I was bound to find out since half of the population in D.C. seemed to know."

Jeremy released the paper, letting it float slowly through the air until it landed at his feet. But he didn't look down. "Babe, I...I can explain."

"There's no need to explain. I know what happened. You were in bed with me one night and you went and screwed Sharonne the next night. And she, got pregnant. Didn't she tell you?"

He rubbed his hands over his head as if he were trying to massage out a good thought, something that could save him. "It's not even like that. It didn't happen like that."

I frowned. "I know how babies are made."

He still didn't look at me. "This is something that just...."

"Let me guess, you just happened to fall into Sharonnne's...."

Before I could finish, he shouted, "No! It's just that...."

"You've been living a LIE," I said, matching his volume. "Our whole damn marriage has been a lie."

"That's not true, you know how much I love you."

"Really?" My voice was one decibel below a scream. I snatched the paper from the floor. "Is this your idea of love?" I mashed it against his face. "Is this how you show someone that you love them?"

"Babe."

"Don't babe me," I said, now feeling totally out of control. "Don't ever babe me again!"

He shook his head as if he didn't accept my words. "Look, we can work through this. We have to work through this."

"Are you kidding me? I'm supposed to just stand by you while you raise a child with another woman? And not only are you a cheater, but you stood here and lied to my face about it."

"No, I've already been talking to her...."

My shoulders sagged and so did Jeremy's as he realized what he'd just said.

"Look, Ginger," his voice was softer now, "I did know about this, not right away, but...Sharonne did tell me."

"When?" I wasn't sure why I was asking for the details. It would just be more torture. But for some reason, I wanted to know. So I asked, "When did you find out?"

"She was about to give birth. She was about to have the baby. She wanted me to come to New Orleans to be with her."

I shook my head, my rage moving aside to make room for all of my sadness.

"But I didn't go!" he said, as if that was some kind of virtue. "I didn't go because I thought Sharonne was lying. I hadn't seen her in months; I'd broken it off."

His words reminded me of Katrina's: *Always talking about breaking it off with her and he never does.*

He continued, "I thought she was just trying to trap me because of who I was. So, I didn't go," he repeated. "I didn't go to New Orleans. I wasn't there when her baby was born," he said as if the child was Sharonne's alone.

"Something must've happened because you knew Andre was your son."

He glanced at me as if he was surprised I knew his son's name. "She said she wanted to do a paternity test and I went along with it because I didn't want her to take it public."

"And so you found out and...what?"

"That's what I'm trying to tell you, Ginger. I've been talking to her. We can pay her off and she'll go away. We're just negotiating the price now."

"The price?" I frowned.

"Yeah, Clyde is working this out."

"Oh, God," I said. "He knows, too?" I threw up my hands. Then, turning to him, I spat, "I guess you didn't learn everything from your mentor. Reverend Robinson kept his mess away from everyone. He was a liar and a cheat, but at least he was a smart one for years."

My words hit my target—his heart. Jeremy was still filled with pain because he'd never heard from the man who'd called him son after that day Reverend Robinson confessed his sin on the altar. There were times when I felt like that was what motivated him to get to where he was today. He wanted to be bigger than his mentor. He wanted to be better. But in truth, they were the same. Both with a family on the side.

"It isn't like that at all," he whispered. "I want to do right by you."

His words surprised me so much, I pressed my hands against my chest. "And what about your child? Don't you want to do right by him?"

"That's what we're negotiating," he said as if that point should have been clear to me.

I shook my head. "There's nothing for you to negotiate. You need to take care of your baby and save that money; you're going to need it."

I grabbed my bag and moved to leave Jeremy and his drama all alone.

But he blocked my path. "What are you talking about, Ginger?"

"I'm out." I paused, wanting to make sure that not only had he heard me, but that he understood me, too. "Tomorrow the children and I are moving out."

"You can't do that. You can't leave me. You can't take my children away from me."

"Watch me."

"You can't do this, Ginger. You will destroy everything."

"You're the one who destroyed everything," I said, punching him in the chest with my forefinger, though I really wanted to use my fist. "I loved you with everything inside of me. I gave you my ALL."

"And now, if you'll give me time, I will make this up to you. I promise you, it will never happen again."

"Damn straight it won't. Not to me."

I marched from the living room and then, toward the stairs, but before I could take a step up, he grabbed my arm, stopping me. My heart was beating fast, my breaths were coming quick as I glanced down to where he held me. When I raised my eyes, I glared at him with all of my rage, trying to bore a hole into his soul. "I don't want to get into anything more with you, Jeremy," I began through clenched teeth, because my children are right up these stairs. But if you don't let me go, I promise you what will happen next, will be Washington Post front page news worthy, Jeremy. Don't try me."

He didn't release his grip. "I just want you to understand. I just want you to give me another chance," he pleaded.

"There can't be a second chance," I said as nonchalantly as I could with a heart that was crashing against my chest, "with an outside child. Now let go of me, or you will pay the price."

It was my words and my tone, I was sure. Slowly, his fingers uncurled from around my arm. With a final glare, I stomped up the stairs, though the strength that I moved with belied the ache that rolled through every bit of me.

My life as I knew it was over, forever. Jeremy thought that I was walking away from $8 million, but I didn't care about that. Jeremy was the one who'd changed because of the money and the power. Not me.

What I was walking away from was the man who'd broken my heart and he didn't have the tools nor the capacity to put us back together. And because of that, there was nothing more that I could do.

Because of that, this was O.V.E.R.

# EPILOGUE

"Well, if it isn't my best friend in the whole wide world."

I looked up from my iPad where I had been engrossed in Michelle Obama's book, to see Dru standing over me with that sunshine smile that I'd missed so much.

"Hey, Girl," I exclaimed as I leapt up to hug her. "How are you?"

She squeezed me tight, then took a step back, her eyes running from my honey blonde pixie cut down to my red bottom spiked boots. "Not as good as you, obviously. You're looking fabulous as always." She snapped her fingers. "Dang, talk about divorce looking good on somebody."

It was meant to be a light comment, but it took away just a little bit of my joy. "Divorce is never cause to celebrate." But I appreciated the compliment and managed a smile. "But, you know I have to stay on point."

We stepped aside to let another Starbucks customer pass to take a seat at the table adjacent from us, then, we slid into

281

the chairs at the table where I'd been sitting. Once she was settled, Dru asked, "How are you really?"

"I'm fine," I said. "I tell you that every time we talk."

"Yeah, but you're all the way in Dallas now and when I can't lay my eyes on you, I don't feel like I know what's really going on for real."

"What are you talking about?" I chuckled. "You were just in Dallas with me last month."

"And? That was a whole thirty-four days ago."

"Well I was good then, and I'm good now." I nodded as that revelation sank in. I really was doing well, even as I had wondered what it would be like to set foot back in D.C. I hadn't returned to the DMV since the movers had backed the 26 foot truck up to our dream home, packed up half of our furniture and everything that belonged to me and the children, and then headed south, the beginning of my nightmare of starting over.

Dru cocked her head and studied me. "I'm glad to hear that, Ginger. Really, I am." She gave me a once-over once again. "Girl, if the First Ladies Council could see you now. Talking about how your life was going to be over if you left Jeremy." She waved her hands as if she was pushing away the words Sonya and Cecily had spoken over my life.

I shook my head as I thought of the First Ladies crew. The women who'd crawled all up in my business and told me we were family...and the women who, when I'd tried to reach out to them once I got to Dallas because I wanted the Dress for Success program to continue, never returned a single call. And not one of them could say it was a cell phone issue since texts and emails went unanswered as well.

That still made me shake my head a bit, though I guess I shouldn't have been surprised. It wasn't like this had come out of the blue, Sonya had warned me:

*You cannot leave your husband because if you do...I'm afraid you will regret it. And that's not a threat, that's a promise.*

I hadn't known what she'd meant by that the day she and Cecily had ambushed me in my office, but I knew now—I'd been voted off the island, which I'm sure wasn't a hard vote for them to take. I guess since I'd shamed them, they shunned me.

"Well, no matter what they said, my life isn't over," I said. "I haven't even been at the ad agency for six months, and I've already secured my first client."

"Really?" Dru clapped. "You didn't tell me."

"Just got the news the day before yesterday. So the way I see it, I may be ten years late getting started, but give me a minute and I'll have my own agency up and running."

"See," she held out her hands as if she were making a point, "divorce is doing you good."

"No, I'm making the best of a bad situation." I pointed toward the barista. "Do you want something to drink?"

"No, I'm good." After a couple of seconds of silence, Dru said softly, "I'm really glad to see you, but I'm surprised you came," changing the tenor of our conversation.

284 | Gizelle Bryant

"If I'm being honest, I am, too." I fingered my chai tea as I replayed Jeremy's request to bring the children to D.C. for the church's eleventh anniversary celebration.

*"I understand if you can't bring yourself to attend, but I really would like the children there," he said.*

Recalling his words when he'd called a month ago, I hadn't made any promises to him then. But last week, I'd returned his call and told him the children would be here. When he kept thanking me over and over, I heard the first moments of joy from Jeremy since our divorce had been finalized five months ago.

It had been a quick divorce for me and Jeremy. Truly, I blinked and our marriage was over. It had been easy since we'd been married in D.C. and the district had such a short process. And it helped that (to my surprise), Jeremy had not contested it and we'd been amicable.

That was a blessing because I hadn't been sure which way this wind was going to blow. When I'd walked away from my husband, Amazon had walked away from him. But a surprise for me was that like me, Jeremy wasn't pressed about Amazon. He cared more about losing his family than losing that deal. It was just too bad that his care had come far too late.

I didn't doubt Jeremy's sincerity. He had begged me just about every day in every conversation we had for another chance. But I was like that tree planted by the water, and when Jeremy finally realized that I could not be moved, he'd told his attorney to give me whatever I wanted. I'd been hurt, but I wasn't vindictive, so through our attorneys, we worked together for a settlement that was fair.

His pleas hadn't ended there, though. Jeremy asked me for another chance right up until the moment I signed my name on those papers, ending our union and his chances.

"So, how was the anniversary celebration?" I asked, bringing my thoughts back to the present.

"It was nice." She nodded. "I'm glad I went. It was a far cry from the drama of the tenth anniversary."

I shook my head as I recalled that fiasco. On the day of the tenth anniversary celebration, my children and I were on Interstate 81, still five hours away from my mother's home in Dallas. But while I didn't show up, Sharonne did. With her baby boy in tow.

Dru had filled me in (and Lizzy had done the same for my mom) on every word and every moment of the debacle: How Sharonne had slinked down the center aisle of the church, wearing one of her signature spandex dresses, while Jeremy gave his sermon of appreciation for all that God had done for him. How he'd started to stutter when he noticed Sharron and even though he'd signaled the deacons, it was too late to stop her. How she'd shouted above the noise (somehow, the church band had begun playing a song in the middle of the madness), telling Jeremy that it was time for him to introduce his son to his congregation.

And how when after Sharonne's announcement and hell had broken loose, Jeremy had broken out. The deacons had shuttled him out of and away from that church and he hadn't been seen or heard from for a week after that. The only way I was sure he was all right was that he called the kids diligently every evening to ask about their day and to tell them good night.

But he didn't show up again in public until the following Sunday, standing on the pulpit before his congregation with tears already sliding down his cheek. He'd cried out his mea culpa, "Forgive me Lord, for I have sinned," taking me all the way back to our beginning.

When Dru had told me that story, all I could do was thank God for making sure the kids and I were already twelve hours into our seventeen hour drive away from D.C.

"I had nightmares about that anniversary for weeks after." Dru shook her head. "That's why I just never went back to New Kingdom, until today."

"Thanks for taking the kids there for me. I just couldn't bring myself to go back."

"I get it. And it was no problem. Everyone was glad to see them and a few folks even seemed glad to see me. It was good to be back, though I wasn't sure I would ever walk through those doors of New Kingdom Temple again."

"You and about twenty percent of the membership, right? That's what was reported on Abundant Life and Abiding Love when Angela Wiley did that follow up show on the fall of Reverend Williams." I shook my head. "She had built him up when she did the show with us, but it seemed like she was just as happy to tear him down."

"But isn't that what so many people do with pastors?" Dru asked. "Sometimes I feel like we, as a society, set pastors up for a fall. And then, we kick them when they're down."

"That's true. But what I say is just don't give people the ammunition to kill you."

"That's true, too," Dru said. "Well, all I know is that the sanctuary was packed today and the way Jeremy set that place on fire," she shrugged, "it won't be long before he takes the membership rolls back up."

"It doesn't surprise me," I said. "Jeremy is a great preacher. He was just a horrible husb..." I stopped myself because what I was about to say wasn't the truth. Jeremy wasn't a horrible man and I really couldn't say he was a horrible husband. He'd just done a horrible thing that I'd been able to forgive, but still had to walk away.

My words brought a small smile to Dru's face. "I really am proud of you."

"Thank you." I took a sip of my tea. "How's your job going?"

She shook her head. "Stella is no Ginger," she said, referring to her boss at the African American Museum, where she'd started working shortly after I moved away. "But since I've gotten that promotion to event coordinator, I'm enjoying it more there."

Just as I lifted my cup for another sip, I saw Jeremy through the glass doors and I hated that my heart quickened a bit at my first sight of him. I had reconciled our divorce in my head a long time ago, really from the moment I read the paternity results. I may have been able to forgive an affair, but once a baby was in the mix, it was deuces. So my head understood; I just needed time for my heart time to catch up.

When he opened the door, Jasmine skipped inside in front of her brother and father.

"Mommy," Jasmine shouted once she spotted me. She'd forgotten all about our talk regarding inside voices. "You should've seen my solo. You were right. Even though I didn't get to practice with the children's choir, I didn't mess up."

I hugged my daughter. "I knew you would be awesome. Auntie Dru recorded it for me, so I'll get to watch it again and again."

Dru nodded as she stood. "Who wants a Frappuccino?"

"Me!" both Jasmine and Jayden sang in unison.

Dru took their hands and led them up toward the counter, leaving me and Jeremy alone. It was an awkward silence which was amplified because of just how crazy this was. Who would've thought the two of us would ever be at a loss for words in each other's presence?

"How are you?" Jeremy finally said as he reached in for a hug.

Inside his embrace, I inhaled the fragrance of his cologne, then stepped back. "I'm well. What about you?"

He began to nod slowly as he glanced over at Jasmine and Jayden at the counter. "I'm well and I'm happy." He turned back to me. "Thank you for letting them come. This was a big day for me."

"You're welcome," I said.

And then, the silence returned. I shifted from one five-inch boot heel to the other, once again marveling at how crazy it felt to be in his presence. But though we talked often about the children, this was the first time we were face to face since I'd rolled out of our driveway heading to Dallas. He'd been to Dallas dozens of times to visit the children and to see them over the holidays, the visits always facilitated by my mother. But even though he'd asked to have Christmas dinner with us, I hadn't been ready. And now that he stood here in front of me, I wondered if I'd been ready even now.

When I glanced back at my ex, Jeremy was studying me and a mist glazed his eyes. "You...look...stunning."

"Thank you." I wondered if the polite thing to do was to ask about his other son, but I decided I definitely wasn't ready for that. It wasn't like he and Sharonne had a relationship. I wouldn't have been able to ever see Jeremy with someone like her; she was exactly what First Lady Eunice had told me all those years ago: Sharonne was good for a roll in the bed, but she'd never stand next to Jeremy at the altar.

Turned out First Lady Eunice had been right. My mother had told me (again, though Lizzy) that Jeremy was taking care of Andre and he was present in his life. But beyond co-parenting, he had no relationship with Sharonne.

Trying to fill the silence, I said to Jeremy, "I heard the sermon today was, how did Dru put it, fire."

290 | Gizelle Bryant

That made him smile and relax his shoulders and I did the same. "I preached from Isaiah forty-four-twenty-two," he said.

It was automatic when I said, "*I have swept away your offenses like a cloud. Your sins like the morning mist.*"

And it was automatic when Jeremy finished for me, "*Return to me for I have redeemed you.*"

The awkwardness was gone now and so with a full smile on my face and in my heart, I could say, "I'm happy things are going well for you, Jeremy."

He hesitated for a moment before he took a step closer to me. "They'd be better if-"

I held up a hand, my palm in front of his face. "I'm here for the kids."

From the look on his face, I could tell that he heard the words I didn't say following I'm here for the kids—nothing more.

Dru and I were still in sync because that was the moment she and the kids stepped into our space with Jasmine and Jayden ecstatic about their Strawberries and Cream Frappuccino's.

"Mom, Dad's taking us to TGI Fridays. Are you coming?" Jayden asked.

"We're going to Fridays on a Sunday!" Jasmine laughed.

Jayden shook his head at his sister and I ruffled her hair that flowed to her shoulders in curls today.

I said, "No, Sweetie. This is Daddy time. But here's what you came for." Reaching into my purse, I handed his Nintendo to him. "We know you can't live without it."

"Thanks Mom," Jayden said, and turning to Jeremy he said, "And thanks, Dad for bringing me to get it."

"Of course, son."

"Okay," I said, "You guys get going. I'll be at the hotel waiting on you guys, so just enjoy your dad."

Jeremy's eyes were filled with longing, his gaze, telling me he wanted me to be there to share their meal. But all he said was, "Okay, we'll see you at the hotel in a few hours." He turned to Dru. "Thanks for coming to the services. We miss you at New Kingdom."

I was glad to see the warmth in Dru's smile. It had taken her a long time, longer than me, really. He'd hurt her best friend, but she did have the heart of Christ—it was time to forgive.

I said my goodbyes to my children with kisses and my ex-husband with one of those church hugs where our hips were miles away from each other, and then Dru and I watched Jasmine skip and Jayden and Jeremy stroll out.

When they were out of our sight, Dru sighed and turned to me. "Did I tell you how proud I am of you?"

"You've mentioned that a time or two."

"You could've destroyed him."

"But I didn't want to, never wanted to."

"That's why you're my She-ro."

I grabbed my purse and slung the designer bag over my shoulder. "Well, my Super Hero powers need some rejuvenating and this tea isn't cutting it. I think it's Dirty Martini Time."

"Now you're talking my language." Dru laughed.

With that, my best friend draped her arm through mine and this time, we were the ones almost skipping out of the door. Outside, I slapped on my oversized sunglasses. I needed to block the glare a bit because the sun was really shining; my future was looking so bright.

# About the Author

Gizelle is the proud co-founder and owner of EveryHue Beauty, a skin care line geared toward women of color. She is very passionate about everyone living in their own beauty from the inside out.

The television personality is a recurring cast member of the "Real Housewives of Potomac," a reality series that follows the lives of woman and currently airs on Bravo. Gizelle has a heart for philanthropy and activism while always embracing her entrepreneurial spirit. Currently, she presides over numerous endeavors geared toward improving the lives of women and children. Whether it's volunteering at a nursing facility, children's hospital or at the Healthy Babies Organization, helping others is what matter most to her.

While Gizelle is very committed to everything that she puts her mind to, her greatest gift and passion is being a mother to her three beautiful daughters, Grace (13), Angel (11) and Adore (11).